ASPECTS OF CAPITAL INVESTMENT IN GREAT BRITAIN 1750–1850

T0300148

ASPECTS OF CAPITAL INVESTMENT IN GREAT BRITAIN 1750–1850

A preliminary survey

Edited by

J.P.P. HIGGINS AND SIDNEY POLLARD

With the assistance of J.E. Ginarlis

Routledge
Taylor & Francis Group

LONDON AND NEW YORK

First published in 1971

Published in 2006 by
Routledge
2 Park Square, Milton Park, Abingdon, Oxfordshire OX14 4RN
711 Third Avenue, New York, NY 10017

First issued in paperback 2014

Routledge is an imprint of the Taylor and Francis Group, an informa business

© 1971 Routledge

British Library Cataloguing in Publication Data
A CIP catalogue record for this book
is available from the British Library

Aspects of Capital Investment in Great Britain 1750–1850
ISBN13: 978-1-138-86484-9 (pbk)
ISBN13: 978-0-415-37852-9 (hbk)
ISBN 0-415-37852-4 (volume)
ISBN 0-415-37850-8 (subset)
ISBN 0-415-28619-0 (set)

Routledge Library Editions: Economic History

*Aspects of Capital Investment
in Great Britain 1750–1850*

Aspects of Capital Investment
in Great Britain
1750–1850

A PRELIMINARY SURVEY

Report of a Conference held at the University of Sheffield,
5–7 January 1969

Edited by
J. P. P. HIGGINS
and
SIDNEY POLLARD
with the assistance of
J. E. GINARLIS

METHUEN & CO LTD
11 NEW FETTER LANE · LONDON EC4

First published·1971
by Methuen & Co. Ltd
11 New Fetter Lane, London EC4
© 1971 by Methuen & Co. Ltd

SBN 416 17690 9

Distributed in the U.S.A.
by Barnes & Noble Inc.

Contents

Editors' Note

The six papers in this book were read to the Conference on the Sources and Methods for the Study of Capital Formation, 1750-1850, which was organised by the Department of Economic History at the University of Sheffield early in 1969. The papers, together with the comments and edited versions of the discussions which followed them appear in the order in which they took place. Despite modifications of approach and the annotation of the text our aim has been to retain as far as possible in published form the style of the occasion.

We would like to record our thanks to the authors of the papers and to those who attended the conference and enriched its proceedings. We are grateful to the University and to the Staff of Ranmoor House for looking after us and also to the Social Science Research Council for providing the financial support without which this exercise could not have been undertaken.

PARTICIPANTS OF THE CONFERENCE

Mr B. Anderson
Mr M. Barratt-Brown
Dr S. A. Broadbridge
Mr E. Butler
Dr J. Butt
Mr C. W. Chalklin
Dr S. D. Chapman
Professor G. Clayton
Professor A. W. Coats
Professor W. Cole
Dr D. C. Coleman
Dr E. Cooney
Mr P. Cotterell
Mr R. Craig
Mr D. W. Crossley
Professor R. Davis
Dr H. J. Dyos
Dr M. M. Edwards

Mr M. Falkus
Dr C. H. Feinstein
Professor M. W. Flinn
Mr J. Ginarlis
Mr J. L. Halstead
Dr J. R. Harris
Mr A. Harrison
Mr N. B. Harte
Mr J. Hibbert
Mr J. P. P. Higgins
Mr B. Hill
Dr B. A. Holderness
Mr D. T. Jenkins
Professor D. S. Landes
Professor P. Mathias
Professor W. Minchinton
Dr B. R. Mitchell
Dr J. Odling-Smee

Dr C. Phillips

Professor S. Pollard

Dr M. Reed

Dr E. Sigsworth

Professor F. M. L. Thompson

Mr D. Tierney

Mr O. M. Westall

Professor J. Whitaker

Introduction

There has never been much doubt about the crucial role of capital formation in the process of industrialization, and particularly in the specific complex of changes known as the Industrial Revolution. Discussion has ranged over the type of capital involved, over the methods of its accumulation and the variations in its ownership. Attention has also been devoted to the social and political consequences of the growth of industrial capital and its redistribution. But somewhere at the centre of the discussion must lie the more basic issue of the quantities of capital actually involved.

Today most countries make elaborate provisions for taking the pulse of their economy at frequent intervals and analysing the data obtained with fairly refined techniques; in this context, it is now usual for all major countries to publish estimates of the rate of their annual capital formation in absolute terms and as a proportion of national income, down to decimal points. This applies even to some of those countries which are in the midst of, or are about to enter upon, their Industrial Revolution. We therefore possess figures of current rates of gross capital formation, expressed as a percentage of gross national income for countries at different stages of development *today*, and it was largely by arguing backwards from these that W. A. Lewis, W. W. Rostow and others developed their working hypotheses on industrialization and the formation of capital. According to them traditional economies have a rate of 5 to 6 per cent and advanced countries a rate of 10 to 12 per cent and over, and the Industrial Revolution brings about, as one of its aspects, a rise from one to the other.

Although the numerical basis was derived from twentieth-century experience, this was considered to be an area in which historical parallels are valid, and the hypothesis of a rise from 5 to 6 per cent to 10 to 12 per cent was intended to apply to the past industrial revolutions of the advanced countries, and specifically to the classic Industrial Revolution in Great Britain. At the time when it was propounded, no statistics existed to check its validity. Since then, however, the first major foray into the statistical framework of the British industrial revolution has been completed, and its results were most damaging to the hypothesis [1]. Far from jumping to double the rates of the 'traditional' economy, capital formation appeared by these figures to have increased from 5 to 6 per cent by only perhaps 1½ per cent to 7

1

per cent by 1800, and it remained there until the great railway booms of the 1830s and 1840s raised it by perhaps another 2 per cent to, say, 9 per cent [2].

The reasoning behind this shattering practical test was well informed and not, by itself, implausible. Yet closer inspection revealed that many of the statistics on which it was based were highly suspect, being derived from contemporary sources which were inadequate and often based on pure guesswork, and which used a very different concept of 'capital' from that current today. Even a cursory reworking of the statistical base to modern definitions revealed a rate of progress somewhat nearer that postulated, though still some way off it: from 6½ per cent in c.1770 to 9 per cent in the early 1790s, to drop to 8 per cent at the end of the war and rise to 11 per cent before the first railway boom [3].

Perhaps the main usefulness of this exercise was to serve as a warning against cursory reworkings, or at least against committing them to paper; for it appears already that several of the sums used there will need some major emendation. However, it has also served a second purpose. It has helped to stake out the area of work required to arrive at some more reliable figures, and by reducing the area of the unknown, has made it that much less terrifying.

For, on the face of it, it is somewhat surprising that the task has not been attempted before. Apart from its own intrinsic interest, it might have been expected to be encouraged by the work on capital formation from 1856 on [4], which in turn was designed to provide a link with the present day official figures, and with which it might be expected to form a consistent and continuous chain spanning over 200 years. If the task has not seriously been attempted before, the reason must surely be, at least in large measure, because it appeared too daunting or, indeed, impossible.

There is one obvious major difference between any series of capital formation (or, for that matter, of national income) running from the 1850s or later, and a similar series covering the century c.1750-1850. For while the former can build on at least some official annual series, largely derived from the inland revenue and other taxation returns, and the problems are chiefly those of interpretation and adjusting taxed property to total property, there are simply no overall figures available at all for any comparable run of years for the century of the Industrial Revolution. Instead of being derived, as it were, from above, the series has to be built up from below. Each annual figure will have to be the sum of all the figures derived separately for each of the relevant sectors of the economy.

The researcher needs, in other words, to have at his disposal something like the bureaucratic apparatus of census takers, and to undertake himself the basic groundwork which is usually the starting point, provided by others, of the high-powered statistical work of the economists who get into print on present day problems. What is more, he has to ask his assistants to enumerate and evaluate data which either have been lost altogether, if they were ever known, or which can, at best, be only inferred from indirect evidence. It would, in other words, require nothing less than the resources of a government department to collate the information, and to invent it where it no longer exists.

No doubt the wiser course would have been to leave it to such a department to undertake the task some day. However, records and archives are destroyed year by year, and meanwhile there was at least some government department able to help. The recently established Social Science Research Council has been most generous in its support for an attempt to provide some consistent figures for capital formation in the period c.1750-1850, and to vary and extend the support promised at first, when the needs of the research project appeared to require such changes. This support included the payment of research assistants at the University of Sheffield; the provision of clerical and similar facilities; and, in a most imaginative gesture, the financing of the Conference, the transactions of which are now between the covers of this book.

It was clear from the start that no Research Council could fully finance the kind of extensive search that was necessary in many separate sectors and that required many specialized skills and much local knowledge. Moreover, it was known that some work was already being conducted in different fields of economic history which would throw up incidentally some of the information which would have to be assembled ultimately to provide a complete picture. Some of this research was so close to the objectives of the project that its results might, with some luck, be incorporated directly or with only minor modifications. This included (to draw some examples from among those attending the Conference) the research concerned with investment in the cotton industry undertaken by Dr Butt, Dr Chapman and Dr Edwards, the work on the woollen industry by Mr Jenkins, the work on agriculture by Mr Harrison, and the work on investment in shipping by Mr Craig. Some scholars were persuaded, after the

inception of the Scheme, to devote their efforts to certain other fairly
self-contained aspects of it: they include Dr Bland and Dr Holderness at
the University of Sheffield. There is also much other work which,
though mainly directed to other purposes, will throw up pieces of the
jigsaw that will be needed to complete the whole picture. These
activities are, of course, going on quite independently in several
different universities and several different cities of the United Kingdom.

Ultimately, the results of all this work will have to be co-ordinated
into a single study. The logistics of such an operation are bound to be
formidable. The director of such a project has not only to keep up a
common timetable and avoid major gaps and wasteful overlaps, but he
has also to try and secure a common approach and common
assumptions by the different members of the extended team. Beyond
this, he would fail in his duties unless he were also able to spread
quickly any newly available information, and to ensure that incidental
information turned up in a search for something else did not get
lost.

Alas, such superhuman qualities are not available to this project. But as
a second best, it was thought that it might be possible to achieve
better co-ordination among all the participants, to make them more
aware of the project as a whole, and to allow them to stimulate each
other, by bringing them together in a Conference at which some
concrete issues would be discussed. This would have the further
advantage of allowing us to call on others not directly concerned with
research on this project, but knowledgeable about some aspects of it
and able to stimulate our thought and contribute their ideas to the
common pool.

This, then, was the first object of the Conference. But we were also
looking for another benefit. If the series covering the Industrial
Revolution were to be linked to the later series, the definitions and
classifications, both of the total and of the sectional series, would have
to be as nearly as possible the same. Theoretically, this could have
been achieved by consulting the appropriate literature, including the
current official handbook describing the conventions used in building
up the statistics of the United Kingdom [5]. In practice, however,
conditions were so different in the period 1750-1850, and particularly in its early decades, that often no easy or obvious identification of
equivalents is possible. We could have made our arbitrary decisions. But
where there was no obvious answer and different interpretations could
be justified, it seemed best to arrive at our classification by the give and

take of discussion which might modify, or even reconcile original positions, by consensus rather than by fiat. If at times our model seemed to lie in ecclesiastical history rather than in the history of scientific progress and the Conference bore the aspect of some of the early Church Councils, the reason is the nature of our task. Nevertheless, the task brought forth some of the most heated, and most fruitful, discussion at the Conference.

Bearing these considerations in mind, the research team at Sheffield was anxious to assemble together three groups of people, though there was not necessarily any clear-cut dividing line between them: those directly concerned with research within the project, those who could contribute mainly by their knowledge of historical sources and research methods, and those who had some practical experience of building up capital formation statistics, or who had contributed to the theory or logic of present-day practices. The time of the year, early January, was chosen to fit in with university vacations. It was not an entirely happy choice, as some members fell victim to seasonal 'flu, and others to the slightly less seasonal snow. But the Conference was sufficiently representative to fulfil the hopes that had been placed on it by the organizers.

The papers read and the discussions which followed them fall clearly into two groups. The first two sessions, introduced by papers by Hibbert and Feinstein, describe the practice and the theoretical and practical problems of current capital formation estimates and of the work on the years since 1856. They therefore represent the theoretical framework into which the estimates for c.1750-1850 ought ideally to fit. The other four papers, by Chapman, Craig, Ginarlis and Holderness, read in the remaining three sessions, discuss some of the work done, or planned, for different sectors of the economy. They are more concerned with practical problems of historical research, but they also refer to some problems of theory and of interpretation. Each of the main papers was followed by one or more prepared comments, and the meetings were then declared open to general discussion. Edited versions of these discussions, with the names of the discussants, are printed below.

The papers should be allowed to speak for themselves, and it would be invidious and foolhardy to comment on them at this stage, but one important point should by made here. The Conference was intended to lead in to the project, rather than conclude it: it was intended to lead in to provide questions and clarify problems rather than produce the answers. It is true that the pilot survey, conducted by Ginarlis on capital formation in canals, turnpikes and other roads, had then been running for two years; but the remainder of the associated workers, including Holderness, had been engaged on the project only a matter of months, and the other four papers arose largely out of work undertaken outside the scope of the project itself. Thus, for the project as a whole, the Conference marked a departure rather than the arrival.

There is, therefore, much that is tentative and unresolved, as well as much that is controversial, in these pages. The original papers and discussion, and their publication now, were and are intended to provoke comment and an exchange of ideas — not to close a controversy. Any reader, whether a participating member of the Conference or not, is therefore invited to contribute further to the discussion, either on issues of principle or on questions of statistical sources and interpretation, by communicating with us at Sheffield. We should, of course, be particularly glad to hear from anyone who is currently working on problems related to, or has brought to light any facts bearing on, the main theme of the inquiry.

Can we justify the Conference? Is there any merit in letting questions without answers re-echo round a circle of scholars; or would we have been better advised to wait until we had a story to tell? What has been gained by the meeting as evidenced by the proceedings now before the reader?

The reader will have to judge the value of the exercise for himself. But we in Sheffield are grateful for the stimulus we have received, and for both the doubts and the certainties which have emerged from the sessions. As illustrations, we may here summarize three areas in which the Conference has left us clearer in our own minds, either about problems or about their solutions.

The first concerns the problem of gross versus net investment, measured, respectively, against gross and net national product. Originally we had been mainly interested in the first, since it seemed to indicate more accurately the burden or effort which the economy was required to carry in the critical years. Yet at the same time we also intended to isolate net capital formation out of the gross figure, since it might have some relationship to the growth rate, and particularly the change in the growth rate which we expected to find in the Industrial Revolution period. Our main problem, it seemed to us, would be to distinguish one from the other, gross from net capital formation, for an age when the actual capital equipment was relatively primitive, and technical change, though rapid by earlier standards, was slow compared with present day innovation.

Our experience so far of searching for actual data had, however, pointed to the likelihood that in many sectors the best figures would be obtained neither for gross nor for net investment, but for 'gross gross' — i.e. investment including the expenditure on running repair and maintenance of capital equipment, as well as its replacement, improvement and extension subsumed under simple 'gross investment'. Where hard data are difficult to come by, the availability of some genuine figures is an important argument, and we had been convinced earlier on that for some sectors we would be well advised to obtain the gross gross figures first, and then reduce them by some appropriate percentage to arrive at gross and net expenditure.

It does appear, however, that even some contemporary series, which presumably do not suffer from quite the same paucity of data, use 'gross gross', and there are sound reasons for such an approach, too. As with all these decisions, the choice would be determined by the questions which the figures were intended to answer. Some of the views emerging from the discussion of the first two sessions in particular seemed to support the notion that as a measure of the burden, effort or shift of resources required in the process of industrialization, this definition might even be preferable, though it was not strictly in line with the Lewis-Rostow hypothesis. But in the comparatively primitive technology obtaining everywhere in the eighteenth century, and in the majority of industries as late as the mid-nineteenth, repair and maintenance of capital equipment loomed much larger than genuine net investment. The vast expenditure on shoeing horses, when measured, for example, against the modest sums invested in cotton spinning machinery, leads to the conclusion that a totally wrong picture of the role of capital in the process of industrialization would emerge unless we also took account of maintenance — though, of course, all the categories would have to be correctly labelled and carefully distinguished. This was but one aspect of the view, expressed several times during the Conference, that there was, in effect, no strictly logical way of applying twentieth-century categories accurately to eighteenth-century conditions.

This conclusion would also hold for a second area of uncertainty, concerning costs which were not necessary in a strictly physical sense, but arose out of the social or political framework of Britain at that time. The discussion centred particularly around the parliamentary and legal costs of obtaining the private acts of Parliament required by Turnpike Trusts, Canal Companies and others needing limited liability or compulsory rights to purchase land. Only a small fraction of those were simply transfer payments in direct bribes to members of Parliament to offer more for land than it was worth in order to buy off any potential opposition — and even some of these were considered to be possibly 'necessary' expenditure for the company concerned. But the rest was expenditure for services rendered — to surveyors, lawyers, witnesses before Committees, etc. A problem of a similar nature was recently raised by Professor Fishlow, who would class the interest paid to subscribers before a railway line was opened, and therefore clearly paid out of capital, as necessary capital cost, since without this incentive the capital would not have been subscribed [6].

From one point of view, expenditure of this kind should not be considered capital formation, since no productive assets were created thereby. Today the similar costs of company promotion would be excluded from this category by the statisticians. But conditions in 1750-1850 were different. These items bulked much larger: the pre-emptive rights and privileges granted to transport companies were then necessary costs, at least in the sense that they were part of the costs of upkeep of the political framework which made this kind of investment possible; a monetary price could be put on privileges thus obtained; and it would certainly be even less realistic to group this kind of expenditure either under current revenue or simply as waste. It has to be seen in eighteenth — rather than twentieth — century terms, and is logically not very different from the expenditure on the management costs, and even the profits, of capital goods producing firms today, which are included in the prices charged to the investing firms and therefore in the total of capital formation as classified by present day statisticians, though they appear equally to add nothing to concrete productive capital.

The third issue concerns the differences in treatment of the various sectors of the economy which the differences in sources and types of information are likely to impose. The range in the type and reliability of information available will be very large indeed. At one extreme, the best series will be found in such areas as canals, where we have the actual figures for well over half the expenditure on capital formation, divided into its main categories, year by year. Some other series, such as turnpikes, docks and some urban road networks will also be well represented, though the actual coverage will be less than half, and the possible errors in the grossing-up process correspondingly larger. Shipbuilding and all other series in which taxation returns are fairly reliable and exist in annual form will also form fairly reliable series: excise duties which permitted the construction of the brick index and the statistics of glass consumption for building, and import figures, for example, of soft woods, are well known in this regard. With some ingenuity, as was recently shown in deriving annual series of corn production [7], other official series of this kind may be found and used. At the other extreme are such sectors as investments in agricultural stocks (a very large item, alas) or increases in work in progress, for which any data will be scarce and yearly figures quite impossible to obtain. In between these extremes there will be the kind of information which is available on house building, on most manufacturing industries and mining and on parish road making. For the cotton industry, for example, we have Dr Chapman's pathbreaking use of the insurance policies of the two large London insurance companies, and these will also be used for other insured properties. There will, therefore, be some reliable information, but this will usually refer to either a tiny proportion of the expenditure, which will have to be grossed-up without much certainty as to how representative the sample is; or it will refer to a more representative sample, but cover only a few years. Fortunately, we do not set ourselves the even more daunting and theoretically even more doubtful task of evaluating the stock of capital at any one time.

Thus it is doubtful if we can ever get a year-by-year series for more than a few sectors, such as investment in means of transport. For the rest, we may get sufficient data for a few key years or groups of years. The rest will have to be extrapolated, or left. And here the danger (not entirely avoided in the preliminary study) is the neglect of the cyclical nature, and possibly the cyclical switch, of investment. If we find years, say, in which the use of bricks on house building is high, and others in which the use of bricks for factory or canal building is high, we may not be justified in taking both sets of figures as typical and adding them together. They may both have been true, but not as simultaneous phenomena, only as alternatives.

Next to the search for the total capital formation ratio, the Conference has shown that this should be our main task: to discover whether cyclical or yearly fluctuations in investment in the adequate series we possess already, reflect fluctuations in total investment, or internal switches within a total which stayed relatively constant. We might thus be able to offer a factual contribution to the discussion on the motivation and sources of investment, and on the degree to which it was a deliberate diversion of resources, or was determined by the total surplus available. We did not set out to answer questions of this kind, but merely to produce total and sectoral figures of quantities. The Conference has forcibly reminded us that even in the production of statistics the answers have no absolute validity, but depend to some extent on the questions originally asked.

NOTES

[1] Phyllis Deane and W. A. Cole, *British Economic Growth, 1688-1959*, pp. 260-4 (Cambridge Univ. Press, 2nd edition, 1967). See also Phyllis Deane, 'Capital formation in Britain before the railway age' *Economic Development and Cultural Change*, 9/3 (April 1961).

[2] Similarly low figures were also found for other early industrial revolutions. Cf. David S. Landes, *The Unbound Prometheus: Technological Change and Industrial Development in Western Europe from 1750 to the Present*, p.69 (Cambridge Univ. Press, 1969); Rondo Cameron, 'Some lessons of history for developing nations', *American Economic Review, Reports*, 57/2 (May 1967), pp. 313-16. Kuznet's figures for other countries are, however, considerably higher: 'Quantitative aspects of the economic growth of nations, VI: long-term trends in capital formation proportions', *Economic Development and Cultural Change*, 9/4 (July 1961), pp. 10-11.

[3] S. Pollard, 'The growth and distribution of capital in Great Britain c.1770-1870' in *Third International Conference of Economic History, Munich, 1965*, pp. 335-65 (Mouton, Paris, 1969).

[4] C. H. Feinstein, *National Income, Expenditure and Output of the United Kingdom, 1860-1960* (Cambridge, 1970).

[5] Central Statistical Office, *National Accounts Statistics, Sources and Methods* (1968).

[6] A. Fishlow, *American Railroads and the Transformation of the Ante-Bellum Economy* (Harvard, 1965).

[7] Susan Fairlie, 'The Corn Laws and British wheat production, 1829-76', *Econ. Hist. Rev.*, 22/1 (1969).

1

Modern Practices and Conventions in Measuring Capital Formation in the National Accounts

J. HIBBERT

This paper deals with capital formation in the context of the national accounts – that is, the accounts of national income and expenditure which are compiled by the Central Statistical Office and which are published in our annual Blue Book.

It may well be that the definitions which we adopt in the national accounts are not appropriate for some purposes, and wherever practicable what we attempt to do is to classify our statistics and provide supplementary data in such a way that they may be regrouped in order to meet particular users' requirements. In deciding how capital formation should be defined in the national accounts, however, it has to be borne in mind that the aim is to construct a consistent set of accounts for the whole economy, so that the definitions we adopt ought to be consistent with those adopted for other economic aggregates in the accounts.

Once we have agreed a satisfactory set of definitions, the next step is obviously to attempt to measure capital formation. We shall see that this presents both theoretical and practical problems, some of which may be very difficult or even impossible to resolve satisfactorily. I will deal with definitions of capital formation as briefly as possible and then turn to these problems of measurement which will probably be of rather more interest.

When we speak of capital formation, then, in general we mean the additions made during a particular period of time to the stock of goods which are for use in future production. These are both fixed assets, such as buildings, items of plant and so on, and work in progress, stocks of raw materials and finished goods. A distinction is usually made between gross fixed capital formation – that is, the addition of new fixed assets to the stock during the period – and net fixed capital formation which takes into account allowances for depreciation of the existing stock of fixed assets.

Capital formation, then, comprises fixed capital formation and increases in stocks and work in progress. These two categories of capital formation are separately distinguished in the published accounts and, as

11

we shall see, they give rise to different problems of measurement and estimation. Generally, in talking about fixed capital formation, I mean gross domestic fixed capital formation – that is, additions of new fixed assets without any allowance for depreciation to the stock of fixed assets which, apart from the exception I shall come to in a moment, lie within the boundaries of the United Kingdom. This is the meaning of the word 'domestic' in the definition. The exception arises in the case of ships and aircraft, which clearly cannot be regarded in quite the same way as other kinds of asset; these are treated as domestic when owned by United Kingdom residents, irrespective of where or by whom they are operated. Otherwise, however, ownership is not the criterion for determining whether or not an activity is termed domestic. With this one exception, the word 'domestic' is used to refer to activities which take place within the physical boundaries of the country, while 'national' is the word used to refer to activities within the ownership of a country's residents. This, of course, is the distinction in the national accounts between what we call 'domestic product' and 'national product'.

I described capital formation as additions to the stock of goods for use in future production. In principle, these additions should include alterations and improvements to fixed assets, but not the cost of repairs and maintenance, which are necessary simply in order to maintain an asset in normal working order. In practice it is usually possible to distinguish only between major improvements and other repairs, and the distinction rests mainly upon whether businesses capitalize their expenditure, or simply treat it as a current operating expense in their accounts. Not all countries adopt this approach to the measurement of fixed capital formation. Some treat repairs and maintenance expenditure as part of capital formation, an approach which does have the advantage of avoiding the difficulty of trying to distinguish between expenditure which adds to the normal life of an asset and that which simply enables a normal life to be fulfilled.

If we think of capital formation as a process of adding to a stock of assets which are to be used in some future period, it seems natural to ask why this stock of assets should be limited to goods of the kind already mentioned. Quite clearly increases in the stock of knowledge or the stock of skilled workers are factors which are available for use in future production. Such additions to the nation's wealth are not in fact treated as capital formation in the national accounts, but changes of this kind could not really be ignored when one came to consider a period of time as long as 100 years. So, presumably, the effects of such factors ought to be examined even if not as part of the study of capital formation defined in the narrower sense.

A further question which arises in considering our definition of capital formation is – where should the boundary of production be drawn? If we say that capital formation is the process of adding to a stock of physical assets which are for use in future production, it seems clear that we need to agree upon what we mean by production. Again, the definitions which we adopt in the national accounts are not necessarily those one would wish to use for all purposes of economic analysis. One example is the treatment of a consumer durable good which typically yields a service to its user over a number of the time periods for which we are constructing accounts. It would not be illogical to regard the purchase of a washing machine, for example, as fixed capital formation, in effect treating the service provided by the asset as output within the production boundary. If we follow this line of reasoning further, however, it becomes clear that we are likely to run into serious practical difficulties. If the washing machine is said to be providing a service which is to be regarded as part of production, so also is the person using it. How should the services of that person be valued both in theory and in practice? In situations of this kind, the general principle followed in the national accounts is to include within the production boundary first of all those goods and services which are actually exchanged for money and, secondly, those goods and services which, though not in fact exchanged for money, are of a kind which frequently are so exchanged. The most important example of this kind of imputation, as we call it, is that of owner-occupied houses. Here, it is supposed that the owner in effect lets the house to himself for a rent which may be estimated on the basis of actual rents paid for similar types of house, and it follows from this definition of the boundary of production that the construction of houses, whether for letting or for owner-occupation, is regarded as fixed capital formation. Likewise, since the use of a consumer durable good is not regarded as within the boundary of production, its purchase is not regarded as fixed capital formation, but as consumers' expenditure. So there is this very clear link between the definition of capital formation and the definition of the production boundary.

One final point which is probably worth mentioning while dealing with definitions is the treatment of work in progress – on goods with long periods of construction. This would include, for example, assets such as ships, power stations, or any type of work where it is customary to make progress payments as the work is carried out. The convention here is to regard the value of work done in any period on projects of this kind as fixed capital formation rather than an increase in work in progress. This has the advantage that the estimates of fixed capital formation approximate more closely in any period to the demands made on the economy by the production of fixed assets than if the value of such assets were included only on completion. Estimates compiled in this way, however, may not reflect changes in productive capacity so well as if fixed capital formation in such assets were measured at the time of their completion.

Having said something about the scope and definition of capital formation in the national accounts, I shall turn to problems of measurement. It is clear that, for most purposes, it is necessary to measure capital formation either in money terms or by means of some kind of index. It might be possible to measure additions to the stock of certain types of asset such as railway wagons or agricultural tractors in purely physical terms, but this is unlikely to get us very far when we actually wish to use such figures. Inevitably, we should want to aggregate capital formation in different types of asset, and would require some common unit of measurement. We usually measure fixed capital formation, at least in the first instance, in money terms by taking the value of expenditure on fixed assets, including virtually all the expenses associated with their acquisition; by this is meant expenses such as transport costs, installation costs and professional fees for architectural or legal services. We do make a distinction, however, between the expenses directly related to the acquisition of fixed assets − that is, those just mentioned − and expenses incurred in arranging the necessary finance, such as the costs of share issues and so on. These are not regarded as part of fixed capital formation, even though they might be capitalized by a business in its accounts.

There are really two methods in general use for measuring fixed capital formation. These are usually referred to as the expenditure method and the commodity flow method, and nowadays, in the national accounts of the United Kingdom, the expenditure method is mainly used.

The approach of the expenditure method is to use data from the records of those purchasing capital goods, and this has two main advantages. First of all, figures can be collected according to definitions, which are generally consistent with the definitions of other statistics for the national accounts derived from the same sources – for example, profits from business enterprises. Secondly, figures of expenditure collected in this way can far more readily be analysed by the purchasing industry and institutional sector than figures derived from the commodity flow method.

By the commodity flow method is meant estimates prepared from the supply side – that is, from statistics of production, exports and imports. This method has the advantage that a more detailed analysis is possible of the type of capital formation taking place – that is, of the different types of asset being installed by producers. But, of course, it suffers from the disadvantages not found in the expenditure method – the difficulties of classifying by type of purchaser and the possibility of inconsistency with other data collected from firms' accounting records. It also presents other problems because transport costs and trade mark-ups have to be estimated in the valuation process, and changes in stocks may need to be taken into account if we are starting with production data, or if the distribution network is fairly complex. Ideally, of course, what we should like to do would be to use both approaches, together with any other supplementary data that may be available, in order to compile a fully reconciled statement of all the various economic flows involved. To a limited extent this is what happens when we construct input-output tables, as we have done for 1963, which are published in the National Income Blue Book. But the approach there in practice has been rather to take the expenditure estimates as given and produce input-output tables consistent with those given totals, which is not really the same as attempting a full reconciliation. However, where this process throws doubt on the plausibility of the existing expenditure estimates this is followed by a reappraisal of those estimates.

These are the two main approaches then – aggregation of expenditure recorded by purchasers or the sum of goods and services provided by suppliers. There are, of course, other kinds of data which might be used, particularly in estimating specific categories of fixed capital formation – for example, statistics derived from administrative records of some kind, such as those for registration or licensing, although nowadays very little use is made of sources of this kind. In attempting to construct historical series, particularly series for some considerable time past, any data of this kind could be extremely valuable.

I should now perhaps say something about the measurement of net fixed capital formation, capital consumption and capital stock, before turning to capital formation in stocks and work-in-progress. We estimate net fixed capital formation by deducting from gross fixed capital formation estimates of capital consumption. A good deal has been written about the concept of capital consumption and its measurement, and it seems to be generally agreed that there is in fact no unique way of measuring it. Most businesses provide for depreciation in their accounts, of course, but there are two main reasons why these figures are unsuitable for measuring capital consumption in the national accounts.

First of all, in general, the depreciation charges made by businesses are based on the historical cost of fixed assets, whereas for the national accounts what we require is a measure of capital consumption which is in terms of the prices of the current accounting period, or at least in terms of a defined set of prices, which can be converted to the prices of a given accounting period. Secondly, as mentioned earlier, we have defined the boundary of production in such a way as to include the construction of assets such as dwellings for owner-occupation in fixed capital formation, and the owners of these assets do not maintain accounts or records in which depreciation is charged. For these reasons, therefore, we find it necessary to make special estimates of capital consumption which in general have been arrived at by first compiling estimates of capital stock, using the so-called perpetual inventory method and assuming that the pattern of utilization of assets is uniformly distributed over their assumed lives — that is, what accountants would refer to as straight-line depreciation.

It would not be particularly helpful to say any more about the estimation of capital stock and capital consumption at this point, but if it seems worthwhile later perhaps we could return to that in discussion.

We ought next to consider the problems which arise in measuring capital formation in stocks and work-in-progress. Some of these problems are of a rather special kind and arise from the fact that the commercial profits and losses measured by accountants include what in national accounting has been termed stock appreciation, which is not regarded as part of the national income.

Stock appreciation is that part of the change in book values of stocks which reflects a change in the level of prices rather than a change in the physical level of stocks, so when prices are rising, stock appreciation is positive and when they are falling, it is negative. Essentially what we are saying is that when goods are taken from stock and used in production, the amount which should be charged to the producer's operating account is the replacement cost of these goods. By contrast, what happens in normal commercial accounting is that the cost of maintaining intact the money value of stocks, rather than the physical quantity of stocks, is charged to operating account.

In order to compile estimates of capital formation in stocks which conform to national accounting concepts, therefore, we have to take commercial accounting data, because these are our only source, and adjust them so that they reflect changes in the physical quantity of stocks valued at the average prices of the period during which those changes occurred. For this purpose we need first of all to make assumptions about the methods of stock valuation which are used by businesses in compiling the figures which they provide. Secondly, we have to make assumptions about the period over which the stocks have been built up. Thirdly, we need to know something about the commodity composition of the stocks to which the data relate – that is, the relative importance of different types of commodities or products included in the stocks of a given type of business. Lastly, we need to have data on the changes in prices of those commodities and products which are known to be important elements in each category of stocks identified. On the first point (that is, the accounting basis of figures of book values of stocks which are to be adjusted) it is thought that the method of valuing stocks most commonly adopted in commercial accounting is that based on the so-called 'first-in, first-out' convention, which assumes that materials are used in the order of their acquisition, the stock at any particular point of time being thought of as that most recently acquired. This stock is then valued at cost or realizable value, whichever is the lower, so if prices are rising, stocks are assumed to have been valued by businesses at the average prices of the period over which those stocks have been built up – that is the second point about which we are required to make an assumption, the time profile, as it were, of the building up of stocks – and if prices are falling, stocks are assumed to have been valued by firms at the prices ruling at the end of the period in question. In order to express the change in stocks during a period at the average prices of that period, we take the level of stocks at the beginning and end of the period, express those stock levels in terms of the average prices ruling during the period – on the basis of our assumptions about the method of stock valuation used in compiling the basic data and the information on the commodity composition of the stocks and changes in the prices of these commodities – and the difference between the stock levels at the beginning and the end of the period (each of them valued at the average prices of that period) gives us the capital formation in stocks valued at the average prices of the period. The difference between the change in book values during the period and the physical change collected in this way is, of course, our estimate of stock appreciation. A short numerical example of a set of such calculations is given in Appendix 1.

This may seem rather a complicated approach to the problem. In fact, in our quarterly statistics the problems of measuring stock appreciation are very great indeed, partly because one is very often uncertain about the method of valuation used by businesses when they provide quarterly figures of stocks, and also because price information is perhaps often inadequate; this is certainly an area of some difficulty at the present time.

So far I have been dealing with the measurement of capital formation in money terms at the prices ruling during the period in which the capital formation has taken place. For many purposes, possibly for most purposes of economic analysis, it is more useful if capital formation can be measured in terms of a fixed set of prices. Although nowadays we have a considerable amount of price data available, collected mainly by the Board of Trade, the problems of estimating capital formation at constant prices are nevertheless quite formidable. It is worthwhile digressing from the principal theme at this point, in order to say something in general about estimates of constant prices. Many people, when they see a table of expenditure figures expressed at constant prices in a publication like the National Income Blue Book, figures which are carefully aggregated to form a total which is carried to some other table in which the arithmetic has been performed just as meticulously – and whatever criticism may be made of national accounts it must be admitted that the arithmetic is pretty good – being unsophisticated users of these estimates, may fail to recognize them for what they are. The estimates of constant prices are essentially index numbers, indicators which have all the limitations inherent in this particular type of statistic. It would perhaps be useful for non-statisticians to give a very simple, and admittedly highly artificial, example of the classic index number problem in is basic form. Details of the example are reproduced in Appendix 2.

The essence of the problem is that the relative prices of the goods and services we are trying to measure have changed and so we obtain different results when we base our constant price estimates on different sets of prices. Let us say that we are measuring two commodities – X1 and X2 – and that Q is their quantity and P is their price; it might be investment in these commodities, consumption or production of them that we are measuring. We are saying that during the period t_0 there are 500 units of X1 consumed at a price of 50, and 100 units of X2 at a price of 100, so that expenditure PQ on these two commodities is 25,000 and 10,000 – which is a total of 35,000. Now, during a later period of time, t_1, we look at these two commodities again, and we find that the first commodity has risen in price to 60 and, perhaps rather surprisingly, a very much smaller quantity is now being consumed – only 50 units, whereas the second commodity is now being consumed at a level of 600, mainly because its price has fallen to 50. This gives us expenditure totals of 3,000, 30,000 and 33,000.

Now, when we come to revalue these expenditure figures at constant prices, what happens? Let us first of all take the second period and revalue these quantities at the prices of the first period, so we are now saying t_1 at t_0 prices. We find that we have 50 units now priced at 50, which gives us 2,500, and we have 600 units priced at 100, which gives us 60,000 – a total of 62,500; so if we are measuring the so-called volume change in the consumption of these two commodities, the change in that volume between the first period and the second period, measured at the prices of the first period, has been from 35,000 to 62,500. But if we measure consumption at t_1 prices we get a very different sort of answer. We have 500 at prices of 60, which is 30,000, and we have 100 at 50, which is 5,000, 35,000 in total, and here what has happened is that in terms of the prices of the second period we find that there has in fact been a fall from 35,000 to 33,000. Well, clearly this can be an unsatisfactory state of affairs. There are methods of getting over this particular problem; one can use, for example, the average prices of the two periods as weights for measuring volume changes, but the illustration may help to show that estimates at constant prices sometimes have very severe limitations. Sometimes the statistician may be criticized and accused of double talk over things of this kind. Some years ago at the Board of Trade, when the estimates were rebased, some volume indicator, which on the old basis had risen over a particular period, fell over that period on the new basis. The administrators in the Board of Trade were really very confused by this because they did not understand the nature of the index number problem and they said, 'Well, surely the volume must either have risen or fallen, how could it have done both?' In fact the question demonstrated that they did not understand the nature of index numbers and the difficulties involved in their compilation.

Bearing in mind the nature of the estimates we can derive at constant prices, and having seen they can be subject to severe limitations, let us see what further problems arise when we set about compiling them. It might seem obvious that if we measure the physical change in stocks in the way described above, there would be no additional problems involved in expressing the change in each period in terms of a fixed set of prices, rather than the average prices ruling during the period in question. We would simply reprice the opening and closing stocks in terms of a fixed set of prices and the change in revalued stocks would provide an estimate of the physical change at constant prices. After all, the relevant information about prices is required for the basic calculation, so no additional information would be necessary.

Life, of course, is not nearly so simple as that. We have already seen that different results may be obtained depending upon which fixed set of prices is used. There is also a range of problems arising from quality changes in the goods or commodities which comprise the capital formation that we are measuring. I would include here the creation of entirely new products which may exist in one period but not in another. These problems arise when dealing with both changes in stocks and fixed capital formation at constant prices. In the case of fixed capital formation, there are further difficulties which arise from the variable nature of capital goods. These difficulties are particularly acute, for example, when attempting to revalue expenditure in building and construction work; the basic difficulty, of course, is that no two assets of this kind are precisely the same. The method of revaluation adopted in practice has been to construct indices of cost rather than attempt actually to measure changes in the prices of the capital assets constructed, and this involves making some assumption about changes in productivity which is clearly unsatisfactory when that measure of productivity ought itself to be based on the volume of building and construction work carried out – that is to say, its value measured at constant prices. So, clearly, this is theoretically unsatisfactory, but one has to resort to this in the absence of anything better. Of course, one might regard the special difficulties arising from the variable nature of capital goods simply as part of this general problem of measuring quality changes.

Discussion of the ways in which quality changes should be reflected in the methods of measuring economic aggregates seems to have flourished for quite a considerable number of years. What does seem to have emerged from this exchange of views is a recognition of the fact that different approaches are appropriate for different purposes. So if, for example, we are interested in the demands on resources made by the production of fixed capital assets, it is suggested that the revaluation of expenditure at constant prices requires the use of a cost index — it is information about changes in the cost of producing fixed assets which is required. On the other hand, if we wish our measure of additions to the capital stock to represent in some sense additions to the volume of future services to be provided by those capital assets, then it is argued that it is necessary to take into account the change in quality of those capital assets. If a new machine which is twice as efficient as an old machine can be produced with the same resources as were required to produce the old machine, the first approach would treat both machines as the same quantity of capital while the second approach would treat the new machine as double the quantity of capital represented by the old machine. However, this line of reasoning does not seem altogether satisfactory. What, after all, is meant by 'demands on resources'? Let us say that, instead of someone inventing a new machine twice as efficient as an old machine which can be produced with the same resources, a technological advance or a reorganization of the producing industry enables twice the number of old machines to be produced with the same resources. There has been no change in the quality of the machine produced, so both methods of measurement at constant prices will yield the same result — a doubling of the quantity of capital formation. But in what sense has the demand on resources doubled? In fact, the increased quantity of capital formation has been made possible by an increase in productivity. But then we are led back to reconsider my first example, and I think it becomes clear that what is really at issue is the point at which increases in productivity should be measured. If we count the new improved machine as double the quantity of capital represented by the old machine, we regard an increase in productivity as having occurred in the industry which produces those machines, rather than in the industry which uses those machines.

This is highly theoretical, of course, and when we come to carry out constant price calculations in practice it is rarely possible to do more than use the price changes of some reasonably representative basket of capital goods as an indicator for the prices of all capital goods included in capital formation. Nevertheless, it has been worthwhile to draw attention to some of these conceptual problems in order to emphasize the very real limitations of constant price estimates.

REFERENCE NOTE

Central Statistical Office, *National Accounts Statistics, Sources and Methods* (1968).

APPENDIX 1

Illustrative calculation of physical increase
in stocks from data on book values

	£
Book value end-September	1,000
„ „ end-December	1,600

Stocks assumed to be built up over 2 months

	index
Price indicator average August/September	127
„ „ end-September	126(a)
„ „ average October/	
November/December	132
„ „ average November/December	133(b)
, „ end-December	135

Value at end-September revalued at December quarter prices:—

$$1,000 \times \frac{132}{126} = 1,048 \quad £$$

Value at end-December revalued at December quarter prices:—

$$1,600 \times \frac{132}{133} = 1,588 \quad £$$

		£
Physical increase	= (1,588 − 1,048) =	540
Change in book value	= (1,600 − 1,000) =	600
Stock appreciation		60

(a) Assumed to underlie the end-September book value figure since it is lower than the August/September average

(b) Assumed to underlie the end-December book value figure since it is lower than the end-December price indicator.

23

APPENDIX 2

*Example of the possible effect of expressing data at
different sets of constant prices*

Time Period	Commodity	Quantity	Price	Value
t_0	X_1	500	50	25,000
	X_2	100	100	10,000
				35,000
t_1	X_1	50	60	3,000
	X_2	600	50	30,000
				33,000
t_1 values revalued at t_0 prices				
	X_1	50	50	2,500
	X_2	600	100	60,000
				62,500
t_0 values revalued at t_1 prices				
	X_1	500	60	30,000
	X_2	100	50	5,000
				35,000

Change from t_0 to t_1 at t_0 prices = (62,500 − 35,000)
$$= +27,500$$
Change from t_0 to t_1 at t_1 prices = (33,000 − 35,000)
$$= -2,000$$

DISCUSSION 1

Discussants: M. Barratt-Brown, S. A. Broadbridge, G. Clayton, P. Cotterell, R. Davis, M. Falkus, C. H. Feinstein, A. Harrison, J. Hibbert, J. P. P. Higgins, B. Hill, D. S. Landes, B. R. Mitchell, J. Odling-Smee, C. Phillips, S. Pollard, F. M. L. Thompson, J. Whitaker.

The discussion fell essentially into two parts. One part consisted of answers by Mr Hibbert to questions put to him regarding the practice and principles of current statistics of capital formation. These questions and answers covered three major themes. The other part consisted of a wide-ranging debate in which several members of the Conference participated actively.

The first question concerned the index number problem and the method of valuation in the current official statistics of capital formation of capital goods showing improved technical performance. In the national income series of the post-war years, the practice had been to start repeatedly from new bases, as in 1948, 1954 and 1963. It was agreed that this repeated forward shift of the base year would tend to produce a slower rate of growth than if there had been a single post-war series, weighted according to the distribution at its beginning. Yet there was no obvious alternative to the present unsatisfactory method: series 'at constant prices' of twenty years earlier would be obviously undesirable; whereas to dispense with actual figures in £ millions and substitute index numbers throughout, which might be conceptually more satisfying, would be confusing to the user particularly where series are broken up into their constituent parts, each in turn represented by an index number – e.g. in the series on consumers' total expenditure and expenditure on groups of commodities. There was also the practical point that the base of such an index, 100, should be ideally somewhere near the middle of a series; but in an evolving series it necessarily had to be at the beginning, leading to greater distortion at its end.

It was difficult to find out what the practice of the Board of Trade was in its series 'at constant prices' when there was a quality change of such items as machinery or vehicles between the beginning and the end of a period. The matter was even more complex when the piece of equipment became a different item altogether – e.g. a steam locomotive at the beginning being turned into a diesel unit at the end. It appears that if, over the period as a whole, a piece of capital equipment

25

which costs no more to produce, gradually improves its performance so that increased, say double, the output flows from it, the capital good is not up-valued on that account. Instead, it is recognized that an improvement has taken place earlier in the productive chain, namely in the capital good producing sector, so that there is, as it were, double the quantity of capital, but at the same value as before, in operation. It was not clear, however, how far this distinction was valid. Further, wherever possible, the normal method would be to value a series for steam locomotives separately over the whole span of years in which any of them were in operation, and do the same for diesels and for all other capital goods *separately*, and then average the costs of all such series to produce an index. But if there were no overlap period in which both were used simultaneously to allow the series to be spliced, and the change-over took place at a single point in time, one would have to value the two items arbitrarily one in terms of the other: x steam locomotives $= y$ diesel locomotives.

The second theme concerned some specific difficulties of definition and classification. The classification of durable consumer goods such as private cars (or before their time of bicycles) would appear to be straightforward and consistent: they are not treated as capital if mainly used for pleasure, and in consequence the flow of services derived from them is not treated as income, either. Yet both these decisions may be seriously misleading for a period in which cars or bicycles are being gradually substituted for public transport services which were covered both in their respective capital and income series. In such cases, or in the reverse change, which is likely to have occurred in the period of the present study, this factor will have to be borne in mind.

The question of the components of the capital stock at any one time was raised first in relation to information on the scrapping of capital equipment. The present practice here had been to assume that equipment was scrapped at a uniform rate over its official life span. However, as the capital stock estimates were being put on a computer, it might be possible, after special detailed enquiry, to make more realistic assumptions about scrapping, and thereby produce more sophisticated capital stock estimates. Meanwhile, the method of measuring work in progress was likely to overstate the capital stock in certain industries. In some cases, as in electricity, this might amount to an error of perhaps 5 to 10 per cent.

There was some uncertainty about the extent to which work on constructing capital equipment, done by farm labourers within their farm, was caught by the statistics. Such work as the erecting of a fence or the enlarging of a barn carried out by regular farmworkers as part of their duties, was likely to have been of greater significance in earlier centuries than today. Nowadays the dividing line was that created by official grant aid: work included in the farm implement scheme would find its way into the statistics whether undertaken by outside contractors or by the farm's own labourers, but not other work by the latter, which would slip through the meshes.

The third theme concerned the rate of capital consumption assumed in the statistics and the extent to which obsolescence was taken account of in the calculation of asset life. Formally, the statistics use the rates of depreciation allowed by the Inland Revenue, except in the case of the nationalized industries for which they are obtained direct. These rates are presumed to include such factors as obsolescence or losses by fire. They are likely to be over-estimates, though in the long run the errors would be offset to some extent, for if too small a proportion of the stock was taken as being consumed each year, the book value of the stock itself would gradually become larger than it should be, and the annual figure being composed of too low a fraction of too high a total might be approximately correct. However, this could mean that the capital stock estimates, as published, might be seriously wrong. Their original purpose had been to form the basis of the series of capital consumption, and for other purposes it might have been better to use other methods of estimation.

The general debate which followed these direct questions on contemporary practice attempted to relate the work of constructing a series for c.1750-1850 to the logic and experience of the construction of the post-war series. It centred, particularly, on the classification of items which were important in the earlier period, but for which no contemporary equivalent existed, or which were so unimportant as to have escaped formal treatment.

One obvious case was repair and maintenance of capital, which was a very large item in relation to capital formation when the latter was 5 to 6 per cent of GNP, but is much smaller now that capital formation is running at the rate of 20 to 21% of GNP. In the United Kingdom the present-day practice was clear: repair and maintenance was not normally included in gross capital formation, though the figures were available, and were sometimes added in to form what was known as 'gross gross' capital formation. Some countries, including the Scandinavian economies, did however include such items, largely for the practical reason that they used the commodity flow method to arrive at their national income estimates, though there may also be some conceptual justification. For the period 1750-1850, it was agreed that it was desirable to collect the figures as well, but to keep them separate from the standard category of gross capital formation.

There was less agreement on the other two main issues debated. Both these concerned classification of two not unrelated items: expenditure on raising finance itself and expenditure on what might broadly be called 'parliamentary costs'. Under this heading would be included the costs of obtaining private acts of Parliament including privileges of limited liability, compulsory purchasing powers over land, rights of way, and so on, indispensable for canal companies, river navigation and dock companies, turnpike trusts and railway companies. These costs might include an element of bribery at one extreme, and elements of surveying costs at the other. Both these types of expenditure, the costs of floating shares and of obtaining privileges, were relatively large items in 1750-1850, but had now so little significance in advanced countries that no clear-cut ruling regarding them can be found. It could be held, however, that they should be treated alike, since they are linked by the fact that parliamentary privileges also included the right to raise money on favourable terms, and that both kinds of expenditure may be subsumed under the heading professional fees.

At present, the costs of raising finance for a capital project would certainly not be included under capital formation, but this was largely for the practical reason that it is not included in the standard forms issued to businesses on which the national accounts are based. There were, however, also some conceptual objections. One was that the costs would vary greatly between industries and sectors and for some (e.g. nationalized industries enjoying Government backing) the cost would have to be artificially imputed. Secondly, it would be hard to separate out costs of flotation for the purpose of creating new assets from the costs of raising finance for other purposes. Thirdly, it would be difficult, in a large firm, to associate the costs of the flotation with particular concrete items of capital. All these objections would become the less valid the further we went back in time, since then the costs of raising capital would become more and more specific. It was in fact the practice of some nineteenth-century firms to treat these costs as capital by carrying them in their books for five or ten years, though this might well be because they did not want to burden the returns of any particular year with the expenditure, and the treatment was still different from normal capital assets which were written off year by year. Moreover, we could not be bound conceptually by the accounting practices of firms. Today, for example, the Airways Corporations treat training costs in their books as capital charges, and other nationalized industries also capitalize some of their initial charges, but all these were reclassified and treated as operating charges in the national income statistics.

The attempt to use capital/output ratios as a touch-stone on this issue brought little light: members on the whole held to their previous convictions. Some considered that such costs (as also parliamentary costs) should clearly in logic be excluded, whereas others felt that they represented necessary costs for railway or canal companies in the reality of the nineteenth century, if not of today, and should therefore figure as capital in capital/output ratios.

There was still less certainty on the question of promotional expenses for companies which never saw the light of day or collapsed within a few years of the boom that had created them. Should they be included among the necessary costs of capital? On the face of it, the arguments in favour were weaker still, for by analogy with surveying costs (in themselves, it was universally agreed, necessary costs of capital formation) for lines which were never built there was great doubt, and certainly today the costs of surveying for oil and gas would not be charged to capital, but be carried as operating expenses. In the eighteenth-nineteenth century context, however, costs of survey as of promotion were more specific to identifiable schemes; they were in total a socially necessary expense, and as they generally preceded incorporation, there were no operating costs that could be charged with these expenses. This tendency to count as capital formation in 1750-1850 certain items which would not be so classified today was to come extent offset by an opposite tendency in the case of much actual equipment built and other installations, e.g. mine sinkings, undertaken. These would clearly be reckoned as capital nowadays, and would normally be purchased from outside contractors; but in 1750-1850 they would frequently be produced by the firm's own staff of maintenance men and other workers, rather like the works of the farm labourers discussed above, and therefore be lost among the current operating costs.

There was a similar division of opinion on 'parliamentary' costs, though here the support for inclusion was much greater from the beginning. These expenses would include the costs of buying land, which were simply transfer payments; but they would also include payments to surveyors, lawyers and other professional men about Parliament, whose earnings must be accounted factor costs and who would presumably, if no parliamentary business had been in the offing, have been otherwise employed. They would also include, more doubtfully, payments that were in effect bribes to members of both Houses of Parliament, to landowners, to corporations, to rival companies or to others who might otherwise have blocked the progress of the private Bill.

From the point of view of the company concerned, these were, of course, necessary costs before it could begin operations, and were booked as such in its capital account. From the social point of view, the issue is less clear, and is more obscure in the case of some of these items than in others. Payments to Parliament might be held to be a tribute paid to the internal peace and security of society. There might be a parallel here to the building of a police barracks, which is counted as capital formation, for it creates assets from which a service is derived – the service of security in which production can proceed. Similarly, the sum total of payments to Parliament created an asset, the favourable social framework, from which the 'service' of security was derived. Some members would go further and note that compulsory purchase and bribery, by making land cheaper than it would have been in the open market and by excluding potential competition, might in fact have saved other capital costs and thus constituted a very worthwhile investment. In some present day developing countries, the substantial costs of bribery were in fact entered in firm's books as initial costs and written off *pro rata* over the life of the asset, and there was a powerful logic behind this. If it is contended that 'assets' of this kind are totally intangible, this expenditure still might be put on a par with, say, the management expenses of firms producing capital goods today, which are included under capital formation in the current national accounts and are, of course, ultimately paid for by the firms installing these capital goods.

A further argument in favour of including these costs was the real savings which occurred when, for example, a general Company Registration Act substantially reduced the actual costs of incorporation, and thereby of capital formation. Unless the costs were included in the first place, the savings in the costs of investment, which ought to appear in the historical series, would not show up.

Against this more liberal interpretation of what should constitute 'capital', the strongest plea on the other side was based on the evidence of the discussion itself, which had shown only too eloquently that the concept of capital was uncertain and fuzzy along the edges. It was therefore most desirable to limit it to concrete, identifiable assets and this was, in fact, the practice now in the forms sent to businesses. If anything beyond this was to be picked out, it should be accounted for in a separate category.

The compromise of a separate category appealed to many. It would include all those items of expenditure for which classification as capital or consumption was equally absurd. One category of 'intermediate' goods was suggested, but as this generally referred to unfinished goods in process of production, it was not necessarily the most apt description of what was required in cases like parliamentary or promotional costs. As it had been established that these costs, which loomed large in the earlier period, had not been properly considered by contemporary statisticians because of their present insignificance, it would be justifiable to ignore present practices and to classify them in accordance with their true role in 1750-1850 in the light of the findings of this project.

Another compromise solution proffered was to recognize the considerable changes in social structure and economic environment between the Industrial Revolution and today, and to look for logical equivalents rather than for identities. It was suggested, in particular, that two separate series might be developed, for the earlier century and for the later, with some kind of linkage between them. This would bring the differences into the open and was preferable to glossing them over by an assumption of perfect continuity.

In the end, presumably, the decision on classification would have to depend on the purpose to which the statistics would be put. If it was intended to discover how much the community was setting aside for the sake of later well-being, the costs of obtaining parliamentary acts would clearly have to be included. If, on the other hand, it was desired to find out how large the stock of capital was that was available for production, and how much was devoted to its increase, the more narrow definition would be more appropriate, and perhaps the difference enumerated and classified separately.

In such a clear-cut confrontation, the decision was relatively easy, but we could enumerate the possible purposes differently. For example we might offer the choice of either (1) establishing the burden on the economy, (2) discovering the distribution of investment among the economic sectors, or (3) being able to make comparisons with present day industrializing economies. In these cases, it might well follow that different definitions should be used for each, but it is not clear what the definition should be in each case.

No easy summary of conclusions is possible. Probing below the surface at a number of points had revealed that the differences in the social and economic framework between the period 1750-1850 and the mid-twentieth century were such as to make a direct use of modern experience and modern detailed classification impossible. If the two series were to have similar definitions and were to be comparable in any meaningful sense at all, the attempt would have to be made to fit them into the same general logic, even if it meant classifying individual items differently in these two periods.

2
The Compilation of Gross Domestic Fixed Capital Formation Statistics, 1856–1913[1]

C. H. FEINSTEIN

This paper provides a detailed description of estimates of gross domestic fixed capital formation in the period 1856-1913 [2]. The results are then compared with an alternative set of estimates. The basic procedure followed in making the estimates was to derive a benchmark for one year (1907), to allocate this to various components, and to extrapolate each component back to 1856 and forward to 1913.

The starting point for the estimates is the 1907 Census of Production [3], and this is the only year for which a reasonably comprehensive figure is available. Unfortunately, there is ample scope for disagreement in the derivation of a benchmark estimate from the Census. Differences arise partly from the absence of data on the extent of duplication in the returns by different trades, partly from the usual difficulties of demarcation between capital and consumer goods and between new assets and replacements, parts, etc., and partly from uncertainty as to the amount to include for items not covered by the census, such as distributive margins and transport or installation costs.

Three estimates of the value of work done in 1907 on the production of capital goods (less net exports) have been published, and there is also an unpublished estimate prepared at the Department of Applied Economics by Miss B. Mercer. The four estimates are compared in Table 1 and range from a low of £148 million to a high of £210 million. Of the four, the most detailed is that made by Cairncross in 1953 and, in my view, it is both the most reliable and the closest conceptually to the estimate required for this chapter. The comparison with other estimates, particularly Mercer's, suggests that it may be somewhat low, perhaps by some £10 million. However, rather than set yet another estimate marching round the world I have accepted Cairncross's figure of £150 million as the benchmark for 1907.

The estimate published with the Census Report by A. W. Flux was discussed by Cairncross [4]. Part of the discrepancy arises because Flux allowed £30 to 35 million for costs of transport, merchants' profits, etc., whereas Cairncross argues persuasively that about £5 million

33

would be adequate. With regard to the remaining discrepancy Cairn-cross observed: 'It would obviously be possible to accumulate the remaining £35 million from the census schedules. But the real difficulty is to know whether this would not be mere duplication' [5]. Since Flux provided no details of his estimate it is impossible to make any further investigation.

TABLE 1

*Comparison of estimates of domestic fixed capital
formation in 1907 (£ million)*

	Total work done			Repairs and maintenance			Domestic fixed capital formation		
	Build-ings and works	*Engin-eering etc.*	*Total*	*Build-ings and works*	*Engin-eering etc.*	*Total*	*Build-ings and works*	*Engin-eering etc.*	*Total*
1. Flux	–	–	342	–	–	132	–	–	210
2. Clark	149	102	251	62	41	103	87	61	148
3. Cairncross	150	125	275	72	53	125	78	72	150
4. Mercer	160	139	299	60	38	98	99	101	200

Sources:
1. *General Report on the 1907 Census* (1908), pp. 30-31. £13 million for naval shipbuilding and ordnance is excluded and the figures represent the mid-point of the range given by Flux.
2. Colin Clark, *Investment in Fixed Capital in Great Britain.* London and Cambridge Economic Service, Special Memorandum No. 38, 1934, as amended in *National Income and Outlay*, 1937, pp. 177-8. To obtain consistency with the other estimates I have transferred £23 million for work done on railways, telephones, etc., from engineering to buildings and works and have added back the £2 million which Clark deducted to exclude Southern Ireland.
3. A. K. Cairncross, *Home and Foreign Investment, 1870-1913*, pp. 120-3 (1953).
4. B. Mercer, *Gross Capital Formation, 1907*, p. 26 (mimeographed, 1964). The figures represent the mid-point of the range given by Miss Mercer.

The next estimate – Row 2 of Table 1 – was made by Colin Clark in 1934 and shows almost exactly the same result as Cairncross for the final total of new work, but there are important differences in the components. In particular, Clark's estimate for total work done on engineering, shipbuilding, etc., contains no allowance either for the tools, brass goods, office equipment and miscellaneous minor items included by Cairncross, or for the costs of transport, installation etc. Part of this omission is repair work, but the balance is reflected in a 15 per cent lower estimate of new work done on engineering, etc. However, this is largely offset by Clark's higher estimate for buildings and works: he arrived at the same estimate for total work done but classified a smaller amount as repairs and maintenance.

The substantially higher estimate − Row 4 of Table 1 − obtained by Mercer after a very thorough exploration of the Census data is due partly to the inclusion of a number of minor items (e.g. casks, pit props, tanks, ropes and cable) which Cairncross either did not treat as capital goods or assumed to be duplicated in the returns of other trades installing or working with these. However, the principal discrepancy is in the treatment of new work and repairs. Mercer considered firstly that a large proportion of the construction work returned as 'alterations and repairs' should be classified for national accounting purposes as new work, and secondly that: 'acceptance of the "accounting" definitions of repairs and new work for railways, highways, public utilities and shipbuilding . . . resulted in the assignment of what appears to be quite unreasonable proportions of total work to the repairs category' [6]. I would not endorse this conclusion, mainly because the use of the 'accounting conventions' is, in my view, both acceptable, and consistent with the estimates for the later periods [7]. Moreover, even if one wanted to adjust the figures there is no objective basis on which to do so, and Mercer's alternative estimates are, as she acknowledges, based on essentially arbitrary corrections and assumptions.

We may, therefore, accept Cairncross' figure of £150 million, with the reservation that it may be slightly on the low side. The next step is to allocate the total in such a way that the components can be related to the indicators for which annual series can be constructed. In the first instance a classification was used which related essentially to the type of asset. The annual series obtained on this basis was accepted as the basic estimate. Alternative estimates were then made [8] to provide a classification of this total by sector and, from 1882 onwards, by industry.

Cairncross provided a table showing the detailed break-down of his estimate of new work [9] and the present reclassification of this into thirteen categories is shown in Table 2. In some cases the 1907 value of the indicator was adjusted to equal the Census data; for others the Census estimate was adjusted to agree with the value shown by the annual series. In most cases, including all the major items such as ships or dwellings, there is a reasonably clear basis for this allocation of the Census data, but for some items the procedure is not entirely satisfactory [10]. However, the items involved are not large and any error introduced at this point (by the use of the 'wrong' indicator to extrapolate the base year value) is unlikely to be significant.

For two of the items shown in Table 2 – dwellings and ships – the 1907 data distinguish between completed units and the change in work in progress over the course of the year. The annual indicators relate only to the completed units, although, in principle, the

TABLE 2
Composition of gross domestic fixed
capital formation in 1907 (£ million)

Dwellings			
1a	Completed dwellings	30.0	
b	Change in work in progress	−2.0	
c	Total work done		28.0
Other new buildings and works			
2	Shops, warehouses, offices, factories, etc.	13.0	
3	Local authorities' capital expenditure*	19.8	
4	Railway way and works	7.3	
5	Docks, harbours, etc.	3.5	
6	Telegraph and telephone lines and works	2.8	
7	Other building and construction work	4.7	51.1
Ships			
8a	Completed ships	21.0	
b	Change in work in progress	−2.5	
			18.5
Vehicles			
9	Railway rolling stock	5.1	
10	Motor vehicles	2.5	7.6
Plant, machinery, etc.			
11	General engineering	24.4	
12	Electrical engineering	6.7	
13	Other items, fittings, installation etc.	13.7	44.8
			150.0

* Excluding docks, harbours, etc.; equipment for electricity supply undertakings and housing. This item includes some expenditure on plant, etc. (e.g. plant used by gas undertakings) but is predominantly buildings (schools, hospitals, etc.) and works (sewerage, roads, etc.).
Source: See text and Cairncross, op. cit., p. 123.

change in work in progress on fixed assets should be treated as part of fixed capital formation. Since no appropriate indicator is available for this I have assumed that it was zero in all years other than 1907. This means that the aggregate series for fixed capital formation is, to this extent, slightly overstated in years (other than 1907) when there was a fall in work in progress, and slightly understated in years when work in progress was rising.

ESTIMATES AT CURRENT PRICES

Dwellings

The 1907 benchmark for completed dwellings is extrapolated by the product of three series. The first is an index of the number of houses built in each year [11]. This is based on house-building in a wide sample of towns and conurbations, but does not cover rural areas [12] or Ireland. The second is an 'index of size and complexity' designed to allow for the increase over time in the size and standard of houses built. It rises by one per cent per annum from 1855 to 1889; and then in order to allow, very roughly, for the effect of the new building regulations introduced in 1890 – by 5 per cent in 1890 and by 2 per cent per annum from there until the end of the building boom at the turn of the century. The rate of increase then drops to 1½ per cent per annum until 1913, and is zero during the war years. The third element is the index of the costs of house-building (labour and materials), compiled by Dr Maywald [13].

Shops, warehouses, offices, factories, etc.

A very approximate indication of the value of non-residential building can be derived from the Inhabited House Duty statistics published in the *Annual Reports of the Commissioners of Inland Revenue*. The significant relevant categories are Residential Shops, and Premises not used as Dwellings. Both numbers and gross annual values are given, and the latter were used because of the wide disparity between the individual units. The annual increase in the gross annual value was roughly corrected for the effect of the periodic re-assessments (working separately with the figures for the Metropolis, the rest of England and Wales, and Scotland), for certain changes in the operation of the Act and for known irregularities in the official statistics. A very rough correction for the fact that the series was obtained from annual values was then made by deflating the adjusted increments by an index of rents given by Cairncross [14]. The resulting estimate of the annual volume of non-residential building was multiplied by Maywald's index of building costs and used to extrapolate the 1907 base-year value of £13 million [15].

The necessary Inhabited House Duty statistics only begin in 1874-5. For 1856-74 non-residential building was assumed to be the same proportion of residential building as it was, on average, from 1875 to 1884.

Local authority capital expenditure

As a reasonable proxy for actual capital expenditure we follow Cairncross in using the local authority expenditure out of loans or, for years before that is available in the *Annual Local Taxation Returns*, receipts from loans. Cairncross's figures are not adjusted to calendar years and cover the period 1870-1914 [16]. The series is easily extended to 1919 by reference to the *Statistical Abstracts*, but it is more difficult to obtain estimates for the period 1856-69. For 1867-8 there is an estimate of receipts from loans of £6 million made for Goschen's *Report on Local Taxation*. For other years most of the components of this total cannot be traced, and the estimate for this period is extremely rough. It is based on such returns as are available, scaled up roughly in proportion to the amounts shown in 1867-8.

This total was then reduced by the estimated loan expenditure on housing, docks, harbour and canals, and on equipment, etc., for electricity supply undertakings [17].

Railway way and works

This series is based on Mitchell's [18] compilation of capital expenditure as shown by the accounts of a large sample of railway companies grossed-up on the basis of data on paid-up capital available for all companies in the *Railway Returns*.

Docks, harbours, etc.

I am grateful for Dr Mitchell for making available his unpublished series for this item. It covers capital (or loan) expenditure as shown in the accounts of the railway companies, local authorities and other port and harbour authorities.

Telegraph and telephone lines and works

Annual estimates for telegraphs and telephones (excluding buildings) were built up from data on public and private capital expenditure. For the Central Government the annual expenditure on extension of telegraphs and telephones and on erection of buildings from 1875-6, and the separate expenditure on telephones under the Telegraph Acts 1892-1907 from 1892-3, is assembled up to 1905-6 in an official return, [19] and from 1906-7 the expenditure on construction of telephones (trunk lines and exchanges) and telegraphs is available annually in the *Post Office Accounts* [20] . For the private sector the estimate covers the capital expenditure of the National Telephone Company prior to its take-over by the Post Office in January 1912. From 1885 to 1904 this was taken as equal to the annual increase in the capital of the Company, [21] and for 1905-11 an estimate of expenditure on exchanges and lines was derived from the summarized accounts in *Garcke's Manual of Electrical Undertakings.*

The cumulated total of the final series for the period 1880-1919 is £49 million and this agrees reasonably well with the £47 million for the value of plant at prime cost as shown in the *Post Office Accounts* at 31 March 1920.

Other building and construction work

This series covers several items, including churches, central government building by the civil and revenue services (including the Post Office) and building and construction work for private tramway, gas, electricity and water supply companies [22] . In the absence of a suitable indicator it was assumed to be a constant proportion of total work done other than on this item and the corresponding item for plant, etc.

Merchant ships

This series is calculated separately for steam and sailing vessels and relates to completed units only. Naval vessels are not included. For the steamers the estimate is the product of the net tonnage built in the United Kingdom for home owners [23] and Maywald's [24] estimates of the cost (in £s) per gross registered ton (multipled by a factor of 1.64 to convert to cost per net ton) [25] . For sailing vessels the annual net tonnage built is valued at Maywald's estimate of the average cost per gross registered ton of 'hulls only' [26] . Unlike the cost indices used for dwellings and machinery Maywald's estimates of shipbuilding costs incorporate an ingenious allowance for the effect of improvements in shipbuilding design and construction, including changes in the materials used to build a unit of registered tonnage [27] . The estimate does not make any allowance for the purchase of second-hand ships from abroad, or any deduction for the proceeds from sales to foreign owners.

General engineeering

This is basically the same as the series which Cairncross devised, and of which he said: 'I had to manufacture an index of output without any figures of machinery produced and an index of machinery prices without any price quotations' [28]. Given the importance of this item it is undoubtedly the weakest link in the pre-1914 estimates of capital formation, but it does not seem possible to obtain a more reliable annual series.

I have followed essentially the same procedure as Cairncross, but have extended the series to cover the period 1856-1919 and have made some minor adjustments, notably the exclusion of iron and steel used by the railway companies (based on information kindly supplied by Dr Mitchell) [29]. The first stage of the procedure is the calculation of the iron and steel available for the production of machinery:

U.K. Production of pig iron
Less Net exports of pig iron
Plus Change in stocks
= Home consumption of pig iron
Less consumption of pig in steel
Plus output of steel ingots
= Home consumption of iron and steel
Less Net exports of iron and steel*
      Iron and steel used for shipbuilding and railways*
= Iron and steel available for machinery*

This series is then multiplied firstly by a 'price index' and secondly by a notional index designed to allow for the increasing complexity and value of a 'ton of machinery'. The price index is constructed by taking a five year moving average of indices of iron and steel prices (average value per ton of iron and steel exports) and of wages in engineering and shipbuilding [30], combined with equal weights; and the 'index of complexity' is arbitrarily assumed to have risen by one percentage point per annum. The product of the three series is then used to extrapolate Cairncross's 1907 figure for the value of machinery produced in the United Kingdom (£50 million). Finally, the net exports of machinery (reduced by 6 per cent to exclude costs of transport and handling) are deducted and the residual is taken as the estimate of the ex-works value of 'machinery' retained for home consumption.

Electrical engineering

This series covers electrical plant and equipment (including transmission cables) purchased by public electricity supply undertakings and also by railways and private concerns generating their own electricity. It is derived by a rather indirect procedure. Firstly, an estimate was made of the accumulated capital expenditure on plant and equipment by public supply undertakings at the end of each year from 1891 to 1919 [31]. Next, the accumulated expenditure on plant and equipment (distinguishing between generation and distribution) were calculated on the assumption that they were a constant proportion of the total (36 per cent and 44 per cent respectively), equal to the ratios shown by the breakdown of the accumulated expenditure at March 1922, given in the *First Report of the Electricity Commissioner*.

Accumulated expenditure on the private supply of electricity was then estimated as a proportion of the expenditure on plant and equipment for generation by the public undertakings. The proportion used was based on the ratio of the generating capacity of industries and other private suppliers to that owned by the public supply undertakings in 1907, 1912 and 1920-4 [32]. The ratio was assumed to have been the same as in 1907 (71 per cent) from 1899-1906 and to have risen to this proportion from a conjectural 50 per cent in 1891-5. The rise to 88 per cent in 1912 was spread evenly over the years 1908-12, and the ratio was then assumed to be broadly stable to 1920 (thereafter it fell rapidly with the expansion of the public supply system, dropping to 57 per cent by 1924).

The accumulated capital expenditure on the public, private and railway electricity supply were then aggregated and the required estimates were obtained from the first difference in this series. The estimate obtained by this procedure for 1907 was £6.7 million and this was substituted for the £6.5 million suggested by Cairncross on the basis of the Census data [33].

Railway rolling stock

The estimates for this item were compiled from the accounts of the railway companies by Mitchell [34]. They include expenditure on renewals.

Motor vehicles

Cairncross suggests that the output of commercial motor vehicles was probably negligible in 1907 and that the motor trade was 'engaged almost exclusively in the production of consumers' durable goods' [35]. However, analysis of the Census date for 1907 and 1912 [36] on production and net imports of cars and motor bodies, together with Prest's estimates for consumers' expenditure on cars [37], indicates that some £2.5 million should be allowed in 1907 and £3.0 million in 1912 for capital expenditure on motor vehicles. Rough estimates for other years from 1900 to 1919 were made by interpolating on the basis of a series obtained by taking the estimated production of cars and commercial vehicles, [38] adding net imports of complete cars and chassis and deducting consumers' expenditure [39]. For 1914-18 a further amount was deducted to cover military purchases of vehicles.

Other items, fittings, installation, etc.

This is a final rag-bag. It covers certain miscellaneous items (tools and implements, colliery wagons, office equipment, brass goods, etc.); the plant installed by gas and water company undertakings; the allowance for costs of distribution, transport and installation of machinery and equipment; and new work undertaken by manufacturers on their own plant. In the nature of the series no suitable annual estimate is available for most of these components, but it seems reasonable to assume that it is a constant proportion of all other capital expenditure.

CLASSIFICATION BY INDUSTRY

From 1882-3 the *Annual Local Taxation Returns* provide a classification of local authority loan expenditure in England and Wales and it becomes possible to go a reasonable way towards a classification by industry, although not to distinguish separately the major private sectors (agriculture, mining, manufacturing, distribution, etc.).

It is easiest to take first the estimate for Transport and Communication. This is based on six series. For four of these – railways, ships, docks, harbours, etc., and the post office – the estimates are those previously described. For roads the estimate is the local authority loan expenditure on highways and bridges and private street works plus the outlays by the Road Fund from 1911. For road goods and passenger transport the previous estimate for motor vehicles is added to local authority loan expenditure on transport services and an estimate for capital expenditure by private tramway and light industry companies [40].

The estimate for electricity combines the 20 per cent of local authority loan expenditure allowed for buildings (p.|38 above) plus the estimate for electrical engineering. The series thus covers local authority and company supply undertakings and also the electrical equipment of industries generating their own electricity.

For gas and water supply undertakings the local authority loan expenditure on these services was combined with special estimates made for company undertakings. In the case of gas companies the estimate was based on the increase in the paid-up share and loan capital of the companies [41] (adjusted for obvious instances of nominal additions to the capital in 1896 and 1899). For the water companies the annual capital expenditure by the Metropolitan companies prior to the formation of the Metropolitan Water Board is readily available in Parliamentary returns. [42] For 1907-14 the overall ratio of company to local authority water supplies was about 20 per cent; [43] capital outlays by the non-Metropolitan companies were assumed to be 20 per cent of local authority plus Metropolitan company capital expenditure from 1882-1902 and 20 per cent of local authority expenditure (including the M.W.B.) from 1903-19.

The series for capital expenditure on social and public services is the local authority loan expenditure less the outlays on housing, roads and trading services, plus the central government estimate for buildings (other than the post office); the series for dwellings is the one already described. The final industry group covers industrial and commercial capital, agriculture, mining, etc. It is obtained by aggregating the original estimates for factories, shops, etc., general engineering, 'other building and construction work' and 'other items, fittings, installations, etc.', and deducting the estimates for the capital expenditure by companies on buildings and plant for tramways, gas and water and by the central government on buildings. It is unfortunate that it is not possible to subdivide this large residual more finely and give, for example, a separate series for manufacturing investment, but with the data at present available there is no reliable basis for this.

ESTIMATES AT CONSTANT PRICES

To obtain estimates at constant (1900) prices, the current price series are deflated by the following indices: for buildings and other construction work the two indices compiled by Maywald [44]; for

general and electrical engineering the index described on p. 40 above;
for ships an unweighted average on indices of the cost of ship plates and
of shipbuilding wages; [45] and for railway rolling stock an unpublished
index constructed by Mitchell [46]. Finally, the two miscellaneous items
are again moved proportionately to all other capital expenditure. The
same indices were used in appropriate combinations for the classification by industry.

COMPARISON WITH OTHER ESTIMATES

There are several estimates with which comparison might be made. Two
of these, by Cairncross [47] and Jefferys and Walters [48], were made
broadly by the same procedure but the present estimates make use of a
more comprehensive range of annual series for extrapolation of the 1907
benchmark, and also have the advantage of improved information on
such aspects as houses built, building prices and ship construction costs.

A more recent, and rather different, estimate is given by Miss Phyllis
Deane [49]. This series completely by-passes the 1907 Census and
instead builds up annual estimates for 1830-1914 from numerous series
for separate categories of capital formation. The resulting estimate of
total gross domestic fixed capital formation is compared with the
present estimate in Table 3 (at 1900 prices) for the common period
1856-1913.

In the decade 1856-64 Deane's series is first above and then below
the present estimate, but the difference is moderate in absolute terms
and the two agree in the mid-1860s. They then move apart, with the
present estimate showing a far more substantial boom in the 1870s, and
at the common peak in 1876 the difference is £30 million (25 per cent
of the higher estimate). Both series again agree on the timing of the
next peak, in 1883, but differ over its scale. The present estimate puts this
peak well below that of 1876, whereas Deane's estimate shows this
boom as the stronger of the two.

The two series again come together briefly at the end of the 1880s,
but from there on the present estimate rises very much more strongly in
the boom of the 1890s, and at the peak in 1902-3 is almost £60 million
(26 per cent) higher. It remains at a markedly higher level until the end
of the period, although the gap narrows slightly in 1911-12.

The discrepancy is actually larger than is suggested by Table 3 since
Deane includes in capital formation the expenditure on new works and
buildings by the navy, army and ordnance departments, as well as new

naval construction of ships and dockyards [50]. The present study follows the standard conventions and classifies these outlays as public authorities' current expenditure [51]. The main item ınvolved is naval shipbuilding; the navy was spending some £2 to £3 million per annum on new ships in the 1870s and 1880s, and then expanded the building programme very rapidly in the 1890s to reach an average of about £9 million per annum after 1900, rising to £13 million in the years immediately before World War I.

TABLE 3

*Comparison with Deane's estimates of total gross domestic
fixed capital formation at 1900 prices, 1856-1913 (£ million)*

	Deane (1)	Present estimate (2)	Discrepancy* (1) as % of (2) (3)		Deane (1)	Present estimate (2)	Discrepancy* (1) as % of (2) (3)
1856	46	41	112	1885	84	91	92
1857	43	37	116	1886	76	83	92
1858	45	38	118	1887	81	83	98
1859	46	42	110	1888	88	88	100
1860	48	44	109	1889	94	97	97
1861	51	53	96	1890	95	99	96
1862	52	57	91	1891	98	109	90
1863	63	69	91	1892	103	114	90
1864	67	80	84	1893	98	113	87
1865	83	84	99	1894	104	120	87
1866	74	75	99	1895	115	121	95
1867	69	66	105	1896	116	137	85
1868	71	65	109	1897	124	157	79
1869	71	63	113	1898	143	181	79
1870	78	66	118	1899	146	197	74
1871	76	81	94	1900	147	199	74
1872	71	83	86	1901	157	207	76
1873	71	79	90	1902	162	217	75
1874	83	94	88	1903	159	222	72
1875	89	109	82	1904	159	210	76
1876	92	122	75	1905	157	202	78
1877	91	120	76	1906	148	194	76
1878	87	114	76	1907	137	162	85
1879	80	98	82	1908	110	142	77
1880	77	99	78	1909	117	146	80
1881	87	98	89	1910	115	148	78
1882	92	99	93	1911	128	141	91
1883	97	107	91	1912	122	138	88
1884	93	103	90	1913	130	157	83

* Column (1) includes, and column (2) excludes, expenditure on new construction of ships, buildings and works for the army and navy.

If we take the estimates (at current prices) for 1907 we find that Deane's estimate, adjusted to a comparable basis, is some £27 million (18 per cent) below the present benchmark of £15 million [52]. In the light of the earlier finding that the estimate for 1907 is, if anything, too low, there would seem to be little reason to substitute an even lower figure.

In order to make a more complete assessment of the two estimates, it is necessary to examine their principal components. Because of the differences in methods of estimation, it is not possible to group the components on a precisely comparable basis, but from 1882 onwards – where the present estimates can be classified by industry – it is possible to distinguish seven broadly comparable categories [53]. The estimates are shown in this form in Table 4 and for the sake of brevity are given as annual averages for four or five year periods.

Of the seven categories, the estimates for four agree reasonably well, but there is one item for which the present estimate is substantially higher and two for which it is much lower. Agreement is best in the case of the estimates grouped together under the heading of transport and communication: railways, roads, ships, docks and harbours, tramways, motor vehicles and post office. This largely reflects the fact that for these series both estimates use essentially the same sources and methods – although there are minor differences arising, for example, in the treatment of renewals of the permanent way or the estimates for roads and bridges.

For *Gas, electricity and water* and for *Other social capital* there is a fair measure of agreement, though Deane's estimates are consistently lower. In the case of *Gas, electricity and water* this is partly explained by the inclusion in the present estimate of capital expenditure on privately owned electrical generating equipment; if this were transferred to *Industrial capital, etc.* it would reduce the discrepancy on electricity at the cost of an increased discrepancy on industrial and commercial capital. The disagreement on *Other social capital* is almost entirely accounted for by the fact that Deane's estimate omits certain categories of local authority capital expenditure which are individually minor but which in total account for capital expenditure of several millions each year [54].

The final item on which the two estimates agree moderately well is *Dwellings*. The comparison can be taken back to 1856 and shows very close agreement (generally within £1 million) until 1891. From there onwards the present estimate is consistently higher and the difference

TABLE 4

*Comparison with Deane's estimate of gross domestic fixed capital
formation, at 1900 prices, by industry, 1882-1913 (£ million; annual average)*

	1882 -85	1886 -90	1891 -95	1896 -1900	1901 -05	1906 -10	1911 -13
1.Transport and communication (a)							
Deane	41.5	33.0	39.2	46.6	57.8	42.6	47.0
Present estimate	40.2	33.2	37.8	45.8	60.6	45.0	43.3
Discrepancy	1.3	−0.2	1.4	0.8	−2.8	−2.4	3.7
2. Gas, electricity and water (b)							
Deane	3.8	3.6	6.2	10.6	14.4	7.2	7.7
Present estimate	4.3	5.0	6.8	12.8	18.6	11.8	8.0
Discrepancy	−0.5	−1.4	−0.6	−2.2	−4.2	−4.6	−0.3
3. Dwellings							
Deane	18.3	17.2	19.4	31.4	32.2	24.0	15.0
Present estimate	17.5	16.8	20.6	35.8	38.2	30.0	18.7
Discrepancy	0.8	0.4	−1.2	−4.4	−6.0	−6.0	−3.7
4. Other social capital							
Deane	6.0	5.8	8.4	10.8	12.6	10.2	9.3
Present estimate	7.2	6.4	11.2	13.0	16.8	12.6	11.7
Discrepancy	−1.2	−0.6	−2.8	−2.2	−4.2	−2.4	−2.4
5. Industrial and commercial capital, etc. (c)							
Deane	14.0	16.8	17.2	18.4	20.6	24.2	23.3
Present estimate	30.2	28.0	38.4	66.2	76.6	59.0	62.7
Discrepancy	−16.2	−11.2	−21.2	−47.8	−56.0	−34.8	−39.4
6. Administration and defence (d)							
Deane	3.8	4.8	7.4	12.2	16.8	14.4	23.3
Present estimate	0.5	0.6	0.6	0.6	0.8	1.0	1.0
Discrepancy	3.3	4.2	6.8	11.6	16.0	13.4	22.3
of which							
Naval shipbuilding	2.4	3.5	4.6	7.1	9.9	9.4	13.3
7. Horse transport (e)							
Deane	4.5	5.8	5.6	5.6	4.6	3.2	1.3
8. TOTAL							
Deane	91.9	87.0	103.4	135.6	159.0	125.8	127.0
Present estimate	100.0	90.0	115.4	174.2	211.6	158.4	145.3
Discrepancy	−8.1	−3.0	−12.0	−38.6	−52.6	−32.6	−18.3

(a) Covers railways, ships, docks, harbours and canals, roads and bridges, tramways, motor vehicles and post office telegraphs and telephones. Horse transport is not included.
(b) The present estimate includes the equipment of industries generating a private supply of electricity.
(c) Covers industry, mining, agriculture, distribution and other services.
(d) The present estimate excludes defence.
(e) Deane's estimate covers horses and carriages, wagons, etc. Horses are omitted from the present estimate but a small allowance for horse-drawn vehicles is included in the estimate of industrial and commercial capital.

averages some £5 million (16 per cent) over the period 1890-1913. There are several factors which could account for this, but it seems that the primary one is the lower average cost per house used by Deane: £215 circa 1900 compared with the figure of some £250 implicit in the present method of estimation [55]. It is easy to find widely varying statements about the cost of new houses and difficult to be certain about their precise content and the extent to which they are representative. The present estimate has its basis in the data collected for the 1907 Census of Production [56]; it is unlikely that the Census would yield an overestimate of new building work — the opposite is far more likely in a trade in which small firms predominate. For these reasons I am not disposed to alter the present estimates for dwellings but recognize the margin of uncertainty attaching to them.

Moreover, if the Census total is accepted, but the allocation between types of building altered in the direction of a lower figure for dwellings, this would mean a higher figure for other building work and so widen still further the discrepancy in the estimates for industrial and commercial capital.

As can be seen from Row 5 of Table 4 the disagreement on this important sector, covering industry, commerce, mining and agriculture, is already very great: over the whole period 1882-1913 Deane's estimate averages only 37 per cent of the level of the present estimate, with annual averages of £19 million and £51 million respectively; over the boom years 1896-1905 it falls to as little as 27 per cent (£20 million and £71 million). The present estimate is derived principally from the series for non-residential building, general engineering and 'other plant, fittings, installations, etc.', all of which are very far from ideal. Nevertheless, I would judge the aggregate to be substantially more reliable than the alternative estimates which, as Deane notes, are 'somewhat impressionistic' and 'give only a very rough overall indication of the levels and trends in industrial capital expenditure' [57]. It seems clear that the errors of omission which Deane anticipated are, in fact, very considerable; the series loses almost all trace of the great upsurge in industrial capital formation in the 1890s, a boom well substantiated from other sources [58].

On each of the components so far considered the present estimate is the higher of the two and the combined discrepancy is thus very large. It is, however, partly offset by the two remaining items. One of these, *Administration and defence,* involves a difference in treatment of defence expenditure. Deane's estimate also includes new works and buildings by the Post Office; in the present estimates these are included in *Transport and Communication*. The other is the estimate for *Horse transport*. The present estimate omits the horses, and the coverage of carriages, wagons, etc., is very poor [59], whereas Deane covers both horses and vehicles. The amount which she has provided for this – an average of some £5 million per year until the last few years before the war – seems very high [60] but it is not an easy item to estimate accurately.

To sum up: the general conclusion which might be drawn from this detailed examination is that the present estimates are defective in certain respects, but almost certainly give a more accurate picture of the trends and cycles in gross domestic fixed capital formation, of its overall level and of its composition by industry.

The final results are set out in Table 5 in the form of estimates at constant (1900) prices classified by type of asset. Corresponding estimates at current prices, and estimates classified by industry and sector, as well as estimates of net fixed capital formation are given in the study referred to in note [1].

TABLE 5

*Gross domestic fixed capital formation at constant (1900) prices
by type of asset, 1856–1913 (£ million)*

	Ships (1)	Vehicles etc. (2)	Plant and machinery (3)	Dwellings (4)	Other new buildings and works (5)	Total (6)
1856	4	2	12	6	17	41
1857	4	2	8	6	17	37
1858	4	2	8	6	18	38
1859	3	2	10	7	20	42
1860	4	2	11	7	20	44
1861	5	3	14	7	24	53
1862	5	3	13	9	27	57
1863	8	3	17	10	31	69
1864	10	4	22	11	33	80
1865	10	5	21	10	38	84
1866	8	5	17	10	35	75
1867	6	4	15	12	29	66
1868	6	3	17	13	26	65
1869	8	2	14	14	25	63
1870	9	3	14	16	24	66
1871	10	4	24	16	27	81
1872	11	4	21	17	30	83
1873	10	4	19	16	30	79
1874	14	5	17	19	39	94

TABLE 5 (continued)

	Ships (1)	Vehicles etc. (2)	Plant and machinery (3)	Dwellings (4)	Other new buildings and works (5)	Total (6)
1875	9	5	25	24	46	109
1876	8	4	30	27	53	122
1877	11	4	29	26	50	120
1878	12	3	26	22	51	114
1879	10	3	20	18	47	98
1880	12	3	25	18	41	99
1881	14	4	24	18	38	98
1882	19	4	20	17	39	99
1883	22	6	20	18	41	107
1884	13	5	22	18	45	103
1885	9	5	20	17	40	91
1886	9	3	20	16	35	83
1887	10	3	19	17	34	83
1888	15	4	21	17	31	88
1889	20	4	24	17	32	97
1890	19	5	22	17	36	99
1891	17	7	23	17	45	109
1892	17	6	27	19	45	114
1893	13	5	25	22	48	113
1894	15	4	31	22	48	120
1895	13	4	32	23	49	121
1896	13	5	38	28	53	137
1897	12	6	46	33	60	157
1898	18	6	46	40	71	181
1899	20	8	57	40	72	197
1900	20	8	56	38	77	199
1901	21	8	55	37	86	207
1902	21	8	58	40	90	217
1903	17	7	64	41	93	222
1904	21	7	59	38	85	210
1905	26	8	57	35	76	202
1906	27	8	54	34	71	194
1907	22	8	46	32	59	162*
1908	12	7	41	29	53	142
1909	14	7	50	29	46	146
1910	17	6	49	26	50	148
1911	19	7	45	22	48	141
1912	21	8	40	18	51	138
1913	24	9	53	16	55	157

*The total is adjusted for the fall in work in progress on ships and dwellings.

NOTES

[1] This is a modified version of Ch. 9 in C. H. Feinstein, *National Expenditure and Output of the United Kingdom, 1860-1960* (Cambridge, 1970).

[2] There is a revised version of the estimates given in 'Income and investment in the United Kingdom, 1856-1914', *Economic Journal*, LXXI, 1961.

[3] *Final Report on the First Census of Production of the United Kingdom (1907)*, Cd. 6320, 1912.

[4] Op. cit., pp. 103-6, 120-2.

[5] Op. cit., p. 121.

[6] Op. cit., p. 1.

[7] See, e.g., C.S.O., *National Accounts Statistics, Sources and Methods*, p. 362 (1968).

[8] See pp. 37-43 below.

[9] Op. cit, p. 123.

[10] In particular, there are problems in reconciling the Census returns with the accounting data for expenditure out of loans by local authorities and capital expenditure by railway companies.

[11] J. Parry Lewis, 'Indices of housebuilding in the Manchester conurbation, South Wales and Great Britain, 1851-1913', *Scottish Journal of Political Economy*, VIII, 1961, pp. 151-2. The index is reproduced by Parry Lewis in *Building Cycles and Britain's Growth*, pp.316-17 (1965).

[12] See B. Weber, 'A new index of residential construction, 1838-1950', *Scottish Journal of Political Economy*, II, 1955, pp. 119-22.

[13] K. Maywald, 'An index of buildings costs in the United Kingdom, 1845-1938', *Econ. Hist. Rev.*, VII, 1954.

[14] Op. cit., p. 213.

[15] This includes a rough allocation of £5 million for structural work undertaken by iron and steel and engineering firms.

[16] Op. cit., pp. 142-3.

[17] this was assumed to represent 80 per cent of total expenditure − see the paragraph on electrical engineering on p. 41 below.

[18] B. R. Mitchell, 'The coming of the railways and the United Kingdom economic growth', *Journal of Economic History*, XXIV, 1964, pp. 334-6. In order to reconcile Mitchell's series with the Census data I have excluded the amount which he added in for renewals to the permanent way.

[19] Post Office Telegraphs and Telephones, *Account Showing the Gross Amount Recived and Expended*, H.C.378, 1913, pp. 4-5, 8.

[20] For 1906-7 see Departmental Committee on Telegraph and Telephone Accounts, *Report and appendices*, Cd. 4520, 1909, p. 23. From 1907-8 onwards see, e.g., 1913, p. 12, and Post Office, *Statement of Account*, e.g., H.C. 218, p. 413 and No. 9, p. 425.

[21] *Select Committee on the Post Office (Telephone Agreement) 1905*, Appendix no. 2, p. 413 and No. 9, p. 425.

[22] Plant and equipment for electricity supply companies is included in electrical engineering, and for gas and water supply companies in general engineering. Estimates for total capital formation in gas and electricity are described below, p. 43.

[23] Board of Trade, *Annual Statement of the Navigation and Shipping of the United Kingdom*.

[24] K. Maywald, 'The construction costs and the value of the British merchant fleet, 1850-1938', *Scottish Journal of Political Economy*, III, 1956, p. 50.

[25] This is the average ratio of gross to net tonnage, calculated from the data for steamers built from 1886 to 1913 when both measures were available.
[26] In compiling his estimates Maywald assumed that the cost of hulls per gross ton for steamers corresponded to the cost of hulls per net ton for sailing vessels (56, p. 46). In the case of sailing ships it is, therefore, not necessary to correct for the fact that the series for ships built is in net tons.
[27] Op. cit., pp. 46-52.
[28] Op. cit., p. 158.
[29] For 1915-18 a deduction is also made for iron and steel used for munitions and other military purposes. See, e.g., F. H. Hatch, *The Iron and Steel Industry of the United Kingdom under War Conditions*, p. 11 (1919).
[30] A. L. Bowley and G. H. Wood, 'Statistics of wages in the United Kingdom during the nineteenth century, Part XIV: engineering and shipbuilding', *J. R. Statist. Soc.*, LXIX, 1906, p. 185.
[31] Based mainly on data in British Electrical and Allied Manufacturers' Association, *The Electrical Industry of Great Britain*, p. 9 (1929) for 1903-19, *The Returns relating to Electricity Supply Undertakings in the United Kingdom for the years 1899 and 1900*, H. C. 1901, 1902 and Garcke's *Manual of Electrical Undertakings*, 1890-8.
[32] 1924 Census of Production, *Part V: General Statistical Tables*, p. 454 and also BEAMA, op.cit., pp.118-21.
[33] Op. cit, p. 114.
[34] Op. cit, pp. 335-6.
[35] Op. cit, pp. 118-19.
[36] *Final Report, First*, pp. 141, 709; and *Third, Part III*, pp. 311-12.
[37] A. R. Prest and A. A. Adams, *Consumers' Expenditure in the United Kingdom, 1900-1919*, pp. 141-2 (Cambridge, 1954).
[38] For 1908-13 the estimated output is given by the Society of Motor Manufacturers and Traders *The Motor Industry of Great Britain*, p. 6 (1947). The series was extrapolated to 1919 on the basis of Hoffman's index, which is supposed to represent the annual output of motor vehicles *(British Industry, 1700-1950*, p. 249 (1955) and the annual production was then valued at the prices per vehicle used by Prest (op. cit, p. 142) for cars.
[39] Prest, op. cit., p. 142.
[40] The estimate is based on the data on accumulated capital expenditure given in the *Annual Return of Tramway and Light Railway (Street and Road) Undertakings*, with adjustments to allow for the effect of acquisition of undertakings by local authorities.
[41] *Annual Return relating to all authorised Gas Undertakings in the United Kingdom other than those of Local Authorities*, H.C. 137 (1914), pp. 102-3.
[42] For 1882-97 see Appendixes P to W of the *Final Report of Her Majesty's Commissioners appointed to enquire into the subject of the Water Supply within the limits of the Metropolitan Water Companies*. Cd. 108 (1900). For other years see *Return of the Accounts of the Metropolitan Water Companies*, H.C. (annual).
[43] This is based on data for England and Wales quoted in Prest, op. cit, p. 99.
[44] Op. cit., pp. 192-3.
[45] As noted above (p. 39) Maywald's estimates of ship construction costs combine an estimate of changes in labour and material costs per ton of hull weight and an allowance for the changes in composition and design of the ships reflected in the average weight of hulls per registered ton. The index prepared for the present estimates for purposes of deflation attempts to

isolate the former element in Maywald's series by reconstructing his index of the change in costs of labour and materials (op. cit., p. 52).

[46] The index was kindly provided by Dr Mitchell. It combines series for engineering wages and costs of iron and other materials.

[47] Op. cit, p. 203.

[48] *National Income and Expenditure of the United Kingdom, 1870-1952,* pp. 34-7 (1955).

[49] Phyllis Deane, 'New estimates of gross national product for the United Kingdom, 1830-1914', *The Review of Income and Wealth,* 14, 1968.

[50] Op. cit., p. 111.

[51] The series that Deane uses for public authorities' current expenditure also covers all defence spending, including naval shipbuilding. Consequently, there is an element of double-counting in her estimates of total expenditure generating gross national product.

[52] Deane's estimate for 1907 at current prices is £132 million (op. cit., p. 105) and we deduct £8 million for new construction of ships and £1 million for new buildings and works (mainly ports) for the navy and army.

[53] I am grateful to Miss Deane for providing the unpublished components of her series and thus making possible this more detailed comparison.

[54] The items of 'social capital' listed by Deane (op. cit., p. 110) do not include the following components of the local authority expenditure out of loans: public libraries, markets, parks, police stations and the residual item 'other works and purposes'. This latter amounted to between £2 and £4 million per annum in the period 1900-14, and the other categories were together responsible for roughly a further £1 million per annum. See *Statistical Abstract,* e.g. No. 58, pp. 56-9.

[55] Before 1891 the effect of this difference must be offset by differences in the estimates of the number of houses built and of the rate of improvement in the standards of building.

[56] See Cairncross, op. cit., pp. 107-9.

[57] Op. cit, p. 111.

[58] See E. M. Sigsworth and J. Blackman, 'The home of the 1890s', *Yorkshire Bulletin of Economic and Social Research,* 17, 1965, especially pp. 85-91.

[59] New construction of horse-drawn vehicles is included in the 1907 benchmark but is not separately extrapolated and is likely to be underestimated in earlier years.

[60] One indication of this is the estimate for 1907, where Deane estimates expenditure on carriages, etc., at about £4 million, of which £2 million is for vehicles. The Census of Production (p. 729) shows some £900,000 for construction of horse-drawn vehicles, but £400,000 of this is for private carriages already covered in the estimates of consumers' expenditure.

DISCUSSION 2

Discussants: S. A. Broadbridge, E. Cooney, P. Cotterell, R. Davis, M. Falkus, C. H. Feinstein, M. W. Flinn, J. L. Halstead, J. Hibbert, J. P. P. Higgins, D. S. Landes, P. Mathias, B. R. Mitchell, J. Odling-Smee, S. Pollard, J. Whitaker.

There was much uneasiness over the great discrepancies between the Feinstein and the Deane figures. These were admittedly constructed from very different inputs, but were attempting to measure the same phenomena. Of the two, the Deane series is much closer in its method of construction to the present scheme than the other, though there are still substantial differences. What was particularly perturbing to some was not so much the divergences in the absolute quantities, though these were substantial, but the fact that in one crucial period the two indices actually moved in opposite directions. Yet the definitions were similar for both series, for example, including imports of capital equipment. Further, while it might appear encouraging at first sight that both series agree fairly closely for the 1860s, since it is with that phase that the projected Sheffield series will have to be spliced; yet the divergences in later phases leave the suspicion that this agreement may be fortuitous. In any case, the Deane series was more plausible in regard to its general level, while it had its gravest weaknesses in the year-by-year figures.

Some members found the absolute levels hard to swallow, even where both series were in broad agreement. In particular, the absolute level of home investments in the troughs of the cycles of the 1870s and 1880s seemed very low on general grounds. Under this sum there had to be included the building of new towns and seaside towns described by Ashworth, for example, more important in the 1890s but strongly in evidence already in the 1870s, and the erection of commercial buildings, as well as industrial buildings, machinery, ships and many other items.

Within these totals no way had yet been found of separating the commercial from the industrial building, in the 'non-residential building' component. Parry Lewis had attempted to isolate commercial building. He began by taking the numbers classified in the Census as being in commercial occupations; he then assumed an improvement in the standard of accommodation of 10 per cent in each decade; and he finally assumed that the annual series showed the same percentage deviation from trend as marriages in England and Wales. His annual series was then obtained as a three year moving average of the first differences in the stock. This is, of course, a very indirect way of measuring annual capital formation in commercial buildings.

In the United Kingdom, the home investment to income ratio has always been low, but when the high and fluctuating overseas investment figures are taken into account, the total investment rate compared with the national income appears to be both fairly stable, and not unreasonably small. It certainly accorded with the widespread view that Britain invested too little at home, even if she invested heavily abroad. The feeling that the overall level had turned out to be too low could not be sustained by the evidence.

If the absolute level of investment recorded in the series elicited some doubt, it was the pattern of cyclical changes emerging from the statistics which caused the gravest uneasiness. The most serious objections were raised against the peak shown for 1876, and Feinstein himself was not too satisfied with this particular result. Virtually all the available independent evidence, such as records of company flotations, the prosperity of the heavy industries, the unemployment figures of the trade unions, particularly in engineering, besides numerous other indices, point to 1873 as the peak, followed by a decline thereafter. Only residential building might be consistent with a peak around 1876. Even if it is borne in mind that machinery prices might be less volatile than prices of iron and coal, and that there would therefore be a less marked collapse of output, measured in monetary terms, for engineering equipment in 1873-6 than there would be for the raw materials, an actual sharp rise to a major peak was difficult to accept for these years.

In defence of such a late boom, it was argued that there might be a considerable lag in the investment industries, following the earlier boom of the final output industries. The overall delay would be the sum of the lags at all stages. Thus there would be a lag in the expansion plans of the consumer goods industries as the boom got under way, and similarly, there would be a lag in the intermediate goods industries, so that by the time the capital goods industries were geared up to a higher output, it might well be 1876 rather than 1873, if the intervening layer of intermediate goods industries was wide enough. Also, the housing boom, which admittedly fits better into the picture, would lead to a subsidiary boom in gas, water works, etc. Perhaps it was only the level of profits which fell sharply, and led to impressionistic reports of a decline after 1873 not borne out by actual output figures, at least in the capital sector. Against this, it was argued that this lag, or echo effect, should have been apparent at every peak, but was in fact not noticeable in the other cycles, where the present series conformed much more accurately to our traditional profile of booms and slumps.

Several explanations were offered for the double peak of 1900 and 1903. This is found in the building figures by themselves, including those collected by Parry Lewis, which therefore lend it a strong plausibility. There was also the Boer War, though it would have to be admitted that by analogy with World War I, the Boer War was unlikely to have consumed much iron and steel; and there was the building of the London Underground, which may have been responsible for increasing the steel consumption: its engineering items were included in the figures for railway investment.

Some members felt that the boom of 1907 should have shown up more sharply than it actually did. In concrete terms, this was mainly a textile boom and relatively little else in Britain, though prices rose steeply and there was a great deal of speculation, spilling over from the U.S.A. But it was possible that, in this case, the effect of the boom was diffused over several years as stocks acted as buffers.

The chances of arriving at a satisfactory series of stocks themselves were considered altogether remote. There are views expressed from time to time — for example, in some reviews of Deane and Cole — that some isolated stock series might be discovered or exploited for this purpose, by being used as a sample and grossed-up. But there is a strong case in principle against using a sample for such a purpose. Inevitably, it will be partial, representing stocks in merchants' hands, perhaps, but not retailers', or in the docks and not in the hands of wholesalers. In such a case, it is perfectly legitimate to make either of two equally plausible assumptions: one can either assume that stocks which are disclosed move in the same direction as those which remain hidden, or one can assume that they move in the opposite way. There seems to be no way of judging which assumption is the correct one, except where it is possible to undertake some special detailed studies, as for example grain stocks in the hands of millers and of merchants.

For the more recent period, balance sheets might be used, and this was done by Feinstein and his associates for the inter-war years, but even here the results were at best very tentative. Far more balance sheets than were actually available would have to be used to provide any degree of certainty.

The conventional assumption from the nineteenth century, but used also by Keynes, was that stocks could be taken as 40 per cent of national annual income. The difficulty about this, even if it were approximately correct, was that it would be far too crude to determine stock changes, which were the operative quantities in a study of investment. Moreover, where more numerous and more reliable statistics are available, as for World War II, the outstanding fact is that all the series of stocks move in completely different ways, so that it was quite impossible to be certain which of the known series represented the missing sections.

3

Fixed Capital Formation in the British Cotton Manufacturing Industry[1]

S. D. CHAPMAN

The problems associated with the calculation of capital formation in the economy vary from one industry to another, more particularly for the period before the middle of the last century. Any attempt to aggregate quantities for the Industrial Revolution must shortly recognize that the source material classifies industries and services in two categories – those that fell within the regular purview of the state for some purpose (such as customs and excise or enabling legislation) and those whose progress was either completely or quite inadequately recorded by the government authorities. There can be a reasonable expectation that economic historians will be able, in the course of time, to assess the quantities and identify the pattern of growth of capital for branches of industry, agriculture, and commerce – like brewing, paper, shipping, railways and Parliamentary enclosure – that the state regulated in some way, but for those that fell into the second category the problems of scarcity and unreliability of data may seem to present insuperable problems. This article considers some methods and problems of calculating fixed capital formation for one important industry, cotton, that was not systematically surveyed until after 1833.

The paucity of records of early firms in the cotton industry clearly makes it impossible to make direct use of this source for the present exercise, and the records of the Board of Trade, the Treasury and other central departments disclose no global assessment of the industry. Fortunately, there is another source which, though badly neglected by economic historians, offers the possibility of a much more comprehensive analysis of the magnitude of fixed capital formation in the first phase of development of the factory system. The numerous valuations of textile firms in the registers of the Sun Fire Office and Royal Exchange have to be interpreted with some caution, but present the patient researcher with a detailed calendar of investment and investors for a limited but critical period at the end of the eighteenth century [2]. After reviewing some possible approaches to the calculation of capital formation in the Industrial Revolution period, this paper

57

considers the ways in which insurance registers can be used to calculate
data for cotton, and links the results with evidence available from
contemporary calculations, technical treatises and literary sources.

1   THE AGGREGATIVE APPROACH

In principle, there are two possible methods of calculating capital
formation in the cotton industry, or for that matter, in any other
industry. The macro-economic approach involves starting with a
statistical series for input or output of the whole industry and seeking
to relate this to capital requirements on the basis of some formula (or
formulae) identified in the technical literature of the industry. The
alternative approach is the micro-economic method — that is, synthe-
sizing totals for capital formation from data on firms or productive
units derived from detailed surveys or local sources. It will be
convenient to consider the macro-economic method first.

The only source available to historians that relates to the cotton
industry *as a whole* is the Custom House records of the total imports of
raw cotton, a long series beginning in 1698 [3]. Since all cotton used in
the industry was imported, we have a reasonably reliable record of the
quantity of raw material used throughout the period under review. The
difficulty is to relate this to capital formation as there are no pertinent
technical manuals of the industry before James Montgomery's *Theory
and Practice of Cotton Spinning* appeared in 1836, and the capital and
labour costs instanced in this fascinating work clearly bear no relation
to those experienced by the British industry in its first phase of
expansion. In the period from about 1780 to about 1825, cotton was
being spun by three distinct techniques; jennies, water frames and
mules, in changing proportions. Each technique called for different
kinds of buildings and a different scale of investment. Moreover, even if
we could make safe assumptions about the proportion of the raw
material taken by the different technical sectors of cotton spinning,
margins of error must be multiplied by the need for further
'guestimates', for the rapid growth of the cotton industry in the early
years of the factory system led to wide differences in input/capital ratios
between different processes and between the advanced and numerous
marginal firms. In 1784, for instance, one of the most advanced firms
(Robinson of Nottingham) reckoned to waste between one quarter and
one third of their raw cotton whilst, by 1817, Manchester merchants
allowed only 10 per cent wastage rate [4]. Clearly it is no use treating

the cost structure of a single firm like McConnel & Kennedy as typical, and so far as we know this is the only firm whose records survive in sufficient detail to make any long-term analysis of raw material and capital investment feasible [5].

Any capital formation series calculated by the macro-economic method would, of course, represent *gross* fixed capital formation and, in the case of cotton, this would be a quite inadequate guide to *original* capital formation – i.e. to new building, as opposed to conversion of existing premises. In the first phase of expansion of the cotton industry it was a common practice to adapt older premises for use as workshops, cotton mills and warehouses, and an extensive contemporary literature is eloquent on this process. So far as workshops are concerned, the classic quotation comes from William Radcliffe, who recalled that, in the years after 1788, 'The old looms being insufficient, every lumber room, even old barns, outhouses and outbuildings of any description were repaired, windows broke through the old blank walls, and all fitted up for loom shops. This source of making room being at length exhausted, new weavers' cottages with loomshops rose up in every direction . . .' [6]. In another centre populated with many small manufacturers, it was said that 'Several of the smallest of the original mills [i.e. jenny workshops] in Oldham and the neighbourhood commenced business with not more than eight or ten hands each, upon an average; . . . in many instances the processes were conducted in large two-storeyed and three-storeyed dwelling houses, or portions of dwelling houses, chiefly in commodious chambers [bedrooms]' [7]. Evidence from Bolton, Keighley and various parts of Derbyshire substantiates the same theme [8].

In all the textile regions there is evidence of existing water mills being converted for cotton spinning, and it is not difficult to trace the earlier use of these mills. Many water mills came from the non-textile industries; there were numerous corn mills and a few iron mills, lead works, potters' grinding wheels and cutlers' wheels, sometimes representing a switch of capital from an industry that was declining locally. There was also a substantial acquisition of mill sites from the other sectors of the textile industry. The spectacular success of cotton in the last quarter of the eighteenth century was made partly at the expense of the demand for worsted, silk and linen, and in centres of these industries like Keighley, Halifax, Stockport, Macclesfield, Glasgow and Warrington numbers of mills were turned over to cotton spinning [9].

Even the warehouses built by substantial merchants did not always represent original contributions to capital. For instance, a description of Chorley, written about 1797, notes that '. . . in this part of the country the gentlemen's old seats, halls, etc., are all converted into warehouses, printhouses, workshops, etc., and new and more elegant ones erected . . .' and the writer instanced Shaw Place, 'formerly one of the country residences of the late Lord Willoughby de Parham', and now rented by Messrs Swift & Co., cotton manufacturers [10]. All kinds of urban premises were converted, for instance in Manchester, Brockle-hurst & Whittenbury, cotton merchants and partners of Arkwright, leased 'part of a building known as the Old Playhouse in Marsden St', while Ralph Kirkham used the cellars under the Catholic Chapel to store £3,000 worth of cotton [11]. Even where original capital formation took place, there are many pitfalls for the unwary. Samuel Unwin of Sutton-in-Ashfield built himself a pretentious mansion in Sutton Park, but not all was vanity. A visitor to the house wrote (in 1779) 'Mr Unwin's house is built of stone and on the outside seems fit for a nobleman, but the best rooms are occupied as warehouses for the cotton manufactory' [12].

These illustrations are sufficient to make the point that it would be rash to attempt to estimate net capital formation from gross capital requirements, even if it were possible to find an equation to relate imports of raw cotton to the buildings and machinery that were probably employed. Clearly we must turn to the more meticulous micro-economic approach if our calculations of fixed capital formation are to inspire any confidence.

2   ESTIMATES FROM INSURANCE RECORDS 1770-1795

Despite the formation of numbers of provincial insurance companies in the last two decades of the eighteenth century, the established London companies, the Sun, Royal Exchange and Phoenix, took the lion's share of the rising textile business. It was not until after the turn of the century that the provincial companies began to undercut their London rivals and take over their business [13]. The fortunate consequence for the economic historian is that cotton mills and workshops, which of course were a very great fire hazard, were generally insured with the agents of the three principal metropolitan companies in the 1790s. Insurance valuations of fixed assets are invariably lower than those found in the handful of surviving balance sheets of cotton firms, but the discrepancy can largely be identified with the omission of land and watercourses, and as there were very few mills on virgin sites, this part of the assets must be regarded as a transfer of capital rather than capital creation. [14]

The evidence of insurance records confirms an impression gained from field work in the Pennines, that there were three basic types of factories in the first major phase of expansion in the cotton industry, from 1770 to 1803. For convenience these may be designated types A, B and C. *Type A* is the small factory employing horse capstans for driving carding machines. The same building frequently included hand operated jennies or mules, and sometimes a few looms. John Sutcliffe, a Halifax millwright who had an extensive practice in the north of England, was pointing to the economic and social advantages of this type of factory as late as 1816: 'A horse would find employment for four spinners, and a room six yards square would be sufficient for the card room; another room containing 60 [square] yards would be sufficient for the [spinning] wheels. Here would be a factory large enough to employ a moderate family and three or four additional hands; and how much better would it be for the children to be employed under their parents than in a large factory as they would be in no danger of contracting bad habits . . . . The capital required would be trifling' [15]. In a few instances the horse wheel was replaced by a steam engine; this development is designated *Type A** in the valuation lists in Appendix 6. These small factories and their machinery never valued at more than £2,000 with steam power and £1,000 is a ceiling figure for horse wheels alone [16].

Type B mills were those operated by water power alone; if a steam engine was employed it was merely to pump back water into the reservoir. Field work, newspaper advertisements for the sale of mills, and plans in the Boulton & Watt MSS. show that the great number of mills built in the first phase of investment (1770-1803) were built to an easily recognizable basic pattern. They were three or four storeyed functional buildings, designed for about 1,000 spindles, and 70 to 80 feet long by 25 to 30 feet wide. The only important variation on this pattern was up to twice the length and about twice the productive capacity, and it will be convenient to refer to this as *Type B2* [17]. The typical valuation of the Type B1 mill was £3,000 and the B2 mill £5,000. The basic similarity of type was not, of course, an accident. 'Sir Richard Arkwright . . . originated the buildings; we all looked up to him and imitated his mode of building', Peel once remarked, and there is abundant physical and documentary evidence to show the literal truth of his observation [18]. Sir Robert Peel built fifteen mills on the successful Arkwright pattern, and was in turn widely imitated [19]. 'I am concerned with some friends with building a cotton mill', John Cross of Leeds wrote to Boulton & Watt in 1792, 'It is 25 yards in length and ten in breadth within the walls, four stories and capable of containing 30 to 40 spinning frames with 84 spindles each in a circular form after the plan of Mr Peel's . . . ' [20].

Another reason for the basic similarity of so many mills is that few millwrights were qualified to build power units for the new cotton mills, and consequently most of the work was done by a handful of specialists. Sir William Fairbairn's autobiography provides the most substantial evidence on this point. Recalling his work on the Catrine mills, Fairbairn wrote: 'The machinery of the mills was driven by four water wheels erected by Mr Lowe of Nottingham. His work, heavy and clumsy as it was, had in a certain way answered the purpose, and as cotton mills were then in their infancy he was *the only person* qualified from experience to undertake the construction of the gearing. Mr Lowe was therefore in demand in every part of the kingdom where a cotton factory had to be built' [21]. The building records of the Louth worsted mill (1784-5) show that Mr Lowe's four visits (at three guineas plus expenses) at intervals of three months were enough to direct the local millwright and carpenters, and clearly he could have had many other commissions on hand at the time [22]. Fairbairn probably exaggerated the importance of Lowe, and it may well be that John Sutcliffe was more important in the West Riding, and Joshua Wrigley in Lancashire, but clearly there were few men capable of undertaking the design of a cotton mill [23].

Type C is a convenient epithet for the taller and generally steam-powered mills that began to be built in the last decade of the eighteenth century. Here again, there is a remarkable similarity between the factories in this category because they were built by one of a small group of itinerant engineers. Major Cartwright's Revolution Mill at Retford, the first spinning mill to rely on steam power alone, was not a commercial success, despite Lowe's ambitious plan [24]. Peter Drinkwater's mule factory at Manchester (1790) used steam power only for the carding machinery until the end of the century. The first really successful designs came from Peter Atherton, the Warrington machine builder who had helped Arkwright during his struggling years [25]. Atherton's mills were of 3,000 spindles and powered by 30 h.p. Watt rotary engines, but only a handful of them were built because steam power was so much more expensive than water power at the period [26]. In the Type C category we should also include a few country water mills built to a comparable scale on a few favoured sites where the water power reserves guaranteed a regular 30 h.p. [27]. Type C mills cost a minimum of £10,000, if the insurance records are to be trusted.

It has been necessary to identify mill types in some detail in order to justify the next step in the analysis, which is to suggest that where cotton mills can be identified by type, it is not difficult to make a fair estimate of the investment they represented. The three cotton spinning regions, the Midlands, Scotland, and the north-west, present problems of varying difficulty to the student of capital formation. The Midlands is the easiest region to deal with as research has already established the total number of factories built up to 1803. The Sun and Royal Exchange registers, and miscellaneous sources, provide valuations of about half these mills, and an intimate knowledge of local literature and archives, together with field work in the rural areas, makes it possible to identify the categories and make fair estimates for the remainder.

Turning to the Midland region first [28], the total number of mills is known from earlier research and the number of jenny workshops was negligible [29], so the only difficult problem is to date capital formation. Land tax records, local newspapers and other local sources often relate when building commenced, but it is seldom possible to be sure how long the process of equipping the mill took. Arkwright's Manchester mill took eight years (1782-90) to reach maximum production, but this was a pioneer experiment and cannot be counted typical [30]. Most country mills were probably completed within a year in a region where limited water supplies prescribed a small type of mill, and where the entrepreneurs were characteristically merchants and tradesmen of ample means [31]. The details set out in Appendix 6 identify 121 mills established in the region up to 1803, for which sixty-three valuations are extant in insurance and miscellaneous records. The remainder of the mills are valued on the basis of the types just described (identification of mill types is a relatively easy matter in a region in which so many eighteenth-century mill buildings still survive, and the dimensions of numerous others appear in sale advertisements and the Boulton & Watt MSS.). Though most of the mill sites had a previous use, the valuations given here are for purpose-built cotton and worsted mills (i.e. original capital formation) and not converted premises, so far as is known. The handful of worsted mills has to be included because most of them were engaged on spinning cotton as well as worsted at this period (a similar problem of indivisible units occurs in Scotland where flax and cotton were sometimes spun in the same factory, and in Rochdale and the West Riding where wool and cotton occasionally shared the same premises). In 1795 net fixed capital formation in cotton and worsted mills in the Midlands can be calculated at £380,700, in 1802 at £452,500 [32]. Figures for any other year between 1770 and 1803 can readily be calculated by the method described here.

Andrew Brown's *History of Glasgow* (1796) contains an estimate of fixed capital formation in the Scottish cotton industry which has been quoted a number of times in the standard works without criticism:

39 water mills, which cost for machinery and buildings £10,000 each	£390,000
1,200 jennies at £6 each	7,200
600 mules at £30 each	18,000
Building for the jennies cost	75,000
	£490,000

The insurance records suggest that Brown was misleading in two respects. There were certainly more than thirty-nine mills in Scotland in 1795, quite apart from mule and jenny workshops. The Sun registers record forty-two firms with forty-eight mills and several other concerns are recorded elsewhere [33]. Secondly, Brown clearly overestimated the amount of capital invested in a typical mill, even when allowance is made for the tendency of Scottish mills of the period to have more power resources than their English counterparts. David Dale's insurance on two mills, warehouses and other properties at New Lanark reached £24,400 in 1795; George Dempster's Stanley Mills at Perth were valued at £10,500 on his policies; and the Ballindalloch Mill Co. (Robert Dunmore and James and Archibald Buchanan) £10,300; but all the other Scottish policies for cotton mills fell below £10,000 and seventeen out of forty-two firms were insured for less than £5,000 (Appendix 5).

The structure of the cotton industry in the three principal regions reflects distinct characteristics, the Scottish industry being distinguished by an emphasis on the large mill [34] and by a series of interlocking partnerships [35]. This is partly because Scots law allowed joint-stock companies for cotton mills, and partly because the Scots cotton industry was for the most part imported from England by wealthy Glasgow and Paisley merchants [36]. Nevertheless, the design of Scottish mills closely resembled the English prototypes, and all the mills identified here appear to be original buildings. The first mills, at Penicuik (1776-9) and Rothesay (1779) [37], were built by former workmen of Arkwright, while the most successful of the pioneer Scottish mills, built by Robert Burns at Johnstone Bridge from 1782, were admitted to be on Arkwright's principle [38]. In 1784 Arkwright and Dale formed their partnership at New Lanark and the major phase of expansion of the Scottish cotton industry was inaugurated [39]. It is not surprising, therefore, to find that Scottish mills fit readily into the classification (B1, B2, C) adopted for England. The more ample water power resources of Scotland encouraged the building of more of the rural Type C mills, but there is no doubt that the cost of building and equipping mills was lower in Scotland, which may be taken to justify the lower insurance valuations for this kind of factory.

The main problem of interpreting the process of capital formation in Scotland, apart from the persistent question of the reliability of valuations, is the number of years that it took to complete a mill. The problem presents itself in an acute form in Scotland because of the large power potential of many sites and the limited financial resources of partners. A partner in Houston, Burns & Co. of Johnstone Bridge mill (near Paisley) declared in 1788 that 'none of the cotton mills in Scotland were set to work all at once, or even at this time perform their full compliment of labour. The conveniences [ample water power] and the circumstances [capital shortage] of this country prevent it; and every manufacturer who attempts so great an establishment contrives his machinery so as to admit of being suited to the gradual extension of the capital, and the increase of hands' [40]. The ground floor, usually the last to be occupied, was often used to accommodate juvenile labour and itinerant workers. The consequence for the calculation of capital formation is that, while the insurance registers allow reasonably reliable estimates of net capital formation in 1795, calculations of year-by-year estimates would involve too many assumptions to be undertaken with any assurance.

The Sun's impressive coverage of Scots cotton mills seems to have been limited to the merchant-manufacturers; there is no corresponding series of policies for the smaller jenny spinners. Andrew Brown's estimates have the particular merit of drawing attention to the amount of capital contributed by the smaller manufacturers, and though the value he places on 'building for the jennies' is rather suspect in view of the widespread practice of converting older premises, no alternative estimate is available. The total fixed capital in the factory production of cotton in Scotland in 1795 can be estimated by adding the insurance totals (Appendix 5), plus a figure for a few omitted mills, to Brown's estimates for mules, jennies and their buildings [41]. The conclusions drawn from these calculations are considered in the final section of this article.

The most difficult problem in approaching the northern cotton industry [42] is that there is no reliable information on the total number of mills before Crompton's survey of 1811. Dr Aiken gives figures for Stockport (23 mills), Macclesfield (10), and Mottram (12) [43]; Butterworth has details for Oldham (23 mills in 1795, the year of Aikin's figures) [44], and two or three local historians have made estimates for peripheral areas [45]; but that is all. The few directories of the period have little value for those interested in capital formation; they list dozens of merchants, cotton manufacturers and fustian manufacturers, but do not say which were building factories and warehouses. Few rate-books have survived for the period – Manchester is the only important centre with a good series [46]. The mills inspected under Peel's Act (1802) are by no means a complete list. Field-work, often so helpful in rural areas, becomes impossible in those parts of the region where nineteenth-century urban development has overlaid the earlier sites.

The four types of mills already identified for the Midlands and Scotland were also common in the northern region. A further type of development was also important in the central part of the region – for convenience it can be labelled the Bolton type of factory, from being most characteristic in that locality. It consisted simply of the accumulation of buildings – warehouses, workshops and factory – around the original nucleus of the fustian manufacturer's house. It was also common in Manchester, Stockport, Oldham, Warrington and the surrounding country areas, and there are obvious similarities with the evolution of country clothiers' premises in the West Riding, described by Crump and Ghorbal in their *History of the Huddersfield Woollen Industry*. Clearly the capital invested in these developments was not so standardized as for other types of factory, and a large range of valuations is found – for example, Richard Taylor, cotton manufacturer, Bolton, insured in 1791 with the Royal Exchange [47]:

House and warehouse adjoining	£100
Furniture (£50) and utensils (£150) therein	200
Workshop in the yard (£50) and utensils (£50)	100
Utensils in warehouse in Abraham's Ct, Manchester	100
	£500

'Memo: the assured only warps and weaves and has no stoves...' indicates the nature of the utensils referred to in the policy. At the upper end of this scale we may instance James Lees of Oldham, the son of the John Lees who invented the carding feeder, and one of the carding mill owners used by Arkwright in 1781. His son began with a horse-wheel mill in 1776-8 and 'raised himself from the extremest drudgery of the spinning room to the position of one of the most opulent inhabitants' of Oldham [48]. In 1795 he insured for £2,050 as follows [49]:

	Sun	Royal Exchange
New Dwelling house, warehouse and spinning factory in one building	£400	£380
Stable, back kitchen and rooms over	100	—
Millwrights work, gears, etc. [horse wheel]	30	—
Clockmakers work, carding and breaking machines	200 ⎫	
Stock and goods	320 ⎭	620
	£1,050	£1,000

The initial point about the northern cotton industry is therefore that capital formation is less easy to calculate than in regions where factory building followed a more uniform pattern. But cotton manufacturers who followed the Bolton course of development invested in water mills in the few recorded instances where their capital rose above £2,000, so that although there were numbers of entrepreneurs investing their capital in factory production in the satellite towns, the total size of their fixed capital was still small in 1795. Oldham is better documented than most of these towns and provides a more precise illustration of this point. Butterworth maintained that there were twenty-two factories in the town in 1796 (exclusive of spinning rooms), and fifteen of them, including all the better known ones, can be valued from the Sun and Royal Exchange registers. The sum of the fixed capital of these fifteen was £22,550 in 1795 (Appendix 4), and it is very doubtful whether the unrecorded seven factories were worth more than £1,000 each, on the average. £30,000 would, therefore, be a generous estimate of the total fixed capital of Oldham's cotton manufacturers in 1795, a sum that falls short of the fixed capital investment of some individual merchants in the north of England. Moreover, this modest capital was only built up slowly by most of the entrepreneurs in the sample. Several of the Oldham men appear to have been men of humble birth, who began their independent career in the late 1770s with the purchase of small machines for twisting silk, known locally as 'Dutch wheels' [50].

The names of the large factory spinners – i.e. those investing in purpose-built Type B2 and C mills – are fairly familiar from the literature, and a list of them drawn from the insurance registers (Appendix 1) appears to be fairly complete, apart from two or three West Riding manufacturers (Appendix 2). A lower limit of £5,000 insurance policy was fixed for the identification of the large factory owners because this figure is the approximate minimum cost (as measured by the Sun and Royal Exchange agents) of a Cromford type mill that was not converted from other premises [51]. In the north of England insurance policies of less than £5,000 show clear evidence of the use of converted premises, and of employing 'utensils' (looms and jennies) in warehouses to make up a valuation approaching that of the group responsible for original capital formation [52]. In the £4,000 to £5,000 policy bracket one encounters the owners of the largest of the Bolton type factories (Leigh, Kinder & Haslam of Bolton, insured for £4,800) [53], and fustian manufacturers like John, James and George Olivant of Manchester, whose manufacturing activities began in their warehouse in Cromford Court and extended by the purchase of a disused forge at Duckinfield (valued as a cotton mill at £750) and a small carding mill with a horse wheel in Garratt Lane, Manchester (valued at £300) [54]. The list in Appendix 1 contains the names of forty-three firms, and allowing for a handful of omissions from the insurance registers, it appears that there were about fifty major contributors to *original* capital formation in the northern cotton industry.

The next step is to relate the total investment of the forty-three leading firms, the vanguard of the industry, to the large but unknown number of small manufacturers. It is impossible to make a precise calculation of the relative contribution of the major and minor investors because, apart from questions of definition, the total number of small firms can hardly be guessed at. The most that can be done is to analyse the contribution of large and small firms for a representative locality where the data are reasonably complete. Stockport makes a good case study for a number of reasons. Aikin reckoned that there were twenty-three large cotton factories in the town about 1795 [55] and the number of small workshops was probably not very different from the fifty-five jenny shops that Samuel Crompton noted a few years later [56]. No more precise estimate is available for any other cotton town at the period, and nearly all the Stockport mills and workshops can be identified in the Sun and Royal Exchange registers (Appendix 3). The Stockport cotton industry took over the town's silk mills in the 1780s and was subsequently noted for the unusual scale of its cotton factories. At the same time the locality was noted – to judge from the accounts of Radcliffe, Crompton and Gaskill – for the large number of workshops and entrepreneurs of artisan origin, a development which was further encouraged by the division of one or two large mills into 'stalls' when their owners became bankrupt or withdrew from the industry [57]. This polarization reflects the structure of enterprise of the regional industry more accurately than any other single centre could do.

The records of insured capital of Stockport mill owners justifies the distinction we have made between the entrepreneurs of large (£5,000+) concerns and those of the small mills; there is a very significant drop in value from the smallest of the former to the largest of the latter [58]. Moreover, it appears that some of the fixed capital of the small mill owners was provided by a Manchester cotton merchant, James Harrison, whose insurance policy of 1790 records his ownership of three mills and three workshops in Stockport, four of which were rented to local men [59]. There are clearly gaps in the insurance records, but the totals for the different groups do serve to give an approximate idea of their relative contribution to fixed capital formation. Very few of the workshop entrepreneurs insured premises, and this probably reflects the fact that few owned the rooms or buildings in which they worked, while from the point of view of the present study, the calculation of capital formation is not inflated by the erroneous addition of converted premises.

The eight leading Stockport firms invested £57,800, according to our source of information, but this is clearly a conservative estimate because the cost of excavating reservoirs and watercourses and building dams and sluice gates might represent an important part of the cost of a water mill. The eight owners of smaller mills contributed a little under £20,000, and forty-eight entrepreneurs in cotton workshops a little over this amount. In round figures, it might be said that on the most conservative estimate the leading group of cotton spinners in Stockport were responsible for 60 per cent of the fixed capital of the industry at the time, while a more realistic appraisal (based on an estimate for uninsured assets) might suggest three-quarters as a more accurate proportion [60]. Inferences drawn from the literary sources would certainly lend support to this conclusion [61].

If the estimates for Stockport may be used for a wider generalization, the total insured capital of forty-three leading firms recorded in Table 1 would represent not less than 60 per cent of the capital of the cotton industry of the north of England about 1795. The total investment would, therefore, be of the order of £1,250,000. An estimate for the cost of development of sites for water power should be added to this total, but it is hardly possible to put a figure on this element of cost – not only because every site presented different problems for the millwright-engineers that planned their development, but also because most sites had been exploited for water power at an earlier date and the value of the inheritance, though considerable, cannot be estimated.

The totals derived from calculations of capital formation in each of the three cotton regions – the Midlands £381,000; Scotland £392,000; the Northern region £1,250,000 – together total £2,023,000. This figure does not take account of some capital formation that paralleled the creation of the factory system, notably the growth of machinery in the domestic (weaving and framework knitting) sector, and the increase in warehouse accommodation by cotton merchants who were not engaged in the spinning branch. The scale of investment in these branches at the period is never likely to be more than informed guesses, and the most that can safely be said is that it is doubtful whether the total British fixed capital in 1795 exceeded £2.5 million [62].

Records of cotton manufacturers in the Sun and Royal Exchange registers do not appear in any considerable numbers until the late 1780s and fall away rapidly after 1795-7, so the final question in this section must be to inquire if the national total for 1795 can be extrapolated either backward or forward by means of reliable guide lines derived from other sources. The mechanics of capital formation in the period up to 1795 have already been outlined in this section, and in this case it is only necessary to state a conclusion. Because of the problems of extended periods of building and equipping mills, and the absence of data on so many northern concerns, the only way to extrapolate backwards would be to make a rough approximation by assuming that the investment pattern that can be identified for the Midlands (Appendix 6) corresponded to that found in the other two regions. There are so many obvious objections to such an assumption that it is doubtful whether the exercise is worth the arithmetic involved. Extrapolation forwards from 1795 involves other and more fundamental questions about changes in technology and productivity within the industry, and they are best treated together in the next section.

3   AGGREGATIVE ESTIMATES 1795-1817

One way of extrapolating forward from 1795 might be to follow the trend prescribed by imports of the raw material. The objections to using such data have been remarked on at the beginning of this paper, and the points already made carry peculiar force in the period after 1796 because of radical changes in the productive resources of the spinning sector. It was in this period that the development of mule spinning accelerated rapidly, not merely because of Kennedy's successful application of Watt's engine to the mule, which effectively terminated the era of expensive steam power [63], but also because of a dramatic switch in the direction of the investment of the 'cotton lords,' the leading company of Lancashire merchant-manufacturers. This point needs a little elucidation and is worth a minor digression from the main theme.

Investment in spinning mills on Arkwright's technique was characterized by a preponderance of merchant capital, by the migration of capital from other branches of the textile industry, and by the expansion of the industry into new peripheral areas in search of water power sites and colonies of handloom weavers. Merchant investment has already been identified as the primary source of capital in the Midlands and Scottish cotton mills [64], and for the northern region it is illustrated by the analysis of occupations of leading factory owners in Table 1. Twelve out of forty-three northern firms were headed by established Manchester fustian merchants and ten of them were drawn from the middlemen manufacturers of Stockport, Preston, Blackburn

TABLE 1
Occupations of principal partners in 43 leading cotton
spinning firms in the north of England, c.1795.

	No. of Firms	Insured Capital (£)	% of total insured capital
Manchester fustian merchants	12	255,960	33
Country factors	10	88,000	12
Calico printers and merchants	4	234,590	31
Former mechanics, management and 'men of humble birth'	3	65,050	8
Migrants from woollen and silk industries	8	64,450	8
Migrants from London and Midlands textile trades	6	57,650	8
TOTALS	43	£765,700	100

(33, 12, 31 grouped as } 76)

Sources: Sun and Royal Exchange Fire Policy Registers and other sources detailed in Appendix 1.

and other 'country' centres of the industry. The only other large category – the calico manufacturers – consists largely of the Peel family and their partners, together with their former partners (the Howarths) and Forte, Taylor & Bury, a firm that bought Peel's Oakenshaw print works. Though the Peels and Howarths began their career as calico printers, they had become Manchester merchants by the early 1780s, and the other calico firm was also an early entrant to merchanting [65]. By 1795 the merchant-manufacturers had largely absorbed the concerns started by the artisan-inventors of the pioneering years of mechanized cotton spinning [66], while the new class of entrepreneurs trained in the school of management was only represented by one firm out of the forty-three [67]. The adaptability and energy of the 'cotton lords' has been underestimated [68], and when Kennedy showed a way they quickly redirected their considerable capitals into the finer and most profitable branches of spinning. Samuel Crompton's neglected mule spindle census of 1811 clearly shows many of the 'old' cotton spinning families asserting a position of leadership in fine spinning, as well as maintaining their position in what might be called the Arkwright sector [69]. The essential point is that after the middle 1790s investment in the peripheral factory colonies appears to have ended in the northern region as entrepreneurs diverted their resources to mule spinning, and the industry rapidly abandoned the Arkwright capital-output ratio for a more productive one.

However, this line of thought suggests another way that might be used to calculate fixed capital formation in cotton during the critical years of development of the French wars. Could we link the 1795 insurance estimate and the data calculated by Crompton and his friends in 1811? Crompton's spindle census is often quoted to show that at the time of his census there were 155,880 jenny spindles, 310,516 water spindles and 4,600,000 mule spindles, but the first two figures are misleading because in general Crompton only counted jennies and water frames where they existed in the same factory as mules and (by definition) he excluded most of the rural areas where the Arkwright type mills were still active [70]. But the figures for mule spinning may be taken as fairly complete in view of the meticulous care with which the lists were compiled and the assistance that Crompton received from the most prominent men in the cotton industry at the period. It seems fairly clear that the relatively small number of mule frames in existence in 1795 were quite obsolete by 1811 and few of them were still in use. 'The machinery of a cotton spinning work . . . is subject to very great and rapid waste, and it requires to be renewed every four or five years', a witness in a Scottish case claimed in 1816 [71]. The same year an English millwright made a similar observation: 'Mule spinning is certainly a very complex business which may still be considered in its infancy, for its machinery admits of endless improvement, and it is one of the disagreeable but unavoidable circumstances attending it that the most ingenious spinner can never say he is spinning upon the best principle for six months together' [72]. In some instances Crompton's MSS. show the size as well as the number of mules operated by various firms, and these are invariably larger than the 144-spindle mules which

Drinkwater was installing in the early 1790s and which represented (according to Robert Owen) the most advanced machines in the industry at the period [73]. The application of power to the first two components of the four-movement cycle of the mule quickly led to the adoption of bigger machines; McConnel and Kennedy were already making them in the range of 180 to 288 spindles in 1795 [74]. So it appears that the mule spindles counted by Crompton were practically all installed after 1795 [75], and if (as I have surmised) new investment in Arkwright type mills dried up about this time, the capital invested in the British cotton spinning industry in 1811 can be calculated by adding the value of the 1811 mule spindlage (including buildings and power units) to the 1795 (insurance) total. In 1811 G. A. Lee stated that the value of buildings, power and machinery engaged in spinning on Crompton's system was between £3 and £4 million [76], and this estimate agrees with our meagre knowledge of the cost of building and equipping mule spinning mills [77].

The most important of a number of possible objections to this simple addition relates to the now familiar problem of transfer of buildings – in this case from roller spinning to mule spinning. If we add the insurance total to the Lee total is there not a risk of counting the same factory buildings twice? The majority of purpose-built (Types B1, B2 and C) cotton mills of the Arkwright era were outside the fine spinning area (as defined in Crompton's survey), so there was little possibility of transfer; in the central areas these mills were soon too narrow for efficient mule spinning [78]. Professor Daniels showed that the number of cotton mills in use in Manchester barely increased between 1803 and 1820 [79], and the same appears to be true of Oldham [80], but these figures speak only of the *numbers* of mills, so that even if the situation was found to be true of other towns [81], they say nothing of the capacity of premises. More than half the 650 firms in mule spinning in 1811 were working over 2,500 spindles [82], and a plant of this size and its steam engines just could not be contained in the converted cottage premises that had so often served the industry in Manchester and its satellite towns in the 1780s and 1790s [83]. Some acquaintance with the technology of cotton spinning between 1796 and 1810 also provides adequate evidence of heavy investment in steam power. Crompton's data suggest that much the greater part of the mule spindles was driven by steam [84], and if 350 mules spindles to each horse power is adopted as a basis for calculation, 13,000 h.p. would be needed to drive the 4.6 million mule spindles. It will not be widely misleading to surmise that in 1811 steam power totalling some 10,000 h.p. was being employed, practically all of which had been installed since 1795 [85]. At Boulton & Watt prices this would represent new capital worth £0.5 million [86], quite apart from the associated engine houses and transmission systems, which could have cost as much again [87]. It is impossible to resist the conclusion that, if the total number of mills did not increase, there must have been extensive rebuilding and enlargement of factory premises in the centres of fine spinning. So far as fixed capital formation is concerned, the lower figure in Lee's valuation range (£3 million) can be accepted as a conservative estimate.

The estimates of fixed capital formation made in the course of this paper, and one made by Kennedy in 1817 [88], are drawn together in Table 2 to provide a basis for some concluding interpretations.

TABLE 2
Estimates of fixed capital formation in the
British cotton industry, 1795-1817

	Water Spindles (millions)	Mule Spindles (millions)	Fixed Capital (£ millions)
1795 (Insurance)	1.25	–	2.0
1811 (Crompton)	assumed same	4.6	5.0
1817 (Kennedy)	assumed same	6.6	6.3

The final figure, £6.5 million, is an estimate calculated from the mule spindlage for 1817 on the basis of Lee's 1811 valuations, as revised in this chapter. (4.6 million spindles cost £3 million, so 6.6 million spindles would have cost about £4.3 million). To the £4.3 million must be added the assumed total (£2.2 million) for water spindles, which has been taken to be approximately constant from 1796 onwards [89].

If the calculations made here constitute a reliable guide, the cost of fixed capital investment in the initial period of 'take-off' in cotton was very modest, primarily because of the ease with which mills, mill sites, power units, workshops, warehouses and craftsmen's skills could be transferred from other industries. Potentially the most expensive item was the mill, but for most of the Arkwright era (1770-95) convertible sites and buildings were plentiful and cheap, largely due to the general improvement of efficiency of water wheels in the Smeaton era [90]. However, convertible premises and sites were limited in their capacity and their supply was inelastic. The further expansion of cotton necessarily involved more investment in original building and mechanical power, and only the rapid transfer of investment to mule spinning prevented a steep rise in marginal costs consequent on the further dispersion of productive capacity and technical skills of the industry. The mechanical genius of Lancashire was directed towards a reduction of plant costs, which fell from £2 per spindle at the height of the Arkwright era to less than £1 a spindle by 1836 [91]. The rapid development of mules was particularly remarked on, as we have already noted, at the close of the French wars, and it was these steadily falling marginal costs (together with the intermittent periods of high profits) that enabled the industry to maintain an investment programme despite the inflation of building costs in the war years.

If the initial stages of transition to the factory system were accomplished with little apparent financial strain, the modest fixed capital requirement was not the only reason. Much of the heavy investment in the first generation was undertaken by established merchant houses in cotton, wool, silk, linen and hosiery sectors of the textile industry, and fragments of evidence confirm the hypothesis that merchants found little difficulty in making the marginal shifts from working to fixed capital necessary for building [92]. With the switch to mule spinning, the isolation of merchant-manufacturers in their remote colonies and the growth of merchant credit provided more opportunity for the rise of the 'little masters', but this development must not lead us – as it led the early commentators – to neglect the role of the hereditary leadership in the process of change. Indeed, the longer one looks at the early cotton industry under the microscope, the less revolutionary the early phases of its life cycle appear to be.

4   THE LINKAGE BETWEEN ESTIMATES FOR 1817 AND 1834

It remains to attempt to establish some kind of link between the calculations of capital formation in this paper and the estimates for the period 1834-86 assembled by Dr Mark Blaug [93]. The relevant part of Blaug's work can be summarized in a short table, as follows:

	1834	1856	1860	1871	1886
Total capital (£ million) at constant prices	22	43	56	85	109
Fixed capital (£ million) at constant prices	15	30	34	56	76
Ten year moving average of real output (£ million)	11	31	24	42	58
Fixed capital/output (constant prices)	1.4	0.9	1.4	1.3	1.3

The £15 million fixed capital in 1834 represents spinning and weaving, but not bleaching, dyeing and printing which, with hosiery and lace, had an additional £5 million in buildings, plant and machinery. Is there sufficient continuity in the development of cotton between 1817 and 1834 to justify a splicing of the two short series?

One way of answering this question is to extend the study of the prototype (or optimum production) cotton mill forward to the middle 1830s to try to identify the essential changes in scale and productivity that had taken place since the end of the French wars. This is possible from data on the cost of building and running mills provided by Montgomery and Ure in 1836 and summarized in the adjacent table. Montgomery's was the mill of the past and present, Ure's of the future. If Montgomery's costing is to be trusted, his smaller mill was much more economical to build and run, while Ure's capital/output ratio was much closer to those maintained (as Blaug shows) with remarkable constancy for the remainder of the century. The middle 1830s were obviously a turning point in mill design, and some interpretation of what was happening is needed.

The Arkwright (Type B2) cotton mill had an annual output of 100,000 lb in a range of counts from 16s to 42s, but mainly concentrated in the middle 20s; as already stated it represented an investment of about £5,000 [94]. The few steam (Type C) mills that were built in the first major period of expansion (up to 1803) produced less in proportion to the investment; Markland, Cookson & Fawcett, whose Leeds mill was built by John Sutcliffe in 1791 and insured for £12,000, produced 150,000 lb. a year with a 30 h.p. Watt engine [95]. Montgomery's mill had different dimensions (in order to accommodate mules) but was precisely the same size, in terms of square feet, as the larger Arkwright prototype and, if we can exclude its power looms, cost a little over £6,000 for an annual production of 300,000 lb in the lower counts (16s to 20s). Clearly the application of power to the mule had produced economies in capital/output ratios to the extent of a trebling of output, but the scale of fixed capital investment in individual productive units had grown very little since the transference of this machine to the factory had necessitated wider buildings from the turn of the century. In 1833 the representative size of the Manchester firm was still 100 to 200 hands, and in the satellite towns it was probably even smaller [96]; Montgomery's mill, a representative factory unit whose costs were 'all calculated from the cost and expense of establishments that have been lately erected', was also about this size [97].

TABLE 3
Size and productivity of cotton mills in 1836
according to data in

(1) James Montgomery *The Theory and Practice of Cotton Spinning*, pp. 248-55 (Glasgow, 1836).
(2) Andrew Ure *The Cotton Manufacture of Great Britain*, Vol. I, pp. 297-313 (London, 1836).

	(1)	(2)
Fixed capital investment		
Mill buildings, transmission system and fittings	£1,520	£30,000
Engine house, boiler house, gas house	–	3,000
Steam pipes (heating) and gas pipes (lighting)	110	2,400
Steam engine(s)	660	8,800
Cleaning and preparation machines	1,795	12,000
Spinning machinery	1,856	11,500
Power looms and ancillary machinery	2,027	18,000
'Contingencies'/'miscellanies'	200	2,300
	£8,168	£88,000
Brief specification of mill		
Horse power of engine(s)	20	220
No. of spindles (a) throstle	2,100	(nil)
(b) mule	4,800	40,000
total	6,900	40,000
Area (sq. ft)	18,000	126,000[a]
Annual output (lb. of spun cotton)	300,000	2,225,000[b]
Gauge of cotton	16-18s.	36s.
Value of annual output of cotton	28,385	£139,062[c]
Calculations from the above data		
Capital cost per spindle	£0.87	£2.1
Capital cost per 1,000 sq. ft	£450	£700
Ratio of capital to annual value of spun cotton	1 : 3.5	1 : 1.5[d]

Notes to items
(a) Calculated from plans provided as end plates to Montgomery, and Ure Vol. I.

(b) Ure's data are incomplete. Capital investment is based on Ure's figures for Fairbairn's design of Bailey's mill at Stayley Bridge, output is calculated from production figures for mules in Ure, Vol. I, p. 311. A mill designed by Fairbairn for mules and throstles at a cost of £85,000 (Ure, Vol. I, pp. 296-304) yields similar conclusions but has not been used here as the fixed capital is not analysed for this concern.

(c) No data given in Ure. The £139,062 is an approximate figure based on 40,000 spindles and an assumption of a price of 1s. 3d for 36s cotton inferred from price lists in J. A. Mann, *The Cotton Trade of Great Britain*, p. 96 (1860).

(d) The value of output from the power looms is not used for comparisons as Ure has no data.

S. J. Chapman and T. S. Ashton in 'The Size of businesses, mainly in the textile industries', *Journal of the Royal Statistical Society*, LXXVII (1914), subscribe to the concept of an optimum cotton mill, identifying it as a private firm with 10,000 to 20,000 spindles and a joint stock firm in the range of 70,000 to 100,000 spindles, in the period 1884-1914.

The explanation of the economic advantages of the smaller unit of production up to the middle 1830s must lie partly in technical factors, and these can be readily understood by the layman. Mules were operated by highly skilled and semi-independent artisans on standard piece rates, and there was no particular economy in a concentration of their numbers [98]. The evolution of the mule was a slower process than has sometimes been supposed [99], while (according to Montgomery) the 'spinning frames that were constructed under the auspices of Arkwright himself were brought to a very high state of improvement, and those that have been generally used since his time are constructed upon the very same principle; any alterations that have been made are chiefly upon the form or framing of the machine, as that which was formerly made of wood is now made of cast iron' [100]. There were few striking economies of scale in steam power to judge from a comparison of Montgomery and Ure; the former's 20 h.p. engine cost £33 per unit horse power, the latter's £40 per horse power. The introduction of faster wrought iron water wheels and the centrifugal governor must have at least maintained the cost advantages of water power for smaller mills [101]. Comparison between Montgomery and Ure also urges the economy of traditional building methods over iron framed buildings, and later nineteenth-century writers recalled that mills were not generally built to be fire-proof until after this period [102]. Even the advantages of steam piping were doubted, for characteristically empirical reasons. 'John Kennedy said that for some time after fire proof mills were used in cotton spinning it is [sic] found that equally good work could not be done in them as in the old wood mills', Marshall of Leeds noted in his diary in 1829 after a visit to Manchester, 'the brick and lime continue to give out moisture some years', so providing the requisite degree of humidity [103]. It was only in the development of transmission systems — the substitution of cast iron for wooden gears, and the gradual improvement of the quality of casting [104] — that technical developments conferred important advantages on the bigger factory. It seems likely that shortage of competent managers, skilled mule spinners, and probably of capital as well, placed a brake on experiments with larger factory units [105].

If this is all true, how and when did the larger iron framed mill become economic? In his first book, published in 1832, Montgomery wrote that 'Self-acting mules have long been a desideratum in the trade and have occupied the attention of intelligent managers and mechanics for some years past; [but] although several have been invented and secured by patent yet none seem to be possessed of sufficient merit to cause any excitement in the trade; in fact they seem so unimportant as to be seldom spoke of . . . [106]'. But the improvements on Roberts's automatic mule were so rapid that it was being extensively adopted in the 1840s and by 1854 it was employed for all counts of yarn below 50s [107]. Roberts's mule introduced a new dimension in spindlage; to Montgomery 'mules containing from 264 to 288 spindles are the most profitable because they generally turn off a much greater quantity of yarn in proportion to their spindles than those of a larger size . . . [108]'. But the perfection of Roberts's work in the early 1830s enabled mills to be doubled in width, so that one man, with the help of two or three boys, could work 1,600 self-acting spindles as easily as he previously worked two 300-spindle hand mules [109]. In Montgomery's mill the wages paid to mule spinners exceeded three-quarters of the gross annual expenditure [110], and a fundamental economy at this point of production must necessarily have had far-reaching consequences for notions of the optimum size cotton mill.

If Roberts's mule was not adopted overnight, it was not merely for reasons of supply and licensing under the patent. The early power loom was only effective for the lower counts of yarn (i.e. coarser cloths), and this restriction undoubtedly inhibited the development of the mule in the 1820s and 1830s, leading to a revival of the older (Arkwright) technique of throstle spinning [111]. At the time when Montgomery and Ure were writing, Marshall visited Houldsworth's mill, one of the largest and most successful in Manchester, and noted 'I think the fine spinners in Manchester are rather backward in replacing their old machinery with new . . . [112]'. Very likely the manufacturers were holding back major re-equipment, waiting to see where technical developments were leading. The depression of 1837-42 probably served to delay much rebuilding until the 1840s.

The conclusion of this rapid survey must, therefore, be that the considerable growth of the cotton industry that took place between the end of the French wars and the middle 1830s was largely based on a productive unit established for mule spinning in the last years of the eighteenth century. Within this prototype there were, as contemporaries observed, innumerable refinements, but major advances in productivity appear to have derived largely from economies in the use of power [113] (expressed in more efficient transmission rather than engine production), while there is little evidence of new economies of scale. In mechanical principles and spindle size, the mule recommended by Montgomery's pioneer technical manual as most productive was the same as those being built by McConnel & Kennedy in 1796. If there was heavy scrapping of obsolete machinery in this period, it was likely to have been the survivals of the Arkwright period and the botched-up engines of the later years of the Watt patent [114]. It seems probable that the estimates of fixed capital formation in 1834, minus that calculated for 1817 earlier in this paper, approach a fair calculation of original fixed capital formation over the intervening seventeen years of growth — subject, of course, to any adjustments that can be made to take account of the changing value of money.

NOTES

[1] This is an extended and annotated form of the paper read at the Conference.

[2] Sun Fire Office Registers and Royal Exchange Registers are in the custody of Guildhall Library, London EC2. The Sun registers are in two series: the 'Old Series' (abbreviated OS here) comprises MS. 11,936 and covers the period 1710 to 1850 in 733 volumes; the 'Country Series' (abbreviated CS) is MS. 11,937 and contains policies for provincial agencies in 527 volumes for the period 1793 to 1863. Royal Exchange Registers (abbreviated RE), MS. 7253, consisting of 98 volumes covering the period 1773 to 1833. There are gaps in all three series, and none are indexed or the policies entered in any systematic sequence. I should like to acknowledge two grants from the Pasold Fund towards the cost of paying assistants for the routine task of extracting policies connected with the textile industries.

[3] Summarized in B. R. Mitchell *Abstract of British Historical Statistics*, p. 178 (1962).

[4] E. Baines, *History of the Cotton Manufacturer* p. 369 (1835); unsigned analysis of 1783 of the costs of running Robinson's mill at Papplewick, Notts. (Portland MSS. DD4P 79/63. Notts. C.R.O.)

[5] McConnel & Kennedy MSS., Manchester University Library.

[6] W. Radcliffe, *Origins of Power Loom Weaving*, p. 65 (1828).

[7] E. Butterworth, *Historical Sketches of Oldham*, pp. 118, 135 (1856).

[8] Great Bolton Poor Rate Books (Bolton Reference Library); J. Hodgson, *Textile Manufacture in Keighley*, pp. 212-39 (1879). M. M. Edwards, *The Growth of the British Cotton Trade 1780-1815*, pp. 186-9 (1967); S. D. Chapman, *The Early Factory Masters*, pp. 56-60 (1967).

[9] Examples are given in M. M. Edwards, op. cit., pp. 186-7; S. D. Chapman,

op. cit., Ch. 5; J. Hodgson, loc. cit.: 'The lightness as well as the cheapness of the calico has rendered it a chief article of dress amongst all classes of people and annihilated the manufacture of many of the lighter kinds of woollen and worsted stuffs formerly so much in demand . . .' (*Rees Cyclopaedia*, art. on 'Cotton'); the decline of Scottish linen was hardly less precipitate.

[10] *Universal British Directory*, II (Chorley).

[11] Sun OS 333/512654 (1785), CS 4/629341 (1794).

[12] Catherine Hutton, *Reminiscences of a Gentlewoman of the Last Century*, pp. 22-3 (1891).

[13] P. G. M. Dickson, *The Sun Fire Office 1710-1960*, pp. 72-7, 144 (1960). After a sequence of losses on cotton mills the Sun, Royal Exchange and Phoenix progressively increased their rates until in 1815 they stood at 15s. per £100 insured. J. & T. Clarke of Trowbridge wrote to the Sun Office, 7 March 1815, 'We beg to state the Norwich Society insures property subject to the same risk for 7s. 6d. per £100 . . .' and listed eight leading mills in the locality insured at Norwich. (Wilts. Arch. Soc. MSS.)

[14]. See Appendix: 'The Reliability of Insurance Valuations as a Measure of Capital Formation'.

[15]. John Sutcliffe, *A Treatise on Canals and Reservoirs . . . with Observations . . . on the best mode of carding, roving, drawing and spinning all kinds of cotton twist*, p. 62 (Rochdale, 1816). Sutcliffe's claim was not prejudiced by limited experience, for in the early 1790s he served Markland, Cookson & Fawcett, the owners of the largest cotton mill at Leeds (Boulton & Watt drawings, Portfolio 91), John Marshall, the pioneer of flax spinning, and, for a time, Benjamin Gott. (Gott MSS. at Cusworth Hall Museum, Doncaster).

[16] Horse powered carding mills were particularly common in the locality of Oldham and Bolton, where water power resources were meagre. E. Butterworth, op. cit., pp. 117, 129-30, 139-40, 147; J. Aiken, *Country from 30 to 40 Miles round Manchester*, pp. 237-8, 262 (1795).

[17] Most of the physical evidence is in Derbyshire, Nottinghamshire and Staffordshire, where the early decline of the cotton industry removed the incentive for rebuilding mills on a larger scale. The width of early mills was prescribed by the practice of accommodating water frames on either side of the central shafting which stretched the length of the mill (Helmshore Museum exhibits; plates in Rees, *Cyclopaedia*). Another factor in prescribing width was the maximum length of an unsupported timber beam, which was about 30 ft. In the first two decades of the nineteenth century water frames and mules grew rapidly in size, and iron framing made greater dimensions possible: Sutcliffe recommended 48 ft. in 1816. J. Sutcliffe, op. cit., pp. 33-4, 37, J. Montgomery, loc. cit.; S. Andrew, *Fifty Years Cotton Trade*, p. 1 (Oldham, 1887). The implications of the obsolescence of mill buildings erected in the first phase of investment (1770-1803) will be noted in Section 3, below.

[18] *Report of Sel. Comm. on Children in Manufactories*, Parl. Papers, 1816, III, 134, 141.

[19] S. D. Chapman, 'The Peels in the early English cotton industry', *Business History*, XI (2), 1969.

[20] Beverley, Cross & Billiam to Boulton & Watt, 23 June 1792.

[21] W. Pole (ed.), *Life of Sir William Fairbairn*, p. 121 (1877) (my italics). Lowe probably gained his unique experience as Arkwright's millwright.

[22] Louth Mill Co. building accounts (Spalding Gentlemen's Society).

[23] Peter Ewart (Manchester) to Matthew Boulton, 12 December 1791: 'I

haven't been able to find a good millwright here. A few good filers and turners, all engaged for terms of years in the cotton mills. Atherton tells me he knows of two good watch toolmakers in London . . . .' (Assay Office Library, Birmingham). I owe this reference to Dr Jennifer Tann.

[24] S. D. Chapman, *Early Factory Masters*, pp. 107-9.

[25] Bibliography on Drinkwater, Atherton and other leading manufacturers in Appendix 1.

[26] 'The trade of Manchester is chiefly mule spinning, whilst the water twist is mostly spun in the country by water mills because the great power it requires is too expensive for steam engines', (Rees, *Cyclopaedia*, article on 'Manufacture of Cotton', c. 1815). It is possible to obtain cost data to give more precision to this point. For instance, Sir Robert Peel's Fazeley (Tamworth) mill was a typical Type B2 mill, built in 1791 at a total cost of £5,000, including £300 for the two 16 ft. high breast wheels. (Sun OS 376/582847, CS 7/640036). Calculations on the site suggest 24 h.p. for the two wheels on the assumption of 60 per cent efficiency, so that each unit of horse power cost £12. To this must be added the cost of excavating and banking a reservoir of 2·226 acres, and masonry, carpentry and ironwork for the sluice, making a total of about £450 if Smeaton's calculations can be adopted. (John Smeaton, *Reports of the late John Smeaton, F.R.S.*, II, pp. 392-3 (1837). The gross cost of the installation would be £750, or £30 for one horse power. A 24 h.p. Watt engine cost £1,200 in 1795 (E. Roll, *An Early Experiment in Industrial Organisation*, p. 312 (1930)) or £50 for each horse power excluding the engine house, and it is doubtful whether other engine manufacturers could produce rotary engines more cheaply (see, e.g., price list of Low Moor engines, Dunn MSS., Sheffield City Library, MD 1747/12). Water wheels were, of course, much less expensive to maintain than steam engines (M. M. Edwards, op. cit., p. 210), while depreciation rates, even on wooden wheels, were lower than on steam engines; for instance, Lowe's wooden wheels at Catrine lasted over forty years (1784-1825) before they became obsolete (W. Fairbairn, loc. cit.), while in the early 1790s Wilkes of Measham allowed 25 per cent per annum depreciation on his Watt engine (A. Young, *Tours in England and Wales* . . . (L.S.E. reprint, 1932), p. 279). Peel's costs were unusually high because he was developing a virgin site in an area with limited water power; in 1795 nearly all cotton spinners occupied sites previously in some other industrial use such as corn mills, forges etc. In more favoured sites in the Pennines and Scotland the cost of water wheels might be similar (the median insured value was £250) but the cost of leats, dam, etc. much less. (See Appendix: 'The Reliability of Insurance Valuations . . .')

[27] Appendix 6 for examples.

[28] The region is defined in S. D. Chapman, op. cit., pp. 12-13.

[29] Appendix 6.

[30] W. H. Chaloner, 'Robert Owen, Peter Drinkwater, and the Early Factory System in Manchester', *Bull. John Rylands Library*, XXXVII (1954), p. 91. Dr R. L. Hills points out that it was not until 1793, or nine years after the beginning of building at Styal, that blacksmiths and clockmakers disappear from Gregg's wages books: *Studies in the History of Textile Technology*, Ph.D. thesis, Manchester (1968), X/5, XII/11.

[31] S. D. Chapman, op. cit., Chs. 5, 6. Records of building in the region survive for Louth Mill (1784), Pleasley Mill (1785) and Cressbrook Mill (1815-16).

[32] Appendix 6.

[33] Notably in Sir John Sinclair, *Statistical Account of Scotland* (1792) and in various records in the Signet Library and in the Scottish Record Office. (See Appendix 5). I owe my references from the last two sources to Dr John Butt, whose help in allowing me to use his transcripts is gratefully acknowledged. Dr Butt's own study of the Scottish cotton industry will throw further light on the points made here.

[34] Compare data in Appendices 3, 4, 5, 6.

[35] E. g. David Dale was a partner in New Lanark, Catrine, Ayr, Newton Douglas and Stanley mills; George Houston in mills at Johnstone Bridge (Paisley), Lochwinnoch and Cartside (Appendix 5); Robert Dunmore was a partner in Ballindalloch cotton mill, Muirkirk Iron Works, Duntocher Wool Co., and the Dalmotter Co. J. R. Hume and J. Butt, 'Muirkirk 1788-1802: the creation of a Scottish industrial community'; *Scottish Historical Review*, XLV (1967), p. 167.

[36] G. M. Mitchell, 'The English and Scottish cotton industries', *Scottish Historical Review*, XXII (1925).

[37] Signet Library 449/23, 209/34, 411/62.

[38] Signet Library 264/2; J. Montgomery op. cit., 292-3.

[39] H. Hamilton, *The Industrial Revolution in Scotland*, p. 123 (1932).

[40] Scottish Record Office, U/P 1 Currie Dal C/9/1. Corse v. Houston (1788).

[41] The insurance policies of Dale, Corse, Burns & Co., Monteath and Crum, contain valuations of jennies or mules, which may be included in Brown's estimates.

[42] The northern cotton region is taken to include Lancashire, the West Riding, Cheshire (Stockport, Macclesfield and other centres), North Wales (Holywell and Greenfield, Flint), Cumberland, Westmoreland and the parish of Glossop in Derbyshire.

[43] J. Aikin op. cit., pp. 446, 458.

[44] E. Butterworth, op. cit., p. 140.

[45] E.g. G. H. Tupling, *History of Rossendale* (1927); J. D. Marshall, *Furness and the Industrial Revolution*, pp. 50-4 (1958); J. Hodgson, loc. cit.; C. H. Hibbert, 'Investigation into Cotton Mills in Warrington' (typescript, 1900. Warrington P.L.).

[46] Manchester Rate Books (Manchester Central Library) do not identify cotton mills and warehouses as such at the end of the eighteenth century. Rate and valuation books have survived for Great Bolton (the original settlement south of the River Croal) but not Little Bolton, where many of the new factories were built.

[47] RE 22/124243.

[48] E. Butterworth, op. cit., pp. 116, 124, 145-6.

[49] Sun CS 8/640326, RE 27/141905. Household goods (£50) excluded.

[50] E Butterworth, op. cit., p. 126, names nineteen owners of these machines, c. 1770. They were properly called twisting mills, and are not to be confused with the much more expensive Dutch smallwares loom. For the twisting mill see Denis Diderot *Encyclopédie* (1751-2), IV (article on 'Filature'), plate II; Rees, *Cyclopaedia*, article on 'Manufacture of Cotton' and plates.

[51] The figures are approximate because of local cost variations.

[52] M. M. Edwards, op. cit., p. 213, maintains that there were few cotton spinners who built original premises at the period.

[53] RE 26/134305 (1793).

[54] Sun OS 362/560926 (1789), CS 4/625510, 10/64045; J. Aikin, op. cit., p. 456.

[55] J. Aikin, op. cit., p. 446.

[56] C. Aspin, *James Hargreaves and the Spinning Jenny* (Helmshore, 1964), p. 51.

[57] W. Radcliffe, op.cit., pp. 65 ff; C. Aspin, loc. cit.; P. Gaskell, *Artizans and Machinery*, pp. 32-3 (1836). Appendix 3 for examples of 'stall holding'.

[58] Appendix 3.

[59] Sun OS 370/572667.

[60] Analyses of costs of 'civil engineering' work at late eighteenth century mills can be found in John Smeaton, loc. cit., and A. J. Sykes, *Concerning the Bleaching Industry*, pp. 114-15 (1925).

[61] See Appendix: 'The Reliability of Insurance Valuations as a Measure of Capital Formation'.

[62] There are no reliable contemporary estimates of the value of looms but some conception of the order of magnitude may be calculated from the estimates of G. A. Lee and Thomas Ainsworth, quoted in G. J. French, *Life and Times of Samuel Crompton*, pp. 279, 281-2 (1859). In 1811 the mule spinning sector employed 150,000 weavers and this sector was responsible for two-thirds of the output of the industry; the other third was presumably the Arkwright sector which would employ about 75,000 weavers at this time, probably about the same number as in 1795. Assuming looms were worth £5 each on the average, and each weaver occupied one loom, we arrive at the following estimate:

> 1795   75,000 looms worth £375,000
> 1811 225,000 looms worth £1,125,000

The numbers of stocking frames rose from 20,000 in 1782 to 29,582 in 1812 (statistics summarized in D. M. Smith, 'The British hosiery industry at the middle of the 19th century', *Trans. Institute of British Geographers*, 1963, p. 129). New frames cost £18 each on the average (G. Henson *History of the Framework Knitters*, p. 385 (1831)), so gross fixed capital formation in this branch in the period of mechanization of spinning would be about £175,000. Dr Edwards's view that bleaching and printing 'probably absorbed as much capital as the spinners' (M. M. Edwards, op. cit., p. 183) is not supported by evidence of 1795 insurance valuations: see S. D. Chapman, 'The Peels in the early English cotton industry', *Business History*, XI (1969), 74, n.2. The leading printers were also spinners and I have included their interest in the finishing section within my estimate of capital formation; but I hope to make a more adequate examination of this sector when time allows. Capital expenditure appears to have been modest in the finishing sector. Roebuck & Garbett's lead chambers cost only £8 each, according to O. Guttmann, 'The early manufacture of sulphuric acid', *Journal of the Society of Chemical Industry*, XX (1901), pp. 5-8, and one of the largest plants in Lancashire (Bealeys of Radcliffe) insured for only £3,000 in 1795 (Sun CS 9/644232).

[63] John Kennedy, *Miscellaneous Papers*, pp. 71-3 (Manchester, 1849). Boulton & Watt reckoned one horse power to 100 spindles for Arkwright's system from the period of their successful experiment with Robinson's cotton mill at Papplewick (letter to Chas. Wyatt, 30 May 1785, B.R.L.) This equation was fairly widely adopted up to the end of the century – see, e.g., R. Buchanan, *An Essay on the Teeth of Wheels*, p. 131 (1808). The power was chiefly absorbed by friction (R. L. Hills op. cit., X/12). The adoption of the rotary steam engine to the first two

components of the mule cycle required one horse power for about 350 spindles in 1814, according to McConnel & Kennedy, quoted in M. M. Edwards, op. cit., p. 188. Data for John Simpson's (late Arkwright's) Manchester mill in 1801 suggest that this equation was already reached at the end of the century in the most advanced plants (Manchester Ref. Library, BR 677/1. B20). The productivity of a water spindle was no greater than a mule spindle.

[64] S. D. Chapman, *Early Factory Masters*, Chs. 5, 6; G. M. Mitchell, loc. cit.

[65] Appendix 1.

[66] Notably those of Arkwright, John Smalley at Holywell, and Buchanan brothers at Stanley mills, Perthshire. Peter Atherton and Robert Burns (of Houston, Burns & Co. and Corse, Burns & Co.) only maintained their place in the industry through merchant partnerships. See bibliography in Appendix 1; Signet Library 368/21, 360/16, 500/89 for Buchanans; S.R.O. U/P Curie Dal C/9/1 for Burns.

[67] Duck & Potts. Appendix 1.

[68] P. Gaskell, *Artizans and Machinery*, p. 33 (1836), R. Owen, *Life*, p. 26 (1857).

[69] James Montgomery, *Carding and Spinning Master's Assistant*, pp. 145-6 (Glasgow, 1832). Crompton's papers, 1811 box (Irving bequest, Bolton Civic Centre Museum) show that a dozen of the forty-three leading manufacturers of 1795 had entered mule spinning on a substantial scale: Peel, Douglas, Drinkwater, Simpson, Marsland, Horrocks, Gregg, Holt, Watson, Phillips & Lee, Daintry and Birley & Hornby. Gregg, Watson, Douglas and Salvin were beginning to install them in 1794-7 (R. L. Hills, op. cit., VII/14-23).

[70] G. J. French, op. cit., pp. 161-2. G. W. Daniels, 'Crompton's census of the cotton industry', *Economic History*, II (1930-33), pp. 107-10, gives 4.2 million spindles, but Crompton's list of firms shows that this total was incomplete. Crompton's summary omits Strutts' mills at Belper, Holywell mills, Peels' Burton and Tamworth mills, and numerous other warp spinning plants.

[71] S. R. O. U/P Shields 1 SH A/7/49. (Arkwright v. Twigg.) James Montgomery, op. cit., pp. 167, 170, implies a much slower rate of obsolescence.

[72] J. Sutcliffe, op. cit., p. 17.

[73] W. H. Chaloner, op. cit., p. 94.

[74] McConnel & Kennedy to Taylor & Heywood, 28 February 1795.

[75] Strutts are probably the main exception in the period. For some unknown reason William Strutt's experiments with the automatic mule were laid aside (S. D. Chapman, op. cit., p. 212).

[76] G. J. French, op. cit., p. 162.

[77] J. Montgomery, op. cit., p. 249-50.

[78] The most efficient transmission of power to mules was achieved by arranging them on either side of the central shafting so that one man could supervise two machines. On this principle, mules of 192 spindles required a building 48 ft wide, though the width 'I recommend will be by some opposed, as it goes, in a great measure, to overthrow the system on which cotton factories are built in Manchester . . .' (J. Sutcliffe, op. cit., pp. 33-7), Crompton's survey suggests that 192 spindle mules were becoming obsolete by 1811. Further data is given in Samuel Andrew, *Fifty Years Cotton Trade*, p. 1 (Oldham, 1887): mule spinning mills 'were built with a view to accommodate the length of the machines then made . . . They

were generally 14 or 21 yards wide, non fireproof, and the rooms were often low overhead and badly ventilated . . . The spinning rooms of a 14 yard mill would hold 27 dozen spindles (i.e. 324 spindles) mules in that width . . .' Compare the dimensions of mills built in the Arkwright era.

[79] G. W. Daniels, 'The cotton trade at the close of the Napoleonic war', *Trans. Manchester Statistical Society*, 1917-18, 18-21.

[80] E. Butterworth, op. cit., pp. 153, 183.

[81] E. Butterworth, *An Historical Account of the Towns of Ashton-under-Lyne, Stalybridge and Duckinfield,* p. 147 (1842) says that there were only two mills in Stalybridge in 1801. In 1811 there were eighteen mule spinning concerns in the town, seven of them with more than 10,000 spindles. (G. W. Daniels, op. cit., p. 109).

[82] G. W. Daniels, loc. cit.

[83] A sketch of 1797 of the dimensions of a spinning room for Ainsworth's Preston mill, quoted in H. Catling, *The Spinning Mule* (forthcoming, 1970), shows a room 46 x 14 ft for four mules totalling 744 spindles. Such a room would be about the size of one created by opening up the top floor of a terrace of four cottages, and conceivably 1,500 spindles could be accommodated over eight cottages, but there are obvious limits to such adaptation, particularly when it is recalled that the other rooms would be needed for the preparatory processes of mixing, willowing, scutching, spreading, carding, drawing and slubbing.

[84] 144 spindles was about the limit for purely manual operation, and there are few mules of such small size in Crompton's lists. Moreover, the geographical distribution of mule factories in 1811 suggests that less water power was being used in England.

[85] Kennedy, proceeding by an entirely different route, calculated 6.6 million spindles and 20,000 h.p. employed in the British cotton industry in 1817. E. Baines, *History of the Cotton Manufacture*, p. 369 (1835). In view of the post-war slump and recession in building, my estimate seems extremely conservative, even though Kennedy's estimate includes water power.

[86] Reckoning £50 per unit horse power, an estimate calculated from data in E. Roll, *An Early Experiment in Industrial Organisation*, p. 312 (1930). There is no evidence of sharp cost reductions after expiration of Watt's patent.

[87] R. L. Hills, op. cit., IX/5.

[88] E. Baines, loc. cit.

[89] Spinning on Arkwright's system was not revived until the 1830s, when the demand for yarns of the lower counts increased with the establishment of power loom factories. James Montgomery, *The Carding and Spinning Master's Assistant* pp. 145-6 (Glasgow, 1832).

[90] D. S. L. Cardwell, 'Power technologies and the advance of science 1700-1825', *Technology and Culture*, VI (1965).

[91] Calculations based on data for Peel's Fazeley mill (cited above) and J. Montgomery, *Theory and Practice of Cotton Spinning*, pp. 249-50.

[92] E.g. Cardwell, Birley & Hornby are said to have had a working capital of £146,740 in 1794 (M. M. Edwards, op. cit., p. 258) but their two mills were insured for a mere £6,200.

[93] M. Blaug, 'Productivity of capital in the Lancashire cotton industry during the nineteenth century', *Economic History Review*, XIII (1961).

[94] Calculations based on data for Robinson's Papplewick (Nottingham) mill in RE 32a/154792; DD4P 79/63 (Notts. C.R.O.).

[95] Sun CS 13/653223 (warehouse omitted); Sutcliffe's drawings of mill in Boulton & Watt MSS., Porfolio 91; calculations based on John Marshall's report of c. 1795 that the 'greatest speed at which they can spin cotton is 15 ft a minute [per spindle] or 12 ft a minute the day through' at Cookson & Fawcett's mill. (Marshall MSS. 57, p. 17, Brotherton Library, Leeds). The calculation assumes 3,000 spindles (for a 30 h.p. Watt engine), production of seventy hours a week and fifty weeks a year, and an average count of 20s.

[96] E. Butterworth, op. cit., p. 119.

[97] J. Montgomery, op. cit., p. 255.

[98] The best evidence for this claim is the widespread persistence of 'stall holding', i.e. small spinners owning their own mules but renting space and power. E. Butterworth, op. cit., p. 183; S. Andrew, op. cit., p. 2.

[99] J. Montgomery, *Carding and Spinning Master's Assistant*, pp. 167-70, and the author's introduction to new edition of G. F. French, *Life and Times of Samuel Crompton* (Adams and Dart, 1970).

[100] J. Montgomery, op. cit., p. 145.

[101] A. E. Musson and E. Robinson, *Science and Technology in the Industrial Revolution*, pp. 462-3 (Manchester, 1969); A. Rees, *Cyclopaedia*, article on 'Manufacture of Cotton'. M. M. Edwards, op. cit., p. 210.

[102] S. Andrew, op. cit., p.1; D. A. Farnie, *The English Cotton Industry 1850-96*, M.A. Thesis, p. 430 (Manchester, 1953).

[103] Marshall MS. 37, p. 1 (Brotherton Library, Leeds).

[104] J. Montgomery, op. cit., p. 167; A. Ure, op. cit., vol. I, p. 301. Iron gearing is referred to in a description of one of Peel's mills in 1783 (A. Rémond, *John Holker*, p. 158) but was not generally adopted until much later. J. Farey, *A Treatise on the Steam Engine*, p. 443 (1827).

[105] On capital shortage see my article 'James Longsdon, farmer and fustian manufacturer: the smaller firm in the early English cotton industry', *Textile History*, III (1970).

[106] J. Montgomery, op. cit., p. 170.

[107] D. A. Farnie, op. cit., p. 18.

[108] J. Montgomery, op. cit., p. 167.

[109] W. Fairbairn, *Treatise on Mills and Millwork*, II, p. 178 (1861).

[110] J. Montgomery, *Theory and Practice of Cotton Spinning*, pp. 254-5.

[111] J. Montgomery, *Carding and Spinning Master's Assistant*, p. 146. Marshall MSS. 37, pp. 49, 62.

[112] Marshall MSS. 37, p. 74.

[113] The number of spindles driven by one horse power increased as follows:

	c.1800	1836
Throstles	100	180
Mules (hand operated)	350	500

A. Ure, op. cit., vol. I, p. 304, and evidence cited above.

[114] Cf. John Marshall, c.1803: 'The steam engines at Glasgow are in general very bad ones, only two or three of Boulton & Watt's . . . .' (Marshall MSS. 62, unpaginated notes of Scottish tour). A local survey of this period showed nine steam engines and eleven horse gins used in Scottish cotton mills ('McTaggart's List', Boulton & Watt MSS., B.R.L. Reference from Dr J. Tann).

APPENDICES
The reliability of insurance valuations as a measure of capital formation.

The records of the Sun, Royal Exchange, and Hand-in-Hand insurance companies at Guildhall Library, though extensive, contain no explicit information on methods of valuation used by the companies' agents, and the following remarks are therefore based on what appear to be reasonable inferences. Insurance valuations might be expected to be realistic, inasmuch as the company would not normally over-value a property while the customer would insist that his property was not under-insured. Occasional mistakes by the companies in valuing goods or negligence of customers in periodically re-assessing the value of insured items should not be allowed to divert attention from the basic truth of this consideration. The tension between company and customer over insurance valuations might, it can be argued, produce a more realistic valuation than those that can be studied in the few surviving balance sheets of the period relating to textile firms.

Basis for valuation. During the period when most spinners employed direct labour, both for mill and machine building, and much time and capital was wasted in fruitless pioneer experiment, costing must have been a difficult matter, even for the handful of managers with training in accounts. Thus Rothesay mill, which is said to have cost £4,892 to build (1778) realized only £1,500 seven years later, when Arkwright type mills were still at a premium (Signet Library, 209/34). The basis for valuation is not made explicit in the surviving records of the insurance companies, but the invariable practice appears to have been to insure at historic cost, subject of course to the approval of the local agent. As a result of a sequence of serious losses by the Sun, Royal Exchange and Phoenix from their cotton mill business, approval of the London office had to be registered after 1806 (Sun Fire Office General Minute Books, MS. 11,931/7, 8).

Depreciation of assets were seldom made on any regular basis as accounting techniques were most elemental. Thus Robert Burns, one of the most successful Scottish cotton spinners, entered machinery in his books at cost and did not allow depreciation for twenty years (Signet Library, 264/2); in their first fourteen years (1786-99) Oldknow Cowpe & Co. only allowed for depreciation of machinery once, and that a mere £57 in 1795 (Hollins MSS.). This is not particularly misleading when it is considered that spinning machinery on Arkwright's principle followed the same basic pattern from the early 1770s to the end of the century, and the introduction of machinery for carding, batting and other preparatory processes during this period displaced traditional handicraft methods rather than other machinery (R. L. Hills, op. cit., IV/24 and V). New water power units, transmission systems and buildings were expected to have a long life, while older converted premises were recorded in insurance policies at cost. Newcomen and Watt engines were often bought second hand (Boulton & Watt 'Engine Book'; M. M. Edwards, op. cit., p. 211) and insurance valuations reflect this transfer with a lower valuation. Quotations in the literature about high rates of obsolescence on cotton mill machinery will be found, on close examination, to refer to the rapid evolution of the mule after c. 1795. Normally the value of an asset was written down in accounts and hence in the insurance records only when its historic value had obviously collapsed – e.g. when a common steam engine failed to meet the promise of its makers, or the original mill on a site was superseded by new buildings. Valuations were normally rounded to the nearest £10, or adjusted so that the total assets insured reached a multiple of £50 or £100.

89

Omissions. So far as the cotton industry is concerned, the main omission is of reservoirs, dams and watercourses that did not have to be insured. In mitigation of this discrepancy it may be fairly pointed out that, in 1795, there were few mills on virgin sites, most cotton spinners taking over the sites of corn mills, forges, lead works, potteries, and silk and linen mills. In such cases original capital formation by cotton spinners will be more accurately recorded in insurance valuations than in any surviving balance sheet or inventory summary. Where a virgin site was occupied, the cost of spade work and masonry was not large, if Holme and Slater's Bolton mill (1792) may, as field work suggests, be taken as typical (A. J. Sykes, loc. cit.):

To little wear and fender	£4	11	0
To 209 yards of banking, walling and puddling @ 3s.	31	7	0
To 169 yards of troughs and fixing at 1s.	8	9	0
To cutting water sluice and soughing	16	8	6
To wear and all work belonging to it	28	18	8
To old wheel trace and sough	4	17	10
To new wheel trace and sough walling etc.	12	17	5
To 11 yards soughing @ 4d., 23¾ yards @ 6.		15	6
	£108	4	11

M. M. Edwards (op. cit., p. 209) instances a larger mill where the cost of 'carrying' the water came to £223.

Other omissions can sometimes be identified, particularly 'social' assets like workers' houses and apprentice houses. These are identified in the following lists where possible.

Comparisons with other business records. There are in fact very few records of textile concerns c. 1795 which offer a satisfactory basis for comparison. In some instances comparison may be reassuring – e.g. J. & T. Clarke of Trowbridge (Wilts. Arch. Soc. MSS.), while in others there may be puzzling discrepancies – e.g. Oldknow, Cowpe & Co. of Pleasley (Notts.):

ANNUAL ACCOUNTS (Hollins MSS.)

Mill, houses, damhead and cut	£2,539
Water wheel, pitwheel and penstock	400
Machinery and utensils	2,760
	£5,699

SUN INSURANCE POLICY CS 11/648272

Cotton mill	£600
Millwrights work	300
Clockmakers work	900
Stock	200
Houses	300
	£2,300
Phoenix policy on mill, machinery and utensils	1,000
	£3,300

Some of the difference may be accounted for by the inclusion of land and site value, as well as dam and cut, in the annual accounts. In terms of accounting for capital formation, these items would represent transfers (Pleasley was a forge site) and the insurance valuation may represent original additions to capital more accurately.

The Rothesay mill case cited above (Signet Library, 209/34) is a reminder that capital losses written off by pioneer mills will not, of course, be recorded in insurance policies. In this instance the insurance valuation (£4,800, 1795) is not far from the sale price (£4,500, 1791), but does not disclose £4,392 lost in 1785 and at this second sale. However, there were probably few mills in this category.

Stock. The valuation of what is termed 'stock', 'stock and goods' or 'stock and utensils' is the most difficult item to interpret. The valuations for the largest mills are often only £200 to £500, and very rarely exceed £1,000, and these figures cannot be realistic estimates for raw material, work in progress and holdings of the finished product at the mill, if other sources of information may be trusted (S. D. Chapman, *The Early Factory Masters*, p. 126; M. M. Edwards, *The British Cotton Trade*, pp. 257-9). The item is probably intended to cover tools and other moveable utensils, and has thus been included as fixed capital, with the totals for the various firms cited in the Appendices to this article.

Multiple insurance of large cotton and worsted spinning mills was common, the Sun, Royal Exchange and Phoenix often sharing the risk. In the Sun policies, the other companies' policies are explicitly allowed by endorsement at the foot of the valuation, very likely as part of the standing agreement between the three London companies. In practice, however, minor omissions and discrepancies occur in the records – e.g. the Backbarrow Co.'s Sun Policy for 1795 records a policy of £3,600 at the Royal Exchange (CS 9/640814) but in fact the additional policy was for £5,000 (RE 29/144296). As the Phoenix policies have not survived it is impossible to check the accuracy of policies imputed to that company. There is occasional evidence of failure to record a second or third policy at all (e.g. Ballindalloch Mill Co., Balfron, Stirling, Sun CS 8/638345) and if this omission were widespread it could cause gross errors in any calculations based on insurance data. Some safeguard against such errors is provided by the existence of a sequence of policies for most firms, and by the student's familiarity with the firms under review which leads to easy identification of obvious inconsistencies between one concern and another.

Summarily, it may be said that the frequent use of converted premises tended to inflate insurance valuations, while the omission of original ground improvements, housing and other items often led to undervaluation. On balance, it may be surmised that insurance policies approached a conservative estimate of what would now be recognized as net fixed capital formation.

APPENDIX 1

Insurance policy valuations of English cotton manufacturers c. 1795
(Policies over £5,000 only – Midlands omitted)

	No. of calico works	No. of mills	Value (£)
Robert Peel, Sons & Partners, Blackburn, Bury, Bolton, Burton, Tamworth	8	23	191,690
William Douglas and the Holywell Co., Manchester and Holywell (Flint)	–	7	80,950
Peter Atherton & Partners, Liverpool, Holywell, Chipping	–	4	43,500[a]
Peter Drinkwater, Manchester and Northwich	–	2	38,600
Joseph Thackeray & Partners, Manchester and Cark-in-Cartmell	–	3	27,760
Simpson & Barton (late Arkwright), Manchester	–	2	22,500
Forte, Taylor & Bury, Manchester and Blackburn	2	1	21,000
Samuel & Peter Marsland, Stockport and Manchester	–	4	20,200[a]
John Horrocks, Preston	–	4	16,350
Samuel Gregg, Manchester and Styall	–	2	16,000
David Holt & Co., Manchester	–	2	15,000
Edmund Lodge & Sons, Halifax and Rochdale	–	2	13,800[b]
Wells, Heathfield & Co., London, Sheffield and Stockport	–	2	13,200
John Parker & Partners, London and Clitheroe	–	4	12,200
John Watson, Preston	–	2	11,850
Markland, Cookson & Fawcett, Leeds	–	1	11,600[b]
Howarths & Smith, Blackburn, Manchester and London	1	1	11,700
Bott, Bower, Birch & Randall, Tutbury (Staffs) and Nantwich	–	2	11,450
Francis Heywood & Partners, Manchester, Macclesfield and Litton	1	2	11,300
Birch, Robinson, Walmsley & Barker, Backbarrow (Furness)	–	2	11,000
Nash & Abbott, Manchester	1	2	10,200
Phillips & Lee, Salford	–	1	10,000
Daintry, Ryle & Co., Macclesfield	–	2	10,000[a]
Gideon Bickerdike, Manchester and (with Buchanan Bros.) Deanston (Perthshire)	–	2	9,700[a]
John Haigh, London and Marsden (Huddersfield)	–	4	9,100
Alexander Hunt, Stockport	–	2	7,700
John Whitaker, Stockport	–	1	7,500
Edward & James Pedder, Preston	–	2	7,500
John & Robert Kirkman, Liverpool	–	1	7,000
Busfield & Co., Bingley (West Riding)	–	1	7,000

Samuel Oldknow, Mellor	–	1	6,950
Salvin Brothers, Manchester and Durham	–	1	6,750
Blesard & Arthington, Leeds	–	2	6,450
David Campbell & Partners, Manchester	–	2	6,400
Paul Tate & Robert Brown, Manchester and London	–	1	6,200
Cooper, Cardwell, Birley & Hornby, Blackburn	–	2	6,200
Abraham Clegg, Oldham	–	2	6,000
Abraham Illingworth, Stockport	–	1	7,100
James Doxon, Stockport	–	2	5,500
Blagborough & Holroyds, Leeds	–	1	5,400
Duck & Potts, Manchester	–	1	5,200
Peter Garforth & Partners, Skipton	–	3	5,200
Atherton & Rawstornes, Huddersfield	–	1	5,000
Totals	13	110	765,700

(a) Valuation known to be incomplete.
(b) Includes wool or worsted works.

NOTES

In general the valuations given here are the original (crude) totals. The only adjustments that have been made are:

(1) Stock at London and Manchester warehouses has been deducted. Stock insured at the mills was invariably at a nominal valuation (£200 to £500 was typical) and in many instances appears to include movable utensils; it has therefore been left in the total.

(2) Household goods, clothes, plate and books have been deducted. Houses have been included as they were invariably used as offices, workshops, and storage space.

(3) The value of Boulton & Watt engines has been added in two instances where their omission can clearly be identified. (Alexander Hunt, Abraham Illingworth).

SOURCES ON THE ABOVE FIRMS:

Manchester fustian merchants

William Douglas & Holywell Co.: Sun CS 7/638223; RE 29/143470; Boulton & Watt MSS. (Birmingham Reference Library); E. J. Foulkes, 'The cotton spinning factories of Flintshire', *Flintshire Historical Society Publications*, XXI (1964).

Peter Drinkwater: Sun CS 7/638222; RE 29/143469; W. H. Chaloner, 'Robert Owen, Peter Drinkwater and the early factory system in Manchester', *Bull. John Rylands Library*, XXXVII (1954).

Thackeray, Stockdale & Co.: Sun CS 9/640660, 10/641765; W. H. Chaloner, 'The Stockdale family, the Wilkinson brothers and the cotton mills at Cark-in-Cartmell', *Trans. Cumberland and Westmorland Antiquarian Society*, N.S., LXIV; J. Farey, *A Treatise on the Steam Engine*, p. 662 (1827).

Simpson & Barton: RE 27/141103; Sun CS 7/638231; S. D. Chapman, *The Early Factory Masters*, pp. 70-1, 128 (1967); Robert Owen, *Life of Robert Owen*, p. 48 (1857).

Samuel Gregg: RE 29/143468; Sun CS 7/638224; W. Lazenby, *The Social and Economic History of Styal*, unpublished M.A. thesis, Manchester, 1949.

David Holt: RE 31/149003, 29/143664; Sun CS 7/638228; Lewis's *Directory of Manchester and Salford, 1788;* E. Baines, *History of the Cotton Manufacture*, p. 346 (1835); *Manchester Mercury*, 26 August 1794.

Francis Heywood & Partners: RE 21/128862 (1792) (merchant stocks), 22/128180 (Litton mill); Sun CS 13/656809; *Manchester Mercury*, 9 July 1799; John Graham, *History of Printworks in the Manchester District* (MS., Manchester Public Library) pp. 369-70; Wm. Smith & Co., *A Select List of Bankrupts* 1786-1806 (1806); S. D. Chapman, op. cit., 199-209.

Birch, Robinson, Walmsley & Barker: Sun CS 9/640814; RE 1442696; J. D. Marshall, *Furness and the Industrial Revolution*, pp. 50-3 (1958); Lewis's *Directory . . . 1788* under Birch & Son and Robinson and Walmsley.

Phillips & Lee: Sun OS 364/564432 (1790) for mercantile interests; CS 10/644316; cf. A. P. Wadsworth and J. Mann, *The Cotton Trade and Industrial Lancashire 1600-1780*, pp. 288-301 (1931).

Gideon Bickerdike: Sun CS 10/640586, 18/666171; W. Bailey, *Western and Midland Directory* (1783); Sessions Papers, 368/21, Signet Library, Edinburgh (I owe this last reference to Dr John Butt).

Salvin Brothers: Sun OS 341/523976 (1786), 362/557527 (1789) for mercantile interests; CS 19/671073 (Durham mill); McConnel & Kennedy MSS. (Manchester University), In Letters, 1795-6, 1797; Bailey, *Agricultural Survey of Durham* (1813); Boulton & Watt MSS. (B.R.L.)

David Campbell: Sun CS 11/651449; Lewis's *Directory . . . 1788*.

Country manufacturers

Robert Peel, sons & partners: S. D. Chapman, 'The Peels in the early English cotton industry', *Business History*, XI (1969).

Samuel & Peter Marsland: RE 26/133474; Sun CS 7/638245, 13/656810; A. P. Wadsworth and J. Mann, op. cit., p. 495; G. Unwin, *Samuel Oldknow and the Arkwrights*, p. 27 (1924).

Samuel Oldknow: Sun OS 341/525204 (1786), 345/531757 (1787), 376/582836 (1791), 8/640361 (1791); G. Unwin, op. cit.

John Watson Jnr: Sun CS 8/638760-2; J. Aikin, *The Country from 30 to 40 Miles round Manchester*, pp. 286-7 (1795).

Alexander Hunt: RE 26/124909 (1793); W. H. Chaloner, 'The Cheshire activities of Boulton & Watt, 1776-1817', *Trans. Lancs. and Cheshire Antiquarian Society*, LXI (1949).

John Whitaker: Sun CS 12/648968; Wm. Smith & Co., op. cit.

Edward & Jas. Pedder: Sun CS 8/638928; C. Hardwick, *History of Preston*, p. 456 (1857).

John & Robert Kirkman: Sun CS 8/638149.

Cooper, Cardwell, Birley & Hornby: Sun CS 10/641162; W. A. Abram, *A History of Blackburn*, pp. 389-91, 398-9 (1877); M. M. Edwards, *The Growth of the British Cotton Trade 1780-1815*, pp. 255-8 (1967).

Abraham Clegg: Sun CS 17/663046; E. Butterworth, *Historical Sketches of Oldham*, pp. 96, 121 (1856 edition).
Abraham Illingworth. RE 22/124217; Wm. Smith & Co., op. cit.

Calico printers

Forte, Taylor & Bury: Sun CS 9/644236, 11/651070; J. Graham, op. cit., pp. 409, 421.
Howarths & Smith. Sun CS 7/638235; S. D. Chapman, 'The Peels in the early English cotton industry', *Business History*, XI (1969).
Nash & Abbott: Sun OS 360/554233 (1789), CS 8/638574 (1795); W. Bailey, *Western and Midland Directory* (1783); J. Graham, op. cit., pp. 424-5; *Manchester Mercury*, 10 September 1782.

Former mechanics, management and 'men of humble birth'

Peter Atherton: Sun CS 9/644220, 11/649218. E. Baines, op. cit., p. 150; E. J. Foulkes, loc. cit.; Boulton & Watt MSS. The total valuation given in Appendix 1 is the sum of the insurance policies for Mold, Flintshire (£13,500), Chipping (£5,000), and an estimate of £10,000 and £15,000 for his two steam mills at Liverpool. Atherton's letters in the Boulton & Watt MSS. show that he used his Liverpool plans for the erection of mills in other parts of the country, including those of Denison of Nottingham and John Peel of Burton, whose policies are extant. On the occupations of Atherton's partners, for Wm. Harrison see Lewis's *Manchester Directory 1788* ('woollen and fustian manufacturer, High St and Piccadilly') and J. & T. Hodgson, Sun CS 7/635634 ('merchants of Liverpool'). In a letter to Boulton & Watt, 11 February 1796, Atherton wrote '. . . instead of Esquiring me, call me Cotton Machinery Manufacturer . . .'
John Horrocks: Sun CS 12/651301; C. Aspin, *James Hargreaves and the Spinning Jenny* (1964); R. S. Fitton and A. P. Wadsworth, *The Strutts and the Arkwrights*, p. 282, note 1 (1958).
Duck & Potts: Sun CS. 9/644231; Robert Peel (Bury) to Boulton & Watt, 20 July 1792, says that both partners were former servants of his.

Merchants transferring capital to cotton

Haigh Bros.: Sun CS 7/638226; Wm. Smith & Co., op. cit.
Wells, Heathfield & Co.: Sun OS 343/527446 (1787); RE 17/112726; Sun CS 8/636393; *Universal British Directory*, I (1790) for Thomas Martin of London; maps and plans of Sheffield mill in Fairbank Collection, Sheffield Central Library; sale of mills *Derby Mercury*, 23 February 1815.
J. & J. Parker: Sun CS 11/651450; Parker, Holland & Garside CS 8/640366. O. Ashmore, 'Low Moor, Clitheroe: A 19th century factory community', *Trans. Lancs. and Cheshire Antiquarian Society*, Vols. 73 and 74 (1963-4).
Tate & Brown: RE 20/118479 (1790), 22/126038 (1792), 24/132338 (1793), 27/138205 (1794).
James Doxon: Sun CS 11/648486; J. Aikin, op. cit., pp. 448, 476-7; Signet Library Sessions Papers, 394.
Bott, Bower, Birch & Randall: Sun CS 11/648079, 13/653824; W. H. Chaloner, 'The Cheshire Activities of Boulton & Watt', loc. cit.; S. D. Chapman, op. cit., p. 90; J. Jaffray, *Hints for a History of Birmingham*, I, Ch. 18 (1857).

Daintry, Ryle & Co.: Sun CS 7/636686; C. S. Davies, *A History of Macclesfield*, pp. 125-6, 141-2 (1961). The partners also ran a calico factory at Leek and a loom shop at Eyam (Derbys.) neither of which is included in their 1795 policy. (S. D. Chapman, op. cit. pp. 89, 207, 234).

Edmund Lodge & Sons: Sun CS 4/629365-9; 10/641547-50. The other six West Riding firms are identified in Appendix 2.

APPENDIX 2

Investment of Leeds merchants in cotton and woollen mills, 1788-1800

	No. of mills	Value of insurance policy c.1795 (£)
Cotton mills built by Leeds merchants:		
Markland, Cookson & Fawcett, Leeds	2	16,000*
Blagborough & Holroyds, Sheepscar (Leeds)	1	5,400
Ard Walker, Hunslett (Leeds)	1	2,400
Blesard & Arthington, Leeds	2	6,950*
Peter Garforth, Leeds and Skipton	3	5,800
William Burrows, Leeds	1	2,850
Atherton & Rawstornes, Huddersfield	1	5,000
Denison & Oates, Nottingham	1	10,000
	12	54,400
Cotton mills built by investors with mercantile connections:		
Gowland & Clark, Far Bank, Leeds	1	n.d.
Wilkinson, Holdforth & Paley, Leeds	1	n.d.
Beverley, Cross & Billiam, Leeds	1	4,000
Cf. the number and valuation Woollen mills built by Leeds merchants:		
Thomas Lloyd, Armley (Leeds)	1	6,700
Benjamin Gott, Bean Ing (Leeds)	1	29,550
Fisher & Nixon, Holbeck (Leeds)	1	1,650
John and Edward Brooke, Leeds	1	n.d.
Nevins & Gatliff, Hunslett (Leeds)	1	10,400
J. Plowes, Leeds	1	2,750
	6	51,050

* Insurance policy does not include country mills owned by partners.

NOTES ON FIRMS AND SOURCES:

1 *Markland, Cookson & Fawcett:* R. V. Taylor, 'Edward Markland Esq. (1749-1832)', *Biographia Leodiensis*, p. 337; Leeds Directory, 1797; Boulton & Watt MSS. (B.R.L.); Sun CS 8/636966, 13/653223, 17/666225.

2 *Blagborough & Holroyds:* MSS. of Holroyds, Dyers and Merchants, Sheepscar (Leeds City Library); Boulton & Watt MSS.; Sun CS 7/638885, 13/653405, 17/666003, 89/840103, etc.

3 *Ard Walker* appears to have entered the cotton industry in 1787 as an executor of John Storey, late of Hunslett oil and cotton mill (Sun OS 343/530723-4) and during the next ten years equipped it with new water

97

wheels, machinery and steam engine (Sun CS 10/646372, 19/671015, 88/833882).

4 *Blesard & Arthington:* Sun CS 12/648558, 17/663499. The partners also had a country cotton mill on the River Nidd; B. Jennings (ed.), *History of Nidderdale*, p. 208 (1967); RE 32a/154777 (1796).

5 *Peter Garforth* was the son of a miller at Skipton (W. H. Dawson, *History of Skipton*, p. 280 (1882)). In 1787 Peter Garforth and William Burrows (q.v.) are described as merchants and scribbling millers of Scot Hall Mills, near Leeds (Sun OS 343/528873). When the partners divided Garforth became partner in cotton mills at Skipton, Carlton and Kirkby Malkamdale (Sun CS 1/620080, 9/646240, 11/648095, etc.)

6 *William Burrows* added cotton spinning to the corn milling and wool scribbling at Scot Hall mills (Sun CS 13/651631, 19/671207).

7 *Atherton & Rawstornes:* merchants and cotton manufacturers at Colne Bridge cotton mill near Huddersfield (Sun CS 9/646209, 19/671055), later known as Rawstornes cotton mill (Lupton Letter Books, 21 May, 1801); appear to have been connected with the Leeds merchant family of Rawstornes ('Extracts from an Old Leeds Merchant's Memorandum Book'. *Thoresby Society Miscellanea*, XXIV).

8 *Denison & Oates:* cotton mill was built in Nottingham in 1793 and burned down in 1801, when it was said to have been insured for £10,000. J. Blackner, *History of Nottingham*, pp 8, 248, 395 (1816); Boulton & Watt MSS., *Thoresby Society Miscellanea*, XV (1909), pp 251-73, XXVI (1924) pp. 102-5. Oates's trading connection with Nottingham is inferred from his account with Smith's Bank, 1780-97 (Nat. Provincial Bank MSS.).

9 *Gowland & Clark:* successive *Benjamin Gowland*s were sea captains and shipowners at Whitby; the partner of this name in the Far Bank cotton mill described himself as 'gentleman', but retained property at Whitby (Gowland MSS. at N. Riding C.R.O.). *Richard Clark* was a roper who owned a house and warehouse on N.E. side of Leeds bridge in 1795 (W. Riding Registry of Deeds, Wakefield). See also Boulton & Watt MSS; and *Leeds Intelligencer,* 27 May 1799.

10 *John Beverley* was a pawnbroker, *John Cross* a cotton manufacturer and former partner of Arkwright at Birkacre, and *John Billiam* a medical practitioner (contracts for steam engines, Boulton & Watt MSS.); Sun CS 11/649649; Wadsworth & Mann, p. 489.

11 *Joseph Holdforth* was a cabinet maker, *Thos. Wilkinson* a cooper, and *Richard Paley* variously described as soapboiler and iron merchant. He was a partner in Fell Ing iron works, Wakefield and Bowling, Low Moor and Birkinshaw iron works, near Bradford (W. Riding Registry of Deeds; W. Cudworth, *Histories of Bolton and Bowling,* pp 205-21 (1891); *Leeds Intelligencer,* 30 May 1796, 15 February 1804).

12 *Thomas Lloyd* rebuilt Armley Mills, near Leeds, in 1788-9 (W. B. Crump, *The Leeds Woollen Industry, 1780-1820,* pp 154-5 (1931)). The plant, including six water wheels, eighteen fulling stocks and seven scribbling machines, was then valued at £4,900 (Sun OS 364/562208); by 1797 the insurance valuation had risen to £6,700 (Sun CS 17/663496).

13 *Benjamin Gott:* W. B. Crump, op. cit.; Sun CS 19/667675.

14 *Fisher & Nixon:* Boulton & Watt MSS.; W. B. Crump, op. cit., p. 5. The power unit and machinery are not included in the 1796 valuation (Sun CS 13/651630) and the 1808 policy for £8,600 (Sun CS 81/822103) is nearer the capital value of the completed mill.

15 *John and Edward Brooke:* W. B. Crump, loc. cit.

16 *Nevins and Gatliff:* Boulton & Watt MSS; RE 32a/155018-9 (1797).

17 *J. Plowes:* Sun CS 5/631846.

APPENDIX 3

Stockport Cotton Spinners c. 1795

MILL OWNERS	No. of workshops	No. of mills	Mill buildings (£)	Machinery (£)	Millwrights work (£)	Steam engines (£)	Total valuation (£)
MILL OWNERS							
Marsland, Samuel & Peter:							
Heaton Norris	2		1,000	5,000	–	–	6,000
Park Mills		2	8,000		–	_500_	8,800*
Oldknow, Samuel		1	3,800	1,200	200	_500_	5,200
Hunt, Alexander		1	3,700	3,500	–		7,700
Whitaker, John		1	2,400	3,000	1,050	–	7,500
Illingworth, Abraham		1	1,800	3,220	–	1,500	7,100
Doxon, James		2	1,600	1,300	400	–	5,500
Bury, Jeremiah & Co.		1				_500_	5,000
Holland & Bridge		1					5,000*
	2	10					57,800
Collier, John	1	3	1,670	510	270	–	3,600
Haughton, Josiah and Mary	1	1	–	1,570 –	300	350	3,480
Everett, Thomas	1	1	1,300	–	300	–	2,600
Lavender, William	1	1	450	1,540	600		2,910
Howard, James		1	530	1,150			1,680
Brown, James		1	530	300	120		1,660
Horsaid, James		1			200		1,000
Prestnall, Oldham & Lees		1	600	600		300	960
	4	10					17,890

* Does not include investment in Manchester mills.

Figures underlined are the author's estimates.

	No. of Work-Shops	Buildings (£)	Machin-ery (£)	Total Valuation (£)
WORKSHOP OWNERS				
Horrocks, Thomas	2		2,000	3,000
Hardy, William & John	1	1240	250	2,400
Collier, Benjamin	1	330	470	1,300
Peel & Ainsworth (branch)	1		200	1,200[a]
Jackson, David	2		1,200	1,200
Cheetham, James	1		750	1,000
Thornley, Robert	1	600	400[b]	1,000
Bradock, John	1	300	380	950
Bancroft, William	1		850	920
Halton, Wm., Thos. & Josiah	1		600	600
Bennison, Thomas	1		720	720
Kershaw, Edmund	1	200	500	700
Allcock, Randle	1		250	530
Dakin, Robert	1		500	500
Howard, Samuel	1	300		500
Hampson & Smith	1		400	450
Stringer, Joseph	1		450[b]	450
Walthall, Richard	1		375	430
Chapman, William	1		400	400
Grantham, James	1		400	400
Bland, Richard	1		260	320
Peers, James	1		250	300
Eardley, Thos., Chas. & Wm.	1		300	300
Williamson, Robert	1		260[b]	260
Stringer, George	1		250	250
Atkinson, Brunt & Turner	1		240	240
Brown, Mary (Exors. of)	1	25	125	225
Cheetham, John	1	– 1200	–	200
Heaward, Samuel	1		150	150
Simister, George	1		140[d]	140
Goulden, William	1		120	120
Alsop, William	1		150	150
Bailey, John	1		150	150
Martin, Thomas (Victualler)	1		120[c]	130
Chorlton, Charles	1		90	115
Pritchard, James	1		100[c]	105
Hankinson, William	1		80	100
Bradbury, Ephraim	1		100	100
Halton, Joseph	1		100	100
Clayton, James	1		100	100
Rowley, Thomas and William	1		100	100
Roper, George	1		100	100
Smith, John	1		80	100
Barker, John	1		100	100
Cooker, James	1		100	100
Grantham, James	1		100	100
Howard, Abraham	1		100[b]	100
Goodyer, Thomas	1		50	50
	50			23,055

[a] Does not include capital invested in mills in Manchester and elsewhere outside Stockport.
[b] includes 'stock'.
[c] Housed in Illingworth's mill.
[d] Illingworth's machinery.

APPENDIX 4
Oldham cotton spinners insured with the Sun and
Royal Exchange Insurance Companies, c. 1795

	No. of 'Mills'	Value (£)	Source
Abraham Clegg	2*	6,000	CS 17/663046
Ralph Kershaw, Copster Hill	1*	3,600	CS 4/629332 RE 30/145921
John Lees, Pit Bank and Acre Mill	2*	3,400	CS 11/648054-5 649240
Daniel Lees, Bank Side	1	2,550	CS 11/648485
James Lees, Mumps	1	2,100	CS 8/640362
Johnathon Ogden	1	1,000	CS 9/644637
Mellor & Cheetham	1	700	CS 17/664463
Joseph Dunkerley	1	700	CS 7/638241
James Whittaker	1	600	RE 22/128418
James Clough	1	600	OS 358/550208
James Travis	1	500	CS 9/640813
John Milne	1	500	CS 9/640813
Robert Whittaker	1	300	
	15	£22,550	

* Steam engine employed

APPENDIX 5

Valuation of Scottish cotton mills by the Sun Fire Office c. 1795

	Location of mill(s)	No. of workshops	No. of mills	Policy valuation (£)	Policy No.
David Dale	New Larrark	—	2	24,400	8/638322
George Dempster & Co.	Perth	—	2	10,500	8/640186
Ballindalloch Mill Co.	Balfron, Stirling	—	2	10,300	1/622252
					8/638345
Claud Alexander & Co.	Catrine, Ayr	—	1	9,900	8/638323
Wright, Mellis & Co.	Perth	—	1	9,500	10/641200
Gordon, Barron & Co.	Aberdeen	—	2[a]	9,300	9/644260
Corse, Burns & Co.	Paisley	1	1	9,000	9/646035
Robert Fall & Co.	Dunbar	—	1	8,400	11/648801
Jas. Monteath & Co.	Anderston	1	1	8,300	10/641197
Douglas, Dale & McCaul	Newton Douglas	—	1	8,200	11/648860
Joseph Twigg & Co.	Paisley	—	1	8,000	7/638674
George Houston & Co.	Johnstone, Renfrew	—	1	7,800[d]	11/651628
Underwood Co.	Paisley	—	1	7,800	11/649006
Gideon Bickerdike & Co.	Deanston, Perthshire	—	1	7,700	10/640586
Archibald Neilson	Kirkland	—	1	7,180	11/648819
Linwood Mill Co.	Paisley	—	1	7,000	8/638346
Houston, Burns & Co.	Lochwinnoch, Renfrew	—	1	6,900[d]	11/651427
John White & Co.	Penicuik, Midlothian	—	2	6,700[d]	13/654879
Leys, Brebner & Hadden	Aberdeen	—	1	6,300[d]	12/648723
Gillespie, Freeland & Co.	Glasgow	—	1	6,200	7/636278
Stewart, Dunlops & Co.	Paisley	—	1	5,700	11/649057
Dale, Clarke & Co.	Ayr	—	1	5,700[b]	8/638324
John Melville & Son	Dysart	—	1	5,300	10/644359
Alex. & Jas. Crum	Glasgow	1	1	5,100	9/644274
Mackerrel, Laing & Co.	Paisley	—	1	5,000	7/636270
Fisher, Buchanan & Co.	Rothesay, Bute	—	1	4,800	8/638331
McLeod, Twigg & Co.	Paisley	—	1	4,700[e]	18/666172
Black, Hastie & Co.	Bridge of Weir, Renfrew	—	1	4,500	11/649005
Crossley Mill Co.	Houston, Renfrew	—	1	4,300	11/649864
Fulton, Buchanan & Pollock	Paisley	—	1	4,000	8/638314

	Location of mill(s)	No. of workshops	No. of mills	Policy valuation (£)	Policy No.
Scott, Stevenson & Co.	Glasgow	—	1	3,700[e]	17/664261
John Austen & Co.	Neilston, Renfrew	—	1	3,500	10/640584
Pat. & Jas. Aytown	Kinghorn	—	2	3,200	11/648851
Campbell, Spiers & Co.	Glasgow	—	1	3,000	7/636268
Reynolds, Monteath & Co.	Glasgow	—	1	2,800[b]	8/638343
Joseph Russell & Co.	Kinghorn	—	1	2,500[e]	19/671076
St. Murren Co.	Paisley	—	1	2,000[d]	12/649737
Ferguss & Russell	Kirkaldy	—	1	2,000[e]	3/625028
John Fergus & Sons	Kinghorn	—	1	1,600[d]	14/653334
Caldwell & Aitken	Lochwinnoch	1	1	1,300	9/646222
Cowan & White	Bridge of Weir	—	1	1,200	9/644273
David Finlay & Co.	Paisley	—	1	1,000	8/638328
TOTAL for 42 firms		4	48	256,280	

Estimates for mills not included above:

	Location of mill(s)	No. of workshops	No. of mills	Policy valuation (£)	Source
Birtwhistle & Murray	Gatehouse-of-Fleet	—	2	10,000	Dr J. Butt
John Cochrane & Co.	Neilston	—	3	13,000	SL 411/62
Thos. Scott & Co.	Gatehouse-of-Fleet	—	1	8,000	SL 264/4
James Doxon	Busby, Glasgow	—	1	5,000	SL 394/4
		4	55	292,280	

(a) One mill in course of erection.
(b) Incomplete valuation
(c) 1794 valuation
(d) 1796 valuation
(e) 1797 valuation
SL Signet Library (Butt transcripts).

Notes:
(1) Twenty jenny shops for which policies are extant are not listed here.
(2) Where duplicating policies were taken out during the year, the higher valuation has been cited.
(3) The policies of six firms mention the spinning of flax as well as cotton: Aytown; Dempster; Fall; Finlay; Leys, Brebner & Hadden, and Melville.

Valuation of cotton and worsted mills
erected in the Midlands, 1770-1803

	Date	Value (£)	Source
Nottinghamshire firms			
John Bacon, Sutton-in-Ashfield	1783	2,500	RE 29/143655 (1795)
Burden, Mansfield	1785	4,000 ⎫	CS 9/641202 (1795)
	1788	4,000 ⎭	
Chambers, Fiskerton		2,000	RE 24/127330 (1792)
Cox & Halls, Nottingham	1791	2,000	Type A*
Davison & Hawksley, Nott'm	1788*, 1791	5,300	CS 7/638827 (1795)
Denison & Oates, Nottingham	1792	15,000	J. Blackner, *History of Nott'm* (1815), p. 395
Killingley & Green, Nott'm.	1792	3,500	CS 9/641089 (1795)
Halls & White, Basford	1787	3,000	? Type B1
	1800	10,000	*Nott'm Journal,* 2/8/1820
Hancocks & Wakefield, Mansfield	1789	4,000	CS 9/640844 (1795)
Handley & Sketchley, Newark		4,500	CS 9/644067 (1795)
Hardcastle, Newark	1791	1,000	RE 18/121267
Harris, Nottingham		1,440	P.R.O. B/3/2119
James & Hargreaves, Nottingham	1769, 1788	4,000	Type B2*
Lambert, Gonalston	1784	3,000	CS 9/644204 (1795)
Markland, Evison & Little, Southwell	1786	2,700	CS 10/646166 (1795)
Morly, Nottingham	c. 1781	2,200	CS 5/635087 (1794)
Oldknow, Cowpe & Co.			
Pleasley	1786	3,790 ⎫	
New Mill	1798	1,180 ⎬ Hollins MSS.	
New Mill	1799	2,530 ⎭	
Pearson & Grimshaw, Nott'm		2,200	RE 22/126459 (1792)
Robinson, Bulwell & Papplewick	1778 ⎫		RE 4/74349 (1778)
	1784 ⎪		
	1791 ⎬	15,700	RE 32a/154792/3
	? ⎪		(1796)
	? ⎭		
Smith, Radford	c.1791	3,500	Type B1*
	1802	6,000	Type C-
Stanford & Burnside, Nott'm	1782	5,500	CS 9/640828 (1795)
	1800	3,000	Type B1
Stanford & Ellcott, Mansfield	1788	7,500	CS 17/663456 (1797)
Stanton, Mansfield	c.1792	3,000	Type B1
Stretton, Thacker & Co., Wilne	c.1781	3,000	CS 10/646116 (1795)
Trueman, Nottingham	1791	2,000	Type A*
Toplis, Cuckney	1785	7,450 ⎫	CS 5/631405 (1794)
Worksop	1792	7,300 ⎭	20/669119 (1797)
Unwin, Sutton-in-Ashfield	1770**, 1784	15,000	Type C variant
Mansfield	1782	3,000	? Type B1
Tansley (Derbys.)		6,000	2 mills, Type B1

Walsh, Bulwell	1793	1,000	? Type A
Willoughby, Nottingham		1,500	RE 25/135163 (1793)
Derbyshire firms			
Arkwright, Nottingham	1770*, 1782	1,500	Type A*
	1790	+ 600	
Cromford I	1771	4,000	Type B2
Cromford II	1777	3,000	RE 4/75060 (1779)
Bakewell	1782	3,000	
Cressbrook	1779*, 1787	1,700	OS 378/588793 (1791)
Rocester	1782	3,000	? Type B1
Wirksworth	1783	4,200	CS 17/664245 (1797)
Masson (Matlock)	1784	10,000	Type C variant
Bradley, Mayfield	1784	12,550	RE 29/143634 (1795)
			(CS 7/638230 (1795)
Cresswell, Edale	c.1791	3,000	(RE 29/143301
			(CS 8/638577
Callow, Derby		1,000	Type A
Cooper, Woodeaves	1784	4,000	OS 377/581502 (1791)
Mayfield	1793	5,000	Type B2
Dakeyne, Darley Dale	1788	3,000	Type B1 (NJ 8 Aug. 1789)
Darley Dale	1802	5,000	Type B2 (NJ 10 July 1802)
Dalley, Fellowes & Co.			
Wirksworth		3,000	Type B1
Evans, Darley Abbey	1783	6,000	CS 9/641470 (1795)
Fox & Pickford, Derby			
Gardom, Pares & Co.	1778*	3,000	Type B1
	c.1803	10,000	Type C
Gooddy, Hartington		3,000	? Type B1
Hewitt & Bunting,			
Chesterfield		3,000	? Type B1
Keeling, Peak Forest	c.1787	550	OS 345/531775 (1787)
Kirk, Bamford	1783	1,000	CS 8/638569 (1795)
Longsdon & Moorwood,			
Gt. Longstone	1785-6	850	CS 7/638234 (1795)
Lowe Shirland	1794	3,000	Type B1
Needham, Champion *et al.*,			
Tideswell		950	CS 20/667941
Needham, Frith & Co., Litton	1782	3,300	RE 22/128180 (1792)
Nightingale, Lea	1784	3,000	Type B1
Pearson *et al.*, Brough		1,500	CS 9/640651 (1795)
Radley & Chapman, Chesterfield		1,800	Derby P.L.MS. 6307 1797)
Stone & Harrison, Winster	1791	2,000	Type A* (DM 20 Oct. 1796)
Strutt, Belper	1779	3,000	RE 4/76867 (1779)
Milford	c.1779	5,000	? Type B2
Belper North	1786	5,600	OS 348/536381
Derby	1793	15,000	Type C

Milford Warehouse	1793	? 5,000	
Belper West	1795	15,000	Type C
Taylor & Haywood, Duffield	c.1794	1,500	Type A
Turton, Crich	1798	3,000	? Type B1
Twigg, Ashover		3,000	Type B1
Watts & Lowe, Matlock		2,200	CS 8/640372 (1795)
Woolley & MacQueen, Matlock		3,000	? Type B1
Wyer, Ilkeston	1792	1,800	Ilkeston Manor Court Rolls, 1793.

Staffordshire firms

Bott, Tutbury	1783	2,000	CS 11/648079 (1795)
Cantrell, Brund	1790	4,000	Type B2
Daintry Ryle & Co. of Macclesfield, Endon (Leek)		3,000	Type B1
Dickens & Wilson, Alrewas	1784	3,000	Type B1
Fowler, Tamworth	1790	3,000	Type B1
Parkes, Sudbury	1783	2,000	Type B1
Peel, Burton	1780	3,210	Numerous Sun
Winshill	c.1787	2,690	policies,
Bond End	1784	3,000	summarized in
	1791	+ 4,250	S. D. Chapman, *The*
Tamworth Mill	1791	5,000	*Peels in the Early*
Tamworth Printworks	1795	5,400	*English Cotton*
Bonehill Printworks	1797	2,950	*Industry*
Thompson, Newcastle	1797	3,000	CS 94/853228 (1810)
Alton	c.1787	2,000	Type B1 variant

Leicestershire firms

Buszard. Lutterworth	c.1800	2,000	? Type A
Churchill, Shepshed	1779	3,000	Type B1 (B & W MSS.)
Miller, Howe & Co., Leicester	1791	3,000	Type B1* (DM 11 Aug. 1796)
Wilkes, Measham	1783	1,700	Phoenix Fire Policies
	1801	6,300	(Atherstone agent's books, Warwicks. CRO.)

Northamptonshire firms

Burdett, Burton Latimer		2,000	OS 343/527766 (1787)
Hayes & Gibson, Northampton		3,000	Type B1. (DM 4 Feb. 1802)

Warwickshire firms

Gill, Birmingham	1788	? 1,000	BG 20 Oct. 1788, 7 Apr. 1794
Parkes, Brookhouse & Crompton, Warwick	1797	10,000	Type C
Smart, Milverton	1792	3,000	Type B1

Other firms in the region

Watson, Bromsgrove (Warwicks.)	1784	3,000	Type B1
Rostall, Claypool (Lincs.)		2,000	RE 24/130776 (1792)
(Name unknown) Isle, Salop.		? 3,000	? Type B1

Worsted spinners not included above as cotton spinners

Cartwright, Retford, Notts.	1788	8,000	OS 369/571244
	1793	+ 4,000	Clarke MSS. Retford.
	1797	+ 2,150	CS 17/664036
Barber, Derby	c.1778	? 3,000	? Type B1
Scott, Wolverhampton	1791	1,000	Type A
Rawson, Leicester	1799	? 500	Type B1 variant
Lane, Bedworth	1788	3,000	Type B1
Louth Mill Co., Lincs.	1784	3,000	Type B1
Chaplin, Raithby, Lincs.	1792	6,650	CS 3/627656 (1794)

*Indicates addition of a steam engine.

** Destroyed by fire. Unwin's 1770 mill has been reckoned at £3,000.
Abbreviations used: NJ, *Nottingham Journal*; DM, *Derby Mercury*; BG, *Birmingham Gazette*; B & W MSS., Boulton & Watt MSS.

For mill types A, B1, B2, C, see pp. 61-3.

Workshops in the Midlands cotton and worsted spinning industry
There were a few 'jenny mills' (i.e. workshops containing manually operated spinning machines) in the region at the end of the eighteenth century, but the total number and their dating is uncertain. Most of them were in the High Peak district of Derbyshire and supplying weavers rather than framework knitters. Fifteen of them can be identified in the parishes of Tideswell, Hope, Chapel-en-le-Frith and Castleton (Farey, *Agriculture of Derbyshire*, III, p. 485, and Land Tax Returns, Tideswell, 1799). The Sun insured six of them for £250, £300, £300, £350, £500 and £650 respectively, and these totals include buildings which were probably conversions. The margin of error introduced by excluding these workshops is clearly very small.

Dr Chapman's paper is very interesting and encouraging because it attempts to provide a financial framework for the cotton industry. Most historians of the industry have been bedevilled by a lack of reliable runs of figures relating to fixed capital formation, especially for the eighteenth and early nineteenth centuries. Therefore we have had to rely very much on guesswork; if the insurance records which we have heard about today are acceptable then it augurs well for the Sheffield scheme.

Dr Chapman is right to distinguish between different types of factories in his paper. There has always been a difficulty of definition. What is a factory in the late eighteenth century? What do we mean by a factory in 1820, and in 1850? Dr Chapman refers to four prototypes in the late eighteenth century. It is quite possible that there were many more than these: there was a remarkable variety of factory premises in the cotton industry. Dr Chapman also stresses the importance of the transfer of capital from the silk, woollen, linen and sailmaking sectors to the cotton industry. This was of great importance and must be taken into account in any assessment of fixed capital formation.

There is also another factor which emerged from the paper which should be stressed. Before 1800 a very large number of the buildings used by cotton spinners, printers and bleachers in Lancashire and in the Midlands had not been constructed specifically for the cotton industry. In the 1770s, 1780s and 1790s there was a tremendous amount of conversion and adaptation going on. For example, farm houses were frequently converted into cotton mills. How far do the insurance records take account of this? To what extent does the value of the farmhouse turned into a cotton factory, assessed by the insurance company, represent a credible figure in calculating fixed capital formation?

There are points of difficulty about the insurance records which were ventilated by Dr Chapman. The first is the tendency for firms to undervalue their assets deliberately, in order to pay low premiums, or the extent to which the insurance valuers might have been misled in the task they performed by astute cotton manufacturers.

Secondly, Dr Chapman's research refers to the water power era. To what extent are the water-driven mills underestimated or not represented at all in the insurance records? The list of firms in Dr Chapman's Appendix 1, for example, has a distinctly urban look about it.

Steam-driven factories had a great need to be protected by insurance cover. On the other hand, water-driven mills standing alongside big reservoirs probably did not have the same need to cover themselves with insurance. For example, a Bolton cotton spinner of the 1790s, very much wedded to water power and not going over to steam power until the 1830s, put it forward as one of his arguments for staying with water that he didn't have to bother about insurance. Moreover, how far do the insurance valuations take into account the capital outlay outside the building of the mill? For example, in 1784, a water-frame mill was built in Eccleston, outside St Helens. It had four floors and was 52 feet long, 31 feet wide and 50 feet high, and it cost £490. There was an additional charge of £240 for road building, constructing a bridge and erecting a water conveyance. Now the water wheel and straps for the mill cost £260. In other words, the preparations for water power and the setting up of the mill cost more than the actual construction of the mill. In 1788 in Perth there were four large five storey mills built and the greatest expenses – far more than constructing the mill – were in road making, bridge building and house building. It seems that in the water power era, and this lasted well beyond Dr Chapman's period, there were relatively heavy demands made on capital investment in improving roads, building bridges, housing the labour force, apprentice houses, and so on. And it seems that not in every case were these covered in the insurance returns, so that any account of capital formation should recognize this.

The analysis made of Stockport is very much the centrepiece of Dr Chapman's argument, but how representative is Stockport? It was essentially a fine spinning centre, and such centres in 1795 were relatively few because the majority of the trade were producing coarser counts. In fine spinning very high profits were being made and the average size of mill was larger in the fine spinning centres than in those where coarse yarns were spun. Perhaps Stockport is itself rather exceptional, and a larger sample of areas will have to be analysed.

Two of the points raised by Dr Edwards would worry anyone using insurance records and valuations. The first is whether the amount insured is a true reflection of the actual value of the fixed capital insured or whether it is an under- or overestimate. The second is whether the firms for which insurance records are available are representative of the industry as a whole.

It would seem that there are two approaches to discussing the problem of the accuracy of the valuation. One is the comparison of insurance valuations with information from balance sheets and other company accounts, where they exist, and the second possible approach is an examination in more general terms of insurance practice at this period.

I have dealt mainly with the woollen and worsted industry in the West Riding of Yorkshire for the period from the 1780s to the early 1830s. The fixed capital of this industry would appear to be very similar to that of the cotton industry. Indeed, many Yorkshire mills were used at different times for cotton and woollen manufacture.

As Dr Chapman has found for the Midlands, in the West Riding there are very few company records, accounts and balance sheets that one can look at. Moreover, the firms for which records do exist are not necessarily representative. However, amongst the records of Benjamin Gott's mills, in and near Leeds, are the 'Accounts of Co-partnership' for the firm and it is possible to compare these with the insurance valuations of the same period.[1]

In January 1801 the 'Accounts of Co-partnership' gave a figure of £23,000 as the value of buildings and machinery at Park Mills, Leeds. In July of the same year the firm took out insurance policies with the Sun and Royal Exchange Fire Offices for a total risk of £64,800, of which about £18,000 was for buildings and fixed machinery [2]. In the insurance policy, utensils and some moveable machinery are valued with the stock and it is not possible to separate them. The value of moveable machinery and utensils is included with buildings and machinery in the Co-partnership accounts, however, and one might realistically suggest that the difference between the two totals may be accounted for in this way. Other comparisons are possible for the Gott mills. At Bean Ing in 1799 a fire destroyed the main mill building. An independent valuation was made of the damage and the loss on the building was put at £3,264 17s. 3½d., which corresponds very closely to the £3,000 insured on the building. The total loss on machinery at the mill, according to the same valuation, amounted to £6,137 16s. 0d., compared with a sum insured of £5,200. Again, a relatively small difference might be accounted for by the moveable machinery and utensils being included in different categories in the two valuations [3].

One can make a similar comparison with another of the Gott mills, Armley Mills, where there was a fire in 1805. The valuation of the loss corresponds quite closely to the sum insured [4]. Other accounts on the whole show a reasonable agreement between insurance values and real values. The prices paid for Boulton and Watt engines, for example, appear to correspond very closely with the sum for which they were insured.

Although comparisons such as these are only possible in isolated cases, where they can be made the results do not suggest gross under- or overvaluation of fixed capital.

Where, as was often the case, mills were let to tenants, it would appear that it was quite usual for the owner to insist that the tenant insured the mill building for a stipulated sum. One might suggest that this sum would be a realistic figure [5].

Another possible means of testing the accuracy of insurance valuations might be to compare them for buildings of similar date, size and construction. If values can be shown to relate to each other quite closely, one could suggest that either the amounts were accurate or were inconsistent to some constant proportion. This exercise was attempted in a rather rough and ready fashion for a number of buildings by calculating the value per square yard of floor space. This method is, of course, only possible where sufficient information is given in the insurance policy as to the size of buildings or where buildings are still standing today in their original state and can be measured. In some cases the insurance data are very helpful. As an example, the policy for a cotton mill at Hunslett near Leeds shows that the mill was stone built, five storeys high and had a floor area of 2,139 square yards. In 1809 this mill was insured for £3,000, or at the rate of 28s. per square yard [6]. Gott's main mill building when reconstructed had a floor area of about 3,000 square yards and was insured for £4,000, or at the rate of 26s. 8d per square yard [7]. A cotton mill at Colne Bridge, slightly smaller in size, was covered to the extent of 24s. per square yard [8]. There is much scope for developing and extending this method of comparing insurance valuations but the first results are encouraging.

The other approach that I suggested was to look in more detail at insurance practice in this period. By the beginning of the nineteenth century the insurance business had become very competitive. There was condiderable growth in the number of local insurance companies – in Sheffield, for example, the Sheffield Fire Office started business in 1808. Another office in this area, the Leeds & Yorkshire, on occasions almost bargained premiums with their clients. This competitiveness possibly reduced rates and made it necessary for the fire offices to pay much greater attention to the risks they were accepting. When industrial premises were being insured, the local agent was instructed to inspect the premises and draw up a plan. In the case of loss an independent valuer was often appointed and the amount paid for the damage would correspond to the loss rather than to the amount insured, should the latter be greater. There would, therefore, seem to be no point in the assurer taking out a policy for more than the actual value of his property.

On the other hand, there is the more difficult question of undervaluation. The insurance companies were, however, concerned about it and from various information that one can extract from insurance company letter books and minute books, it would seem that they were unwilling to accept proposals for anything much less than the real value of the property. Part of one letter from the Head Office of the Leeds & Yorkshire Assurance Company to their Oldham agent in the late 1820s, referring to the insurance of a cotton mill, reads:

> This amount, if one may judge by the size of the mill, will not be one tenth of the real value and therefore if a fire were to happen in the scutch and carding rooms, for instance, we might suffer a loss equal to the value of the whole amount insured and be receiving only one tenth of the proper premium [9].

Much more consideration needs to be given to the reliability of insurance data before they can be used with confidence but there are good indications, however, that insurance valuations could provide a very useful source for the study of capital formation in many branches of manufacturing industry.

The other question that Dr Edwards raised was whether the insured mills were representative of all mills in the industry. Being rather suspicious of this as well, I have attempted to test it for the 1830s when a check is possible. For the West Riding of Yorkshire the Sun Fire Office policy registers cover about 10 per cent of all the woollen and worsted mills recorded by the 1836 Factory Inspectors Report. Using the data in this Report and in the previous Children's Employment Commission Report on the number of employees and the amount of power used, one can show that there is a bias towards the larger firms in the registers [10]. This is possibly explained by the fact that the national fire offices were more willing to take large risks than were the small regional offices, which tended to have less assets to back them. The local Yorkshire companies appear to have had a ceiling of £5,000 on any one risk [11]. In this case, an adjustment is possible as one can correlate mill valuation, number of workers and the amount of power and thereby adjust the aggregate figure arrived at by using the sample of mills provided by the insurance records.

It should, therefore, be borne in mind when using the insurance figures for a few premises as a sample of the total industry that the insured premises might not be accurately representative of the industry as a whole.

However, my work so far in the wool textile industry supports Dr Chapman's optimism for the use of this vast and relatively untouched source of data for estimating fixed capital formation. There are a great many problems to be solved about the data and, although much more work is required, all indications point to a successful approach to the problem by this method. There are also some papers amongst the insurance records. One can obtain certain details about the money paid out to firms after fire loss and also in some of the older letter books – that of the Leeds & Yorkshire Assurance Company for example – one may follow the discussion between directors of the company, the local agent and the mill owner after fire loss as to the cause of the fire and the amount to be paid.

NOTES

[1] Gott Papers, Leeds University MS. 193, Documents 20 and 21. Accounts of Co-partnership 1786-1839.

[2] Sun CS, Guildhall Library, MS. 11, 937, Vol. 40, Policy 719778, 1 July 1801.

[3] Gott Papers, Document 89. Particulars of the Loss by Fire at Bean Ing, 11 August 1799. Sun CS, Vol. 23, Policy 679117, 27 June 1798.

[4] Gott Papers, Document 119. Valuation of Damage and Loss by Fire at Armley Mills, 20 November 1805. Sun CS, Vol. 61, Policy 766081, 13 August 1804.

[5] This was the case, for example, with mills on the Earl of Dartmouth's estates at Slaithwaite, Morley and Honley. In the tenancy agreements for his many mills insurance was stipulated. See the Dartmouth Estate Terriers at the Estate Office, Slaithwaite.

[6] Sun CS, Vol. 86, Policy 831406, 5 May 1809, C., R., F. and E. Coupland's mill.

[7] Sun CS, Vol. 40, Policy 719778, 1 July 1801. The size of the mill building calculated from plans and sections dated April 1806. Gott Papers, Documents 232-3.

[8] Sun CS, Vol. 82, Policy 822890, 31 October 1808. Atherstone Rawston's Mill.

[9] Leeds and Yorkshire Assurance Company, Secretary's Book No. 1. Letter dated 29 August 1828. The 'Average Clause' does not appear to have been introduced into this type of policy until at least the 1840s and possibly even later. C.Walford, *The Insurance Cyclopaedia*, Vol. 1, p. 232 (1874).

[10] Parl. Papers 1834 (167) XX, pp. 799-1080. Parl. Papers 1836 (138), XLV, pp. 98-129.

[11] Leeds and Yorkshire Assurance Company, Secretary's Book No. 1. Letter dated 13 August 1825 states a maximum of £5,000 could be accepted on any mill or on any one special risk.

Discussants: S. A. Broadbridge, J. Butt, S. D. Chapman, D. C. Coleman, P. Cotterell, R. Davis, M. M. Edwards, M. Falkus, M. W. Flinn, A. Harrison, J. P. P. Higgins, D. T. Jenkins, D. S. Landes, P. Mathias, B. R. Mitchell, S. Pollard, O. M. Westall.

Most of the discussion followed the papers in concentrating on the cotton industry, particularly in relation to the evidence obtainable from the insurance records, but it was made clear that those records could be used for other industries also. Mr Higgins reported some of his findings arising from his search among the insurance records, extending over two quinquennia, some fifteen years apart. He was of the opinion that, provided a satisfactory statistical technique could be developed, some useful and sensible information would emerge, even on a sample basis, regarding a whole range of other industries, including the other textiles, brewing and malting and various manufacturing trades, such as paper and printing and housing.

The best information available so far, however, was clearly that relating to investment in the cotton industry. A great deal of work has now been completed on this, using other records as well, which allow a more accurate appraisal of the value of the insurance records. Inevitably, much of the discussion was concerned with the uncertainties surrounding the latter.

Perhaps the most serious problem was that of a systematic bias in one direction, which appears to have emerged from the investigations of Dr Butt into the Scottish cotton industry. He could quote the statement of Thomas Belling, a London silk merchant who appeared in the Court of Session as assignee in the affairs of a firm operating in Paisley and London which had raised some capital from Richard Arkwright Jr. He stated that 'insurance cover on the building is not more than one half or one fourth of the true value of the property'; Butt's own findings generally bore this out. He had looked into the affairs of nine large Scottish cotton spinning firms, representing fifteen mills and, for the period 1795-7, about one third of the total capacity in Scotland. For all of these, independent information was available to check against the insurance figures obtained by Dr Chapman, generally derived from the court cases in which the facts were not in dispute. In every case, the insurance figure represented an undervaluation, at a rate which varied very widely, but usually amounted to less than half the true value. In addition, there were the deficiencies of current capital

115

accounting to bear in mind. For example, what meaning could one attach to the £24,400 valuation of Dale's New Lanark Mills in 1795, when Owen soon after bought them for £60,000? Were stocks, that most important variable, taken into account? Dr Chapman himself found that Oldknow, Cook & Co.'s mill was insured for £600, but an independent valuation put it at £2,400. There is the further factor that often a considerable proportion of the fixed capital, as Dr Edwards had pointed out, was represented by expenditure on water courses, reservoirs and dams, which would normally not be insured at all.

The causes for this undervaluation were not difficult to find. In most cases, insurance companies were well aware of the high risk of fire, and indeed few large companies escaped one or more fires in every mill in the early decades, and they would therefore be reluctant to insure to anything like 100 per cent of the value. Secondly, it did not necessarily follow that the object of the insurance was always to provide funds for rebuilding the mill. In the Paisley case quoted above, the firm was very short of capital and took out an insurance, at least in part, in order to have a policy to assign to Arkwright as security for a loan.

A further problem raised was the change of values over time. Unfortunately, we have little information on how far valuation allowed for depreciation and obsolescence of machinery and other equipment, though it was evident that in the main centres at least, agents like Robert Dock for the Sun Company in Manchester, and Messrs J. R. Buchanan in Scotland, were highly experienced and qualified men. The latter firm estimated four to five years for obsolescence on machinery in Scotland in the late 1780s and early 1790s.

Apart from the uncertainty about depreciation, there was also the uncertainty arising from changes in the price level, particularly in the French wars, and uncertainty about the age of the equipment at the time of taking out the insurance policy. Without corroborating evidence from elsewhere it was therefore not possible to convert the known insured values directly into yearly investment figures. In point of fact, most cotton firms appeared in the books of the insurance companies by the late 1780s, and the high point was reached around 1795, the year on which Dr Chapman concentrated. By the end of the century, both the Sun and the Royal Exchange had made such losses that they were putting up their premiums and insisting on approval by London before agreeing to policies on cotton mills, while local companies were beginning to make substantial inroads into provincial business. In the case of some firms, such as Oldknow of Stockport, the Peels, or the

Sheffield Silk Mill, quite long runs of years, perhaps fifteen to twenty, were available; in a few other cases there were other details. Thus the running down of the value of a Boulton & Watt steam engine from £500 to £200 in two or three years might be found, but against this there were often compensating improvements in the equipment.

It was therefore highly desirable, wherever possible, to check or expand the insurance figures by other information. Some would be found in Scotland in the Statistical Account. The high survival rate of buildings also allowed a different kind of check on the nominal insurance values, but might not be available in England. There were also other difficulties. One of the most striking, relating to the motive power, emerged from the insurance policies themselves, which showed insured values, for similar water power units, ranging perhaps from £50 to £1,500. In Dr Chapman's table of millwrights' work, there were thirty-five mills in the range of under £100, twenty-six of £100-199, sixteen of £200-250, twelve in £300-350, and some small numbers above that. These differences were not accounted for by exceptionally large power units, or by the use of iron instead of timber, or by difficult sites which increased the costs of leet or reservoir construction in the more expensive wheels. Dr Chapman's guess was that these differences may spring from the fact that some large merchants recruited itinerant millwrights for their work and paid heavily for the privilege, while others, resident locally, made do with local craftsmen who were very much cheaper, though some of them, inevitably, were incompetent. As a result, it would be unsafe to judge the capital value of a power unit, even of a known type, simply by the horse power generated.

Another independent check could be provided by other official records, particularly records of litigation, which might include disputes on insurance claims. In Scotland, the records of the Court of Sessions had proved very useful, and although there was but a single centralized court, it was not too difficult after some acquaintance with the material to isolate the files likely to contain relevant cases. In England, the most promising records were those of the Court of Chancery. Other sources found useful by various participants were letter books of companies, the records held by local solicitors handling cases of this kind, and bankruptcy papers in the Public Record Office, which holds the residuals, and in the various other registries.

Some participants thought that the incidence and consequences of fires themselves might be worth investigating. Deliberate arson was not unknown, and there might also be some influence on the rate of innovation, since a mill was likely to be re-equipped with up-to-date machinery after a fire. In the early decades machinery was built of wood, while the first 'fire-proof' buildings did not arise until the turn of the century, and were not typical for many years more; at the same time, re-equipment, because of the lack of durability, was also rapid in that period even without losses by fire. In any case, it could not now be established to what extent, if any, any firm was able to salvage equipment in a fire and use it again. This might be on a par with the widespread practice of the leading firms of selling off their out of date equipment to poorer or smaller firms when installing new machinery, and there was always a lively market in second-hand machinery. Unfortunately, the records as a rule give no clue on these matters, though in some cases – in the West Riding for example – insurance policies include floor descriptions of machinery in some detail.

The small entrepreneur who would start with second-hand machinery would usually also start with borrowed money, and would rent room and power in a large mill rather than build his own. Such arrangements were common. One famous case was that of Robert Owen; Salvin Brothers of Manchester deliberately built their mill larger than they needed in order to rent some rooms to others, and in the early 1790s a Manchester merchant called Harrison built three mills and three workshops in the city, four out of the six units being rented out to small entrepreneurs. Local papers like the *Manchester Mercury* are full of advertisements for this kind of property, and there seemed also to have arisen a type of hire-purchase system of finance. In all of these cases, the values, ownership and fate of different items of capital would be extremely difficult, if not impossible, to trace.

Finally, insurance records could not help much in the vexed and interrelated questions of stocks and trade credit. Even by the early nineteenth century, stocks still formed a very large proportion of total capital invested, particularly the highly valued finished stocks of manufacturers, but in view of the possibilities of trade credits and debits, changes in stocks would be difficult to estimate for an industry as a whole, and would not emerge from insurance policies. There was a series of estimates, made by a Manchester merchant for the period c.1770 to 1800 of stocks of raw cotton held in merchants' hands, and this might be a beginning, but in the case of finished goods, the values were so large that slight variations in them would seriously affect the total estimates. Thus, in Dr Chapman's list for 1795, Hornby, Birley &

Cardwell appeared as having an insured capital of £6,000; Dr Edwards had seen their stock figures for the year before that, and they amounted to £93,000. These were merchants rather than manufacturers, so that the example was extreme, but by no means unique.

Credit terms themselves probably changed significantly. Certainly, in the earlier eighteenth century, trade credit would run for six months and up to twelve months, although the period could be much shorter in certain years. If this change occurred at different times in different sectors of business, it would create an imbalance whereby tradesmen giving shorter credit, but receiving the same credit as before from their own suppliers, could get access to a great deal of new capital in the form of stocks. In the aggregate, there would be no difference in the capital needs, but sectorally there might be substantial shifts. One particular case of a firm, described by Dr Chapman, concerned some partners who began trading directly with St Petersburg in 1782 or 1783, hoping for ready cash sales. Instead, they were forced to give credit of up to a year and as a result were so short of cash that their manufacturing operations were inhibited. Such cases were by no means rare, and it became the task of a new set of intermediaries, such as merchants and brokers, to bridge precisely such export finance gaps.

4

(1)   Capital Formation in Road and Canal Transport [1]

J. E. GINARLIS

Previous estimates of capital invested in canal and road transport during the eighteenth and nineteenth centuries have tended to rely on the examination of the amounts of capital authorized [2]. Individual private acts of Parliament were necessary for most transport undertakings in this period and usually stipulated a limit on the amount a navigation company or turnpike trust could borrow [3]. The first major objection to estimating capital expenditure on the basis of such legislative enactments lies in the assumption that the passing of an act was always followed by the commencement of construction activity by the undertaking. Such was not always the case and the scale and extent of railway and canal works were such that acts lapsed and companies failed. These circumstances are usually well documented. In the case of roads, however, it is often very difficult to discover if the passing of an act was followed by turnpiking or whether nothing was done, as sometimes happened when the trust faced continued local opposition [4]. Moreover, where construction activity can be traced it cannot be assumed that the sums specified in acts were actually spent, since it appears that turnpikes seldom approached their permitted limits of borrowing, while canal engineers often underestimated construction costs. Navigation companies in this situation either returned to Parliament for fresh powers to borrow more money, or resorted to doubtful financial expedients in order to avoid the necessary expense and publicity of the parliamentary process.

The second problem in forming construction estimates from capital authorized is that, in the case of outlays on such items as interest, dividend, rent, taxes and land, which are classified as transfer payments since they do not represent the creation of new assets, it was the practice of canal companies and turnpike trusts to make payments from the capital raised. The full extent of the consequent exaggeration of investment expenditure can be clearly seen in the case of the Kennet & Avon Canal Company. The capital authorized by successive acts of Parliament during the construction period 1794 to 1810 amounted to some £950,000. But with the transfer payments deducted the sums

121

spent on construction come to only £770,000 [5] in the same years. Such analysis reveals similar discrepancies in many canal and river navigation companies.

The third criticism of the method of formulating construction estimates from authorized capital is that it omits all improvements or new construction paid for from current revenue. The creation of new assets constitutes investment, whether it is paid for from current revenue or from raised capital. The problems of distinguishing new construction from repairs and maintenance on current account are substantial, as is often the case in modern accounting procedure, and in formulating estimates for civil engineering works the difficulties are magnified by the absence of a specific life cycle [6]. Thus the essential requirements for a set of figures illustrating capital formation in roads and waterways from 1750 to 1856 include a benchmark capital stock estimate for transport undertakings, in order to calculate depreciation and data from original accounting sources which distinguish between repairs and new works. Eighteenth − and nineteenth − century accounts do not always lend themselves readily to such definitions and distinctions since the concepts underlying them were hazy and ill defined.

It is clear that any estimates derived from examination of capital authorized suffer from some of the defects discussed, and the present investigation has therefore concerned itself with sums spent as recorded in contemporary account books or parliamentary papers. However the difficulties of attempting to fit the historical data into modern national income accounting classifications proved so difficult that the figures collected contain both new works and maintenance. Thus they do not represent a true net investment series because current repairs are normally not included in net capital formation − but equally the figures will not be those of a gross investment series because it has proved possible to deduct transfer payments. The figures have, therefore, been termed a quasi-net investment series [7].

Previously the other important method of capital estimation employed for transport undertakings has been to calculate the cost of construction and maintenance per mile [8]. In the case of turnpikes total mileages are known from the 1820s onwards [9] and thenceforward the crucial factor is the average cost per mile. Figures such as John McAdam's £1,760 per mile for construction in 1836 and other averages for maintenance imply derivation from aggregate totals of road expenditure, but the actual basis for the estimates of Macadam is clearly quite superficial. In Bedfordshire (on the Dunstable-Hockcliffe

Road) net expenditure in 1824-5 was £1,426 for four miles, whereas the Riseley road of that county spent £187 on ten miles the same year. In Somerset in 1827-8 the Wincanton road spent £1,882 on forty-two miles, whereas the Yeovil road spent £2,919 on twenty-five miles. Similar examples can be found in all counties of such enormous variations in expenditure, clearly indicating that a large sample of accounts is necessary for any area before estimates of cost per mile can be arrived at with confidence.

The dubious reliability of eighteenth and early nineteenth century accounts is a further complication and, in discussing his estimates of capital formation in railways, Kenwood [10] has pointed out that the railway companies were frequently implicated in questionable financial procedures which render some accounts untrustworthy. Nevertheless, he does not consider this as an important factor affecting his overall estimates, because of the relatively small extent of the corruption. Since turnpike trusts and navigation companies seldom had the opportunities for fraudulent financial practices, which were in large part a function of the scale of the railway companies, it is probable that their accounts are more reliable. Being very much smaller concerns than the railways, they often possessed much stronger ties with the localities which they traversed, and were generally accused of ineptitude and incompetence in the application of their funds rather than conscious peculation.

SOURCES AND METHODS

Turnpike Trusts

There is very little parliamentary material in the form of expenditure returns available for the period 1750 to 1822 [11], and it has, therefore, been necessary to examine such original account books as have survived. These ledgers seldom contain any form of annual statement or summary and the minute books usually record only that the treasurer's account books were examined and a balance was struck. The account books are merely cash books of payments day-by-day, among which figures for land can generally be distinguished by their size. Such payments are frequently the only indication that a new piece of road is to be constructed, because the pages of crabbed figures for carting, gravel and day labour could equally be for old road or new. Where minute books do record authorization of payments their usefulness is limited by the resolutions having been passed either months before or after construction activities, and by the duplication of authorizing resolutions. Generally payments for interest, rent, taxes, and so forth, can be identified in the ledgers because they occurred regularly once a year. This material accounts for approximately 800 miles of turnpike roads out of 14,000 in 1820; this constitutes 17½ per cent in terms of mileage and about 10 per cent in terms of expenditure.

From 1822 onwards every trust was required to file annual statements of income and expenditure with the clerk of the peace. This procedure was standardized in 1833 and thenceforward returns were totalled and published in detail each year [12]. 'Improvements' is derived from the expenditure sheets of those trusts which did attempt to separate 'new works' from maintenance. However, even where apparent distinction is made, the journals of individual trusts show increases for expenditure both under team-work indicating maintenance and under contract-work indicating 'improvements'. Between 1822 and 1833 the only returns presented to Parliament and public were those of 1822-3 [13] and 1828-9 [14] and most of the remainder have been left undisturbed among Quarter Sessions Papers throughout the country [15]. An earlier parliamentary return of 1820 [16] gives, with other details, the mileages and dates of origin of every trust in the country. From 1822 to 1856 there is little difficulty in forming reliable estimates of English trust expenditure. Prior to 1822 it should be possible to construct estimates based on four sets of information: the mileage of each trust, the date of origin of each trust, detailed expenditure figures for each trust from 1822-33, and a sample of eighteenth and early nineteenth century turnpike accounts. For Scotland and Wales there is some parliamentary material available after 1833, but for the earlier period a series may have to be extrapolated backwards on the basis of the English figures as a percentage of the English post 1833 parliamentary returns.

Parish Roads [17]

There is apparently no parliamentary material giving details of expenditure on parish roads prior to 1811 [18] and it is therefore necessary to use the account books which every parish was supposed to keep [19]. It appears from the Warwickshire and Essex parish surveyors' accounts examined so far that statute labour does not constitute a problem when dealing with eighteenth-century roads. Even in seventeenth-century highway accounts, it was the practice to commute statute labour into money terms in the ledgers. This was probably necessary to discover how much a parish had spent in order to arrive at a rate assessment, for highway rates were apparently far more common than has been assumed. The 1775 Highways Act [20] set out explicit rates of composition to apply uniformly to the whole country, although whether money was paid or labour performed was left to the individuals liable. A number of enterprising publishers produced books for surveyors setting out the requirements of the Act, complete with tables of composition for statute duty, definitions of surveyors' powers, and so forth. The parish surveyors' own account books are in many cases easier to use than the turnpike trust account books. Annual summaries were often provided and the detailed accounts for each year seldom occupy more than a page. It is unusual to find any transfer payments to deduct, because there were generally no interest charges and only very occasional payments for land or damages. The accounts were supposed to be examined and approved by at least one Justice of the Peace and the frequency of signed statements to this effect testifies that this was generally carried out. This primitive system of auditing seems to have contributed towards the reasonable clarity of the surveyors' accounts, and is no doubt responsible for some of the annual summaries. By contrast, turnpike accounts were subject to examination only by Parliament [21], and although the individual trusts were supposed to examine their treasurers' accounts they frequently neglected to do so, and accounting standards suffered accordingly.

The obscurity of the accounting methods used by parish surveyors is, therefore, not the primary obstacle in formulating national estimates of expenditure on parish roads. The difficulties arise from the large numbers of parishes, because many account books still remain with the incumbents in the villages, and from the fact that many of the parish ledgers have been lost or destroyed. However, a few counties have a good coverage of parish surveyors' account books and, with extrapolation from the parliamentary figures for total mileage and expenditure of 1812, it should be possible to formulate estimates giving some idea of the orders of magnitude involved.

Urban Streets

Street maintenance was legally the responsibility of the parish throughout the period under review, but parish inefficiency had led to private acts of Parliament for the establishment of bodies of improvement commissioners for individual urban localities [22]. They superseded parish responsibilities for repairing and improving pavements and road surfaces, for cleaning and lighting the streets and sometimes for providing a rudimentary police service. When a turnpike road entered a built-up area the trustees might maintain their authority over the whole road surface and pavements or might permit improvement commissioners varying degrees of jurisdiction. Therefore three bodies: the parish, turnpike trustees and improvement commissioners shared responsibilities for urban streets [23]. The situation was of course further confused by the laying out of new estates. The builders generally appear to have been responsible for constructing the new streets fronted by new houses, although in practice they frequently seemed to have done their best to evade this responsibility. There are no parliamentary returns listing the expenditure of improvement commissioners, and unfortunately their records take the form of minute books rather than account books; nevertheless, this aspect of urban streets would bear further investigation. There is no parliamentary material on the construction of streets by private builders before 1850, and few records of such outlays remain except for large urban estates.

Bridges

The maintenance of bridges in the period 1750 to 1856 was commonly the responsibility of the county [24], and from 1792 county rate returns exist detailing bridge expenditure [25]. Prior to this date there is a series for the West Riding from 1740 [26], and it should be possible to construct estimates for England for the period 1750 to 1792 by extrapolating these figures. The county authorities would maintain bridges but would not construct new ones, and the larger outlays necessary for new bridges led to the formation of bridge trusts and other companies which were similar in many respects to turnpike trusts. The records of many of these have survived, possibly because toll bridges have tended to persist longer than toll roads. Parliamentary sources do not give details of the total number of bridge trusts because those without stretches of road have been omitted from the post-1833 turnpike returns. This is a serious obstacle to estimating bridge expenditure on the same basis as turnpike expenditure.

Canal and River Navigations

There are no comprehensive parliamentary statistics available on canal expenditure before 1850, although various parliamentary reports after that date list in detail most waterways and their mileages. The relative lack of parliamentary attention paid to canals before the coming of the railways may be due to the fact that they were regarded as private commercial concerns, while turnpikes — as trusts to improve roads and not to make profits — attracted considerable parliamentary concern. Thus, estimates of canal construction and maintenance costs must rest almost entirely on examination of original company records.

The ledgers and journals of canal and river navigation companies which were subsequently merged with railways have survived substantially intact, and there is a considerable quantity of material for other waterways in various record offices throughout the country. Since navigation company account books enjoy a much higher survival rate than comparable turnpike material, it may be possible to derive annual expenditure figures for almost 60 per cent of the waterway mileage of 1850. Many canal companies produced detailed annual revenue and expenditure sheets, and even where they did not the surviving ledgers are generally easier to use than those for the turnpikes. Canal committees often seem to have examined their accounts more regularly than road trustees, and this may well have had its effect on the relative clarity of canal accounts. Payments for land, interest, sinking funds, dividends and so forth, have all been subtracted from total expenditure wherever encountered, but separation of new works from maintenance proved as difficult a problem for canals as for roads. Where 'new work' is separated, it does not, of course, distinguish the improvement factor in 'repairs', and although some navigation company accounts might allow of such a distinction, it would be difficult to apply and may well yield dubious results.

The varying concepts of capital and current costs in the early nineteenth century are well illustrated by examples derived from the Wiltshire & Berkshire Canal and the Driffield Old Navigation. The expenditure statement of the Wiltshire & Berkshire for 1830 [27] clearly distinguishes 'new works' among payments for interest, salaries, water, ice-breaking and sundries. Out of a net total of £4,949 [28], £688 is entered under the heading of 'new works' and £2,623 is under 'repairs'. The improvement factor in the last figure could only be distinguished by a formula derived from accounts which contained a more detailed breakdown. The Driffield Old Navigation statement for 1821-2 [29] is a more typical example of a navigation account. Like the Wilts. & Berks. this account details outlays on salaries, rent and incidentals. However, instead of distinguishing 'repairs' from 'new works' it lists 'dredging, labour, carpenters' work, iron work, brick-layers and masons' work'. This being the more common method of canal accounting in which expenditure could apply equally to repairs and improvements, it presents a major statistical problem.

There is in addition a dearth of financial records for several important canals such as the Trent & Mersey, Staffordshire & Worcestershire, and the Grand Junction. For others material has been discovered for only a few years, and it is necessary to estimate for the missing years on the basis of sets of figures for contemporary canals which were similar in scale. Preliminary estimates based on approximately 50 per cent of the mileage in existence in 1797-8, for that year and for 1820-1, indicate a quasi-net expenditure of £331,184 in 1797-8, and from a coverage of the same mileage a total of £334,854 in 1820-1. It is hoped to formulate reliable annual figures of the total fixed capital outlay on canals from the mid-eighteenth to the mid-nineteenth century from benchmark estimates such as these, based on material from large representative samples of canal company accounts.

Vehicles and Horses

For carts, carriages and horses, there are some tax statistics covering a few years among the parliamentary papers for the period 1750 to 1856 [30]. The original detailed returns have been destroyed, and there is difficulty in using the parliamentary material because tax rates and classifications fluctuate. It should, nevertheless, be possible to use this material as a basis for estimates of capital formation, and since the horse tax returns distinguish horses employed in farming, double counting with agriculture should be prevented.

State Transport Enterprises

In the eighteenth century the principal government investment in transport was in the Scottish military roads for which some figures are available. The policy of investment in transport undertakings in Scotland continued in the nineteenth century with the Commissioners for Highland Roads and Bridges, the Caledonian Canal and the Crinan

Canal. In England and Wales direct government intervention was largely confined in the first half of the nineteenth century to the Royal Military Canal, the Holyhead Road, the Carlisle Road and the Metropolitan Turnpike Commissioners. Figures for most of this work survive. The Exchequer Loan Commissioners lent money to both canals and turnpikes on a considerable scale but their figures can be misleading. There was frequently a time lag between the granting of money and its expenditure. They frequently allotted a large sum which construction works took two or three years to absorb. Much of their lending is also accounted for in the expenditure of individual undertakings and the Commissioners' records can be used as a check on this more detailed material.

NOTES

[1] This discussion is based on work carried out as a Junior Research Worker on the S.S.R.C. Capital Formation Project and towards a Ph.D. thesis at Sheffield University.

[2] A. Gayer, W. Rostow and A. J. Schwartz, *The Growth & Fluctuation of the British Economy* (Oxford, 1953); P. Deane and W. A. Cole, *British Economic Growth* (Cambridge, 1964).

[3] For a discussion of powers conferred see T. S. Willan, *River Navigation in England 1600-1750* (London, 1964) and W. Albert 'English turnpike roads 1660-1830', unpublished Ph.D. thesis, London University, 1968.

[4] A. Cossons, 'Warwickshire turnpikes', *Trans. Birm. Arch. Soc.*, Vol. LXIV.

[5] B.T.H.R. RAC 2/9a, 9b.

[6] C. H. Feinstein, *Domestic Capital Formation in the United Kingdom, 1920-1938*, pp. 8-10, 156 (Cambridge, 1965).

[7] Although not fully in agreement with the definition of this term used in Fishlow, *American Railroads and the Transformation of the Ante-Bellum Economy*, pp. 356-63 (Harvard, 1965).

[8] Carter Goodrich, *Canals and American Economic Development*, Chapter IV, passim (Columbia, 1961).

[9] P.P. 1833, H.o.L., Vol. X.

[10] A. G. Kenwood, 'Railway investment in Britain 1825-1875', *Economica*, 1964, p. 314.

[11] There are some totals for 1812-14 in P.P. 1818, XVI 255, but the detailed returns on which these were based have not survived.

[12] P.P. 1836, XLVII 297.

[13] P.P. 1824, XX.

[14] P.P. 1833, X.

[15] Although they have been lost or destroyed in some counties, notable Leicestershire, Norfolk and Cornwall.

[16] P.P. 1820, IV.

[17] Parish roads comprised all those not under the authority of a Turnpike Trust or Improvement Commissioners.

[18] P.P. 1818, XVI 255.

[19] The best account of the parish surveyor and his responsibilities remains S. and B. Webb, *The King's Highway*, Ch. 3, passim (London, 1913).

[20] 13 Geo. III c. 78.
[21] Parliament examined the accounts of a few London trusts spasmodically in the 1750s and 1760s, but thereafter little was undertaken until the systematic requirements of the 1820s.
[22] The best general account of these bodies is S. and B. Webb, *Statutory Bodies for Special Purposes*, Ch. IV, passim (London, 1922).
[23] For a discussion of this see F. H. W. Shepherd, *Local Government in Marylebone 1688-1835, a study of the Vestry and the Turnpike Trusts*, unpublished Ph.D. thesis, London, 1953.
[24] S. and B. Webb, *The King's Highway*, Ch. VI, passim.
[25] P.P. 1839, XLIV.
[26] P.P. 1839, XLIV.
[27] Berkshire Record Office, D/EFBI.
[28] Net total = total minus transfer payments.
[29] East Riding Record Office, DDX 40/19.
[30] P.P. 1812, IX 243; P.P. 1819, XV 423-5; P.P. 1821, XVI 323; P.P. 1830, XXV 225, 231.

4

(2) Capital Formation in Shipping

R. CRAIG

There can be little doubt that the capital invested in shipping represented one of the most important forms of fixed (although floating and moveable) capital in Britain in the period of industrialization. There are major problems, however, in making reliable estimates of annual capital formation in shipping before the 1786 Navigation Act [1], which made sweeping changes in shipping registration procedure. The first part of this discussion examines some of the pitfalls which are encountered in the assessment of pre-1786 shipping statistics, upon which any estimates of capital formation will have to be based, followed by some tentative observations upon the methods by which investment in shipping may be quantified in the new era for the British merchant marine which was ushered in by Charles Jenkinson's great 1786 Act. Modern registry procedure began in that year, and although the system was subsequently modified in certain respects, the quantitative data provided as a consequence of the 1786 Act permit almost continuous measurement of the British merchant marine from 1789 [2] up to the present day. Despite the abundance of the quantitative data, this paper is exploratory in character, but it is intended that estimates of capital formation in the British merchant marine will form part of a history of the shipping industry between 1750 and 1914 which is now being prepared for publication.

There are two basic types of pre-1786 statistical series relating to British shipping. The first provides aggregates, often on a port-by-port basis, of the number and tonnage of vessels which annually entered and cleared British ports. Such returns exist in respect of both the coastwise and foreign trades, but not as a continuous annual sequence until the 1770s [3]. The second type of return indicates the number and tonnage of vessels 'accounting each vessel but once' which annually entered and cleared their home ports in the foreign, coastwise and fishing trades [4]. These latter returns, like the former, are discontinuous, and no long series appears to have survived. The second type of return omits the coasting and fishing fleets of the ports of London, and there are various other anomalies in both sets of statistics, which have tended to erode the confidence of those who have sought to

131

use them for specific studies of the trade and shipping of individual ports [5].

The statistical series which aggregate entrances and clearances may possibly suggest changes in the utilization of tonnage in the period before 1786, but they tell us nothing whatsoever about the aggregate size of the merchant marine, nor do they permit us to calculate changes in the annual stock of shipping from which annual capital formation may be determined. The second series of returns might be thought to have some value in calculating capital formation, at least at the various outports of Britain, but the returns were inadequately kept, and are in any case only likely to be comprehensive on the quite unrealistic assumption that vessels always traded from their home ports. It is doubtful if either type of return provides an adequate basis for determining the size of the British merchant marine, even supposing it was possible to make an estimate of the size of London's coastal and fishing fleets. Several kinds of British vessel might escape the annual returns prior to 1786, including the following:

(1) Vessels absent for more than one year on foreign voyages – for example, vessels in the whale fishery, or in the East India trade.
(2) Vessels which, although British owned, were engaged in trades not touching British ports.
(3) Vessels absent from their home ports for a year or more.
(4) Vessels laid up, under repair, being lengthened or rebuilt.
(5) Vessels trading within the administrative limits of a single port.
(6) Vessels carrying cargoes in the coastwise trade which did not require coastwise clearances – such as lime, chalk and manure.
(7) Vessels not carrying cargo.
(8) Vessels employed in government service as transports [6].

Even if we were to regard as negligible the sources of possible error implicit in this list, there are other formidable problems which have to be faced. Capital formation in shipping must, it would seem, be based upon figures of *tonnage*, since clearly the *number* of vessels afloat at any time does not enable us to calculate investment. But the major problem of pre-1786 shipping returns resides precisely in the method by which tonnage was calculated. The second problem is related to the first. Before 1786 there was no universal system of registry; certain well-defined categories of shipping were required to be registered, but it is unlikely that more than a minority of vessels was ever registered at any time.

It is not possible here to rehearse the complex history of tonnage measurement, but the deficiencies of the law in respect of tonnage is a factor which has to be borne in mind. The first official rule for the measuring of vessels by Customs officials appeared in 1671 [7] and this rule, variously modified, survived until 1786, when the Navigation Act of that year enforced the measurement of all decked vessels of over fifteen tons if they were to be entitled to the privilege of British registration. During the preceding century, however, measurement was only applied to limited categories of shipping, and clearly the owners and masters of vessels had a vested interest in under-declaring the tonnage of their vessels for many purposes, particularly where the dues or tolls were levied on the measurement on the hull. Dock authorities were among those to impose rules for the measurement of tonnage for the assessment of dock and harbour dues [8], but such rules were purely local in their effect, and had no general application. Other tonnage rules were applied to particular kinds of vessel, such as those carrying brandy [9], or vessels engaging in the whale fishery which were entitled to a tonnage bounty granted by act of Parliament, but here again such requirements were the exception rather than the rule and most British shipping escaped official measurement.

There is a mass of material on eighteenth-century shipping which records the tonnage of individual vessels. Such records include certain eighteenth-century exchequer port books, the plantation and wool shipping registers of Liverpool [10], the Colonial Office naval lists, Seamen's Sixpence returns [11], and three other types of record which would be well worth systematic analysis. These are the lists of vessels issued with Mediterranean Passes [12], the Letter of Marque declarations [13], and the lists of vessels given protection against impressment [14]. There is also one other annual publication of intermittent value, namely, the early series of *Lloyd's Register of Shipping* [15]. So far, efforts to compare the tonnage of individual vessels found in these sources do not reveal any consistent pattern, except – as might perhaps be expected – the tonnage affirmed under letters of marque tends to be greater than the tonnage declared in other records [16]. It may well be that the letters of marque declarations record tons 'burthen', approximating to what in a later age would be called deadweight tonnage – i.e. the actual capacity of the vessel for cargo.

Great care has to be taken in the use of these records for purposes of comparison since so many vessels were lengthened, altered, or 'raised upon' (that is, were built up above the original deck level), and often this could occur more than once during the lifetime of a vessel. Thus, the tonnage of a vessel could, and often did, change genuinely over time, but almost invariably upwards. Secondly, the names of vessels were also changed with bewildering frequency, and since the name of the master may be the only confirmatory element in identification, and since very large numbers of vessels bore identical names, it is a very real problem to be sure that (for example) the *Mary Jane (Smith)* of 1772 was identical with the *Mary Jane (Smith)* of 1774. Frequently, shipowners gave the same name to successive units of their fleets, and the place and date of building, where given by *Lloyd's Register*, is often an imperfect guide.

The extent to which shipowners and shipmasters habitually under-declared the tonnage of their vessels was a phenomenon well attested by contemporary observers of trade and commerce. Thomas Irving, one of the most perspicacious and certainly the most efficient of the Inspectors General of Imports and Exports generally added one third to contemporary aggregates of British shipping in order to arrive at what he regarded as a true indication of the size of the merchant marine [17]. Only by this expedient was he able to reconcile pre- and post-1786 shipping statistics.

We must now turn from the problems associated with tonnage to those associated with registry. Before 1786 the registration of shipping was very far from being universally applied. Registration of foreign built, British owned vessels was made compulsory in 1660 [18], and legislation extended this provision to all English owned vessels engaged in the plantation trades from 1695 [19]. A new category of registered vessels was created in 1739 when vessels employed in the wool trade from Ireland were subjected to a similar law [20]. But apart from these quite limited classes of merchant shipping, there was no need for other shipping to be registered, although this came to be required of vessels requiring Mediterranean Passes as a consequence of the prevalence of fraud at the time of the American War of Independence [21]. Before 1786, then, most shipping was not registered and consequently there cannot have been any satisfactory official method by which vessels were assigned to specific 'home' ports. This renders highly dubious those existing returns noted above [22] which record vessels 'belonging' to individual ports and 'accounting them but once' each year. Thus any generalizations about the character of pre-1786 shipping rely heavily upon the few surviving examples of plantation registry, wool registry or references in the numerous secondary sources to which reference has been made.

Much of the pre-1786 legislation in respect of the registration of shipping was ineffective and fraud was not uncommon, particularly after the beginning of the American War of Independence. It does not appear that there was any very effective enforcement of the provisions of the Registration Act to ensure that changes in property and ports of registry were enrolled on the registers at the respective outports, and although the Registrar of Shipping in London received duplicate oaths of registry, little attempt was made to collate the data thus provided. If aggregate figures of registrations were compiled, they do not appear to have survived the disastrous Custom House fire in London. Because there was inadequate control of registry, and because the information furnished was really insufficient to render positive the identification of individual vessels, it was possible for documents relating to one vessel to be transferred to others for which no registration had been obtained. A brisk trade developed in plantation registers in the 1770s, not least because there was inadequate control of the registers of vessels which had been sold, lost, or captured by enemies of the Crown. Sir George Clark, who was among the first to investigate the part played by the General Registers of Shipping in the creation of eighteenth-century shipping statistics concludes that the office holders were mainly sinecurists and the history of the office towards the end of the century 'obscure' [23]. This may account for the ambiguities and confusion of shipping statistics in the period before 1786 which more recent research has, as yet, done little to dispel.

The 1786 Navigation Act made registration mandatory for all vessels which were decked or measured more than fifteen tons. By the end of September 1789, therefore, by which time virtually all the vessels eligible for the privilege of British registry had undergone the necessary formalities, there had been created a reasonably accurate and very comprehensive record of every British merchant ship then afloat. However, registration depended not a little upon the zeal and competence, not only of the Registrar General of Shipping and his central staff in London, but more particularly upon the efficiency of the Collectors of Customs and their subordinates in the many outports. There is some evidence for believing that there was inconsistency in the recording of registry particulars between some outports, particularly in the early stages of registration, as might be anticipated in a period of change when the officers of the Customs service were faced with complicated new documents and instructions.

Many of the anomalies occured in the closing of registers after vessels were sold away from their first port of registry, or were lost or taken prize. Many registers were kept open for several years after the vessels to which they referred had been lost, broken up, or sold to foreigners. As a consequence, the yearly aggregates of shipping remaining on the register in the period between 1789 and 1826 tended to over-state the tonnage actually remaining under the British flag. In 1826 and 1827, however, there was a general inspection and reappraisal of the registrations at British ports, and vessels which had ceased to exist for one reason or another were eliminated [24]. The extent of the problem at Liverpool may be illustrated from the records of shipping registered there. Of the vessels registered at Liverpool from 1786 up to 1805 only, more than 20,000 tons of shipping was eliminated as a consequence of the enquiries instituted in 1826 and 1827. Further-more, the Liverpool registers between 1786 and 1805 fail to record the year in which no less than 34,000 tons of shipping were lost or re-registered at other ports [25]. Since Customs officials were expected to maintain 'running balances' of ships remaining on the register of each port as at 30 September of each year [26], the nature of the problem in a major port such as Liverpool may be readily understood.

The wars which disrupted the commercial life of Britain in the late eighteenth and early nineteenth centuries were one of the main causes of the discrepancies which occurred: large numbers of vessels were captured by the French and other belligerents, and, of course, a substantial number were recaptured. Not a few vessels were captured and recaptured several times during the course of the wars and changes of name under foreign flags must render that much greater the possibility of the double and treble counting of prizes taken by both sides in the conflicts. Considerable numbers of wartime captures by the enemies of Britain were resold to neutral subjects under different names, and repurchased by British shipowners quite different from those from whom the vessels had originally been captured. Such circumstances rendered the link with the preceding British registry tenuous and difficult to establish. Moreover, there can be little doubt that the sale of shipping to foreigners was often a device whereby British shipowners could operate under neutral flags during wartime, and for these reasons, it is doubtful whether it is possible to draw up an accurate balance-sheet to determine whether or not Britain gained or lost tonnage in the course of hostilities [27].

So far as the capture by Britain of foreign ships is concerned, we are on firmer ground, however, since there are returns of such tonnage in official papers [28], and the records of the Courts of Admiralty survive in the Public Record Office. It seems probable that Britain gained more merchant tonnage than she lost during the Napoleonic Wars, but lost more tonnage than she gained from the war with America in 1812. Much of the tonnage captured by British men-of-war or letters of marque would require extensive repair and refitting before it was fit for trading purposes; perhaps it would be reasonable to include a notional sum to cover such costs in the aggregate figures for capital formation in the shipping industry in these wartime years. Although the defective method of eliminating tonnage which had ceased to exist was mainly a wartime problem, its influence upon the aggregate returns continued until the nineteenth century was well advanced. But clearly this was a factor of diminishing importance by the mid-nineteenth century, since the collection and dissemination of maritime intelligence had by then greatly improved.

So far we have assumed that British investment in shipping was confined to registrations at British ports. However, some account must be taken of shipping registered in the plantations and colonies, and also of foreign shipping owned by British nationals. Enough colonial registration material survives to permit some reasonably accurate figures of British investment in Empire shipowning, but it will be much more difficult, if not impossible, to quantify British investment in foreign shipping. Perhaps as much as one quarter of Empire shipping was owned in Britain, but against this we should have to offset a smaller but perhaps significant proportion of British registered shipping which was owned by persons resident in various parts of the Empire. British investment in foreign flag tonnage is almost impossible to calculate. British firms and individuals with interests in the East Indies had recourse to investment in Danish and Ostend shipping [29], and it is certain that the British shipowner was not averse to putting his shipping under the flag of Prussia in the early nineteenth century [30]. British legislation concerning merchant vessels, their masters and crews, encouraged British shipowners to operate tonnage under foreign flags in the nineteenth century and beyond. It is perhaps worth remembering that it was the British shipowner, not the Greek, who pioneered the flag of convenience.

An important consequence of the 1786 Navigation Act was that it facilitated the introduction of an entirely new type of shipping returns – statistics of shipbuilding. From 1786 until 1808 the trade and navigation ledgers provide very comprehensive shipbuilding data for all British ports [31]. There is also another series, officially compiled, which provides somewhat different figures for the ports of England and

Wales between 1786 and 1813 [32]. These two series may be supplemented by other tables of shipbuilding which may be found among the printed Parliamentary Papers, covering the years 1790 and 1791, and the years 1804, 1805 and 1806 [33]. Certain shipbuilding returns were lost in the fire which destroyed the old London Custom House in 1814, but from that year onwards there are excellent national shipbuilding statistics which continue in an unbroken series to the present day. From 1814 to 1865, however, the statistics of shipbuilding at individual ports do not appear to have survived in official returns, although such were apparently compiled and may be found as discontinuous statistics in various secondary sources. Port-by-port data appear again from 1865 onwards.

Since the most important increment to the stock of British shipping has for long been the volume of domestic shipbuilding destined for British ownership and registry, annual figures of British shipbuilding have hitherto apparently been the only basis for estimates of capital formation in shipping [34]. However, any calculations based only on British shipbuilding are bound to be sadly lacking in accuracy, since additions to the stock of shipping were by no means only the product of new tonnage from British shipyards. Other very important accessions to British registry have to be included (less certain deductions). The first hitherto excluded is shipping built abroad for British shipowners. In the eighteenth century such shipping formed an important, but by no means predominant, proportion of the total tonnage owned in Britain. America became an active supplier of new tonnage early in the eighteenth century [35], and it was not long after America had won independence that the Canadian Maritime Provinces provided many thousands of tons of shipping for British shipowners [36].

Before 1786 a considerable number of very large merchantmen were built in the Baltic for British owners [37]. The Baltic ceased to supply Britain with tonnage after the passing of the 1786 Registration Act, since such tonnage could no longer claim the privilege of registry, but tonnage then afloat and genuinely owned in Britain was given registration for employment in what was called the 'foreign European trade' – that is, such tonnage was permitted to ply only between Britain and the Baltic [38]. Since such vessels were mainly built of softwood, and could not be replaced thereafter from Baltic sources, tonnage registered for the foreign European trade formed a rapidly declining proportion of British registered shipping after 1786; but before this date, such shipping was of considerable importance and cannot be neglected. There were few other opportunities for British owners to acquire foreign tonnage for British registry between 1786 and the repeal of the Navigation Laws in 1849 except for vessels taken prize and legally condemned. Thereafter, however, it was possible for British shipowners to purchase foreign-built tonnage, either new or, as was more often the case, secondhand. Any accession of tonnage from this quarter, however, was by far outstripped by the number of British vessels which were sold to foreigners. There are comprehensive figures distinguishing the number and tonnage of sailing ships and steamships sold to foreigners from 1865 onwards [39].

Another category of tonnage needs to be mentioned here, although it has already been referred to elsewhere in this discussion. Considerable numbers of vessels were taken prize in wartime, and after condemnation in the Admiralty Court, were made free and registered as British vessels. From aggregates of tonnage acquired in this way would have to be deducted the tonnage of British vessels taken by belligerents and permanently lost to British registry. Finally, other parts of the British Empire contributed in some measure to the strength of the merchant marine. Vessels were built in the East and West Indies for registry in Britain, and secondhand tonnage under colonial registry often passed into British hands. From the annual totals of such tonnage added to the British merchant marine has to be deducted the possibly greater amount of tonnage sold by Britain for registration in the colonies. There are adequate statistics of such transfers from 1865 onwards [40].

Calculations to determine the age distribution of the 1789 merchant fleet are greatly facilitated by the survival of the registrations of shipping at a number of British ports. Some of this material has been transcribed and printed [41], and an analysis of the age distribution of shipping from the stock of tonnage afloat in September 1789 at three or four major ports — for example, London, Liverpool, Whitehaven and Greenock — should permit generalizations of tolerable validity. However, it has been noted by R. C. Jarvis that the age distribution of shipping varies greatly between different ports [42]. The reasons why this should be so are not altogether clear, but it seems likely that a number of influences were at work. It is reasonable to suppose that ports in which trade was expanding vigorously would tend to assemble merchant fleets of low average age. The opposite supposition may be made for ports in decline. But the nature of the employment in which tonnage was deployed might have a countervailing influence, since a rapidly expanding coal or timber trade would not necessarily call forth new tonnage if secondhand tonnage was readily available. Much would depend upon prevailing expectations of long-term profitable utilization undisturbed by the uncertainties of the trade cycle. Predominantly coal shipping ports, such as Whitehaven or Newcastle, tended to possess much rather elderly shipping, despite the hazardous nature of the traditional deployment of such tonnage. Although major shipbuilding ports might be supposed to possess predominantly up-to-date shipping, this was not always the case. Much of Whitby's shipping was superannuated despite the importance of the shipyards there; on the other hand, the small port of Chepstow, which also had shipyards, possessed a younger than average fleet. The often assumed relationship between coastal trades and old vessels receives little confirmation from registry material examined so far. Only the East India trade provides reliable evidence of consistently younger than average tonnage and this was the consequence of East Indiamen being broken up after they had accomplished a fixed number of round trips to the east, thus keeping the age of the fleet low, as well as furnishing Thames-side shipbuilders with conspicuously profitable employment.

Because it is possible, for those ports where registry material survives from 1786, to classify shipping by the year of build, some trends in the level of activity of the shipbuilding industry in the preceding decade are apparent. There was at least one shipbuilding boom, which appears to have run its course between 1781 and 1784, with its peak about 1783. More ·extensive analysis of the registers would unquestionably permit more certain generalizations, perhaps extending to the 1760s and 1770s.

Finally, the vexed problem of depreciation has to be taken into account. Leaving aside all questions of wear and tear, the best estimate for the eighteenth century is that of Professor Ralph Davis, who reckons an annual rate of 4 per cent [43]. It would be profitless to attempt any more sophisticated method than to assume straight-line annual depreciation at this rate for eighteenth-century tonnage. Such calculations may, however, be at variance with reality in a later period, since all the evidence at our disposal suggests a widening gap between the best and worst constructed tonnage. This disparity was perhaps encouraged rather than discouraged by the early nineteenth-century methods of marine classification for insurance purposes. For the better class of tonnage an annual depreciation rate of 4 per cent would be appropriate, but there was an increasing volume of shipping which could not be expected to last twenty-five years. Early nineteenth-century depreciation rates, therefore, might vary from 4 per cent to as much as 9 per cent per annum dependent upon the quality of construction and materials. The early nineteenth-century trend was in the direction of declining quality, and by mid-century considerable numbers of vessels could not expect to remain afloat for more than ten years. Building standards improved and quality became more uniform as the century progressed, and 4 per cent depreciation becomes appropriate again well before 1900. Nearly all tonnage remaining afloat had a substantial breaking-up or scrap value, and this may well have exceeded Dr Feinstein's allowance for shipping in the present century [44]. Secondhand and scrap values were highly volatile, however, depending crucially upon the prevailing levels of freight rates [45]. The well-developed secondhand shipping market furnishes abundant data on prices from the 1850s.

So far, we have discussed the methods by which aggregate tonnage figures may be calculated, the various ways in which the stock of British shipping was supplemented or depleted, and the means by which the age distribution and depreciation of the fleet may be measured. But the only acceptable way in which investment in the industry may be quantified is to establish some notion of the value of shipping on the basis of its tonnage, and it is to this complicated matter that we must now turn.

Once the total quantum of British shipping had been established as the result of new legislation, several writers hazarded guesses as to what average value might be imputed to the aggregate tonnage afloat. Lord Sheffield [46] and William Irving [47] both hit upon eight guineas a ton as an appropriate valuation. Nathaniel Atcheson, an active polemicist in the shipowners' interest, thought that £12 per ton was a'low valuation' in 1808 [48], whilst Robert Edington, writing in 1813, thought that the North-East coast collier fleet might be valued 'on a moderate calculation' at £10 per ton. Edington concluded that the coal vessels belonging to the ports between Blyth and Scarborough were worth over £3½ million [49]. Utilizing the 1812 tonnage statistics, Patrick Colquhoun calculated that the shipping of Great Britain and Ireland (including vessels on the stocks) was worth £27 million to which he added a further £10 million as the value of the fisheries [50]. Estimates made in 1819 valued Newcastle shipping, both coastal and foreign-going, at £10 per ton register, while the same source gives the value of vessels in the North American timber trade a little more than £9.10s.0d. per ton. This latter valuation was 'taken upon a very low scale, being a depreciation of more than 50 per cent since the conclusion of the war [51]. Because there was a vigorous commerce in secondhand tonnage, it is not difficult to accumulate data on secondhand shipping values, but the extreme fluctuations in this highly volatile market, and the great disparities in quality of construction and generosity of outfit make quantification somewhat speculative.

The main component of additions to the total stock of British shipping was newly built shipping, constructed in British shipyards, and fortunately there is an abundance of material on the cost of shipbuilding in the late eighteenth and early ninteenth centuries. However, the copiousness of the data is confused by difficulties in interpretation which are only summarily considered here. Construction costs were typically based upon prices per ton, and we have already observed that the ton was an ambiguous term in the period before 1786. Construction costs are, therefore, easily misunderstood before this date. Although it might be supposed that accurate measurement of tonnage after 1786 resolves some of the problems, this is far from being the case, and some brief generalizations may help to eliminate some of the errors which occur in the calculation of capital formation in new tonnage, based upon the available shipbuilding returns. Sail and steam tonnage have to be considered quite separately, and it is fortunate that the official annual returns distinguish these main categories.

There were two main components in the construction cost of sailing vessels and both were based upon a price per ton. Although shipbuilders' quotations are often based upon measurements which differ to some degree from the register tonnage, it is perhaps reasonable to regard pre-1786 costs per ton as being based upon tons burthen, and the post-1786 costs as being based upon tons register, despite the fact that carpenter' and builders' measure were both used in the earlier as well as the later period. There are additional problems which arise in the 1830s when tonnage measurement rules were substantially altered [52]. Taking the merchant fleet as a whole, we must necessarily adopt some such rule of thumb, in the hope that the variations more or less cancel one another out in respect of the very considerable aggregates of tonnage with which we are concerned. The two main components were the price per ton of hulls and the price per ton of vessels fitted out complete and ready for sea. There can be no possible justification for regarding the former figure as representing capital formation, since often it represented only half the cost to be met by shipowners. Costs of hulls varied a good deal between London, the outports and the colonies, and there were also substantial annual fluctuations in prices, caused by the volatile nature of the market which itself was an accurate reflection of current trading and commercial conditions. We offer here some typical prices of hulls in the 1770s and 1780s:

Place of building	1770s	1780s [53]
London	£7 7 0 to £8 8 0	£8 8 0 to £9 9 0
Outports	£5 5 0 to £7 10 0	£6 5 0 to £8 10 0
Colonial American	£4 0 0 to £5 0 0	no longer built for British registry

It must be made clear, however, that these prices are intended to be characteristic of the typical bulk carrier of from 50 to 400 tons burthen. East Indiamen cost a good deal more than this, but for such tonnage, which was predominantly Thames-built, we have comprehensive figures which illustrate the yearly fluctuations in costs. East Indiamen were by no means typical of the British merchant fleet, and they were, of course, substantially larger than most other vessels then afloat. The price per ton for 800 ton hulls was £14.14s. 0d. per ton in 1781 falling to £12.10s.0d. per ton in 1790-2, rising almost continuously thereafter until 1801 when the price reached nearly £22 per ton [54]. We may compare such figures with those of a typical outport merchant shipbuilding yard, such as Brockbank's establishment at Lancaster, where average quality merchant vessels rose in price from about £7.15s.0d. per ton in 1791 to £13 per ton in 1804 [55]. Thus it can be seen that it is necessary to exercise care in assessing capital formation in new tonnage, bearing in mind the variations in cost between different types of vessel and the marked fluctuations in cost over time. The differential in price noted by Lord Sheffield, when he compared British and American-built tonnage in the colonial period, is matched by an equivalent disparity in costs when the British North American shipbuilding industry became an important source of British tonnage in the 1820s and 1830s. By this time, the disparity in construction costs in British shipyards was, if anything, becoming wider, with River Wear-built tonnage representing the cheaper end of the market; the best British-built vessel could cost twice as much as the worst.

The second component in the cost of sailing ship construction was the cost of fitting ready for sea. Costs include such items as masts, yards, standing and running rigging, possibly sheathing, and all the other innumerable fittings, such as anchors, chains, cables, windlasses and the like, without which no vessel could proceed to sea. These costs were also expressed in a price per ton, and these costs have to be added to the hull costs to arrive at the capital investment in shipping. Virginian-built vessels of the late colonial period which cost as little as £4 per ton for hulls, might cost £8 to £8.10s.0d. per ton fitted and ready for sea [56]. It was estimated that vessels built at Saltcoats (Scotland), which cost £5 per ton for hulls, cost as much again fitted for sea in the early 1790s [57]. In the late 1830s, Plymouth shipbuilding costs were typically £11.10s.0d. to £12 per ton for high-class hulls; oufits for such vessels, including sheathing, then cost about £6 per ton more [58]. The anticipated employment of the vessel would determine the fitting out cost in the majority of cases. The Plymouth-built vessels quoted above were quite small, intended for short-distance voyaging, but most vessels employed in deep sea trade required a more elaborate outfit which would require an outlay of more than £6 per ton.

The foregoing remarks, it is hoped, indicate some of the relevant considerations to be borne in mind in assessing capital formation in newly built sailing ship tonnage. It remains to consider the methods by which steamship investment may be computed. The first steamship came on to the registry in 1813, and therefore some of the tonnage problems associated with eighteenth-century shipping are happily avoided. However, steamships pose some particular tonnage conundrums of their own which require some comment. In 1819, the owners of steamships were permitted a concession in respect of tonnage measurement which was to have important repercussions upon shipping statistics in the ninteenth century. The new regulation applied to steamships in 1819 permitted the deduction of engine room space (including space for boilers and bunkers) from what became known thereafter as gross tonnage. The allowable deductions were substantially modified by subsequent legislation. The tonnage calculated after deducting engine room space, which itself came to be a deduction of all 'non-earning' spaces below the tonnage deck, was known as net tonnage (the concept of deadweight tonnage for steamships, which was to become so important in calculating shipbuilding costs in the later nineteenth century, was rarely employed before 1850). The published shipping statistics for the nineteenth century almost invariably aggregate the net tonnage of steamships and, until certain 'non-earning' spaces were allowable as a deduction from the tonnage of sailing vessels as well after the 1850s, the gross tonnage of sailing ships were aggregated in these returns. Because sailing ships had little or no machinery space, it was only after legislation permitted the deduction of crew accommodation and the like that sailing ship gross and net tonnages were distinguished.

Generally speaking, the difference between the gross and net tonnages of sailing vessels was not great, but for steamships the difference was substantial [59]. Thus, there is a sense in which tonnage comparisons between sail and steam in the nineteenth century are very misleading, since we possess, for much of the period with which we are concerned, the gross tonnage of sail and the net tonnage of steam. This creates some difficulties in assessing the values to be assigned to steamships, newly built and registered. The problem is perhaps at its most acute in the case of steam tugs, which formed an important, though generally disregarded, part of the nineteenth-century steam tonnage fleet. Since the machinery space of tugs comprised practically their entire internal space for tonnage measurement, there was a large category of nineteenth-century shipping for which the net tonnage was extremely small in relation to the gross. Steam tugs might well measure between 5 and 50 tons net, as compared with 50 to 150 tons gross, and since they might typically cost from £2,000 to £5,000 each, any cost per ton on a net ton basis would be highly misleading, since the prime cost per net ton would, for this class of tonnage, considerably exceed the price per ton of the highest class ocean passenger liner. With regard to such ocean liners, there are problems, too, since their prime cost – with the very heavy fitting out costs deemed necessary for the passenger trades – greatly exceeded the cost of the (perhaps more typical) dry cargo carrying tonnage which was beginning to form an important component of the British merchant marine by the 1850s. Once these difficulties are recognized, however, it would not be impossible to make reasonably realistic calculations of the annual aggregates of steam tonnage built in the nineteenth century. Different criteria would have to be applied, however, to the three main categories of steamship – tug, passenger liner, and cargo vessel. Once an accurate breakdown of the tonnage of these types annually constructed has been assembled, it would be quite simple to assign to each category an appropriate prime cost based upon the data available in the records of shipbuilding firms, now happily preserved.

NOTES

[1]   26 Geo. III, c.60.

[2]   The returns were made up each year ending 30 September. The Act permitted vessels in distant trades to be registered up to thirty months from the date of the legislation. Because of this, the first annual return which included all the tonnage then afloat was that for 30 September 1789.

[3]   See the summary table in R. Davis, *The Rise of the English Shipping Industry*, p. 26 (London, 1962). To the sources there cited may be added PRO Cus. 17/1-9, covering annual entrances and clearances from 1772 to 1786.

[4]   Ibid., p. 27

[5]   The problem of shipping statistics has been explored by A. P. Usher, 'The growth of English shipping, 1572-1922', *Quarterly Jnl Economics*, XLII (1929), pp. 465-78; L. Harper, *The English Navigation Laws*, Ch. XXII (New York, 1939); and by Davis, op. cit., Appendix A. The last discussion is by far the best.

[6]   This last category was, of course, extremely important during the American War of Independence.

[7]   22 & 23 Car.II, c.11. The most authoritative discussion of tonnage measurement in this period is by W. Salisbury, 'Early tonnage measurement in England, Part III: H.M. Customs, and Statutory Rules,' *Mariner's Mirror*, 52, No. 4 (November 1966), pp. 329-40.

[8]   For example, under the Liverpool Docks Act of 1709 (8 Anne, c.8).

[9]   13 Geo. III, c.74.

[10] See R. C. Jarvis, 'Liverpool statutory register of British merchant ships', *Trans. Hist. Soc. Lancs. & Ches.*, CV (1963), pp. 107-22.

[11] R. Davis, 'Seamen's Sixpences; an index of commercial activity, 1696-1828', *Economica* n.s., XXIII (1956), pp. 328 ff. The London returns are in PRO Adm.68/194-218.

[12] PRO Adm.7/75-132.

[13] PRO HCA 25 and HCA 26.

[14] PRO Adm.7/363-389 & 650.

[15] Recently made available in facsimile reproduction by Gregg Press.

[16] Two historians have recently made comparative studies of tonnage measurement. J. J. McCusker, 'Colonial tonnage measurement: five Philadelphia merchant ships as a sample', *Jnl Econ. Hist.*, XXVII, No.1, (March, 1967), pp. 82-91, examines the evidence in respect of a very small sample, but nevertheless draws valid conclusions. G. M. Walton, 'Colonial tonnage measurement: a comment', *Jnl Econ. Hist.*, XXVII, No. 3 (September, 1967), pp. 392-7, provides a bigger sample, but the basis upon which the tonnages are compared is not altogether without ambiguity.

[17] *Jnl H. of Commons*, XLVII, 356.

[18] 12 Car.II, c.18.

[19] 7-8 Will.III, c.22.

[20] 12 Geo.II, c.21.

[21] John Reeves, *A History of the Law of Shipping and Navigation*, p. 423 (London, 1792).

[22] See above, p. 129.

[23] G. N. Clark, *Guide to English Commercial Statistics, 1696-1782*, pp. 45-51 (London, 1938). See also E. E. Hoon, *The Organization of the English Customs System 1696-1786*, pp. 117-18 (New York, 1938).

[24] About 230,000 tons of shipping were deducted.

[25] R. Craig and R. Jarvis, *Liverpool Registry of Merchant Ships*, Table 7 (Manchester, 1967).

[26] A typical 'running balance' table is transcribed by G. E. Farr, *Chepstow Ships*, Appendix B (Chepstow, 1954). It was easier, of course, to draw up such a table for a small port like Chepstow than for a major shipping centre like Liverpool or London.

[27] An interesting set of calculations may be found in C. Wright and C. E. Fayle, *A History of Lloyds*, pp. 182-7, and Appendix A (London, 1928).

[28] The early annual returns of shipping registered at British ports distinguishes prize tonnage from British-built tonnage. BPP *Accounts & Papers*, IX (1812-13), p. 449 gives the cumulative aggregate prize tonnage admitted to British registry between 1792 and 1812.

[29] Holden Furber, *John Company at Work*, Ch. IV (Cambridge, Mass., 1951).

[30] Examples abound in the evidence to Parliamentary Select Committees. See, for example, *S.C. on Manufactures, Commerce and Shipping*, BPP VI (1833), cv. of H. Nelson (Q. 6569); J. Astle (Q. 6857); and W. Richmond (Q. 7319).

[31] PRO Cus.17/12-30.

[32] Library of H.M. Customs & Excise, London, Cus.36/5.

[33] BPP *Accounts & Papers*, XIII (1806) and IV (1806-7).

[34] For example, by A. K. Cairncross, *Home & Foreign Investment, 1870-1913*, Ch. VI (Cambridge, 1953); P. Deane and W. A. Cole, *British Economic Growth, 1688-1959*, Table 62, p. 234 (Cambridge, 1962); and C. H. Feinstein, *Domestic Capital Formation in the U.K., 1920-1938*, pp. 170-6 (Cambridge, 1965).

[35] Some colonial American shipbuilding returns appear in *Jnl H. of Commons*, XLVII, pp. 273, 356-7. These figures may also be found in Lord Sheffield, *Observations on the Commerce of the United States*, pp. 84-5 (London, 1784).

[36] See R. S. Craig, 'British shipping and British North American shipbuilding', in H. E. S. Fisher (ed.) *The South-West and the Sea*, pp. 21-43 (Exeter, 1968).

[37] For Baltic-built vessels registered at Liverpool, see Craig and Jarvis, op. cit., pp. 3-4.

[38] The preamble and section XXVIII of 26 Geo. III, c.60 permitted the registration of foreign-built vessels which belonged to British subjects before 1 May 1786. Employment of such tonnage in European trade was allowed to be continued 'until the same shall be worn out'.

[39] The annual tonnage of secondhand shipping sold abroad is available from 1865 onwards, not from 1886 onwards as stated by A. H. Imlah, *Economic Elements in the Pax Britannica*, p. 46 (Cambridge, Mass., 1958). He is correct in supposing that British purchases of new colonial tonnage were negligible by the 1880s, but British purchases of foreign tonnage cannot be ignored.

[40] Capital formation in British shipping thereafter may be expressed as:

$$a + a_1 + (b - b_1) + (c - c_1) + d - e - f,$$

a = annual aggregate value of new British vessels, first registered,
a_1 = annual aggregate value of new colonial vessels, first registered in Britain,
b = annual aggregate value of vessels purchased from the colonies,
b_1 = annual aggregate value of vessels sold to the colonies,
c = annual aggregate value of vessels purchased from abroad,

c_1 = annual aggregate value of vessels sold foreign as secondhand vessels,

d = annual aggregate value of tonnage added by the rebuilding and lengthening of the existing shipping,

e = vessels wrecked or otherwise lost,

f = vessels broken up or otherwise destroyed.

The data are available from 1865. Before 1865 there were two major changes in the stock of shipping owned in Britain which have hitherto been neglected. First, some allowance has to be made for the loss of British tonnage which, because it was partly owned by American citizens, failed to qualify for the privilege of British registration after 1786. Second, in 1863, over 600 vessels of 329,000 tons were sold by American to British shipowners and placed under British registry. This was as a consequence of the American Civil War. A conservative valuation at £5 per register ton suggests that this transfer represented about £1½ million additional investment.

[41] G. E. Farr, *Records of Bristol Ships, 1800-1838* (Bristol, 1950), and his *Chepstow Ships* (Chepstow, 1954); R. Craig and R. C. Jarvis, op. cit. Other studies utilizing registry material include R. Weatherill, *The Ancient Port of Whitby and its shipping* (Whitby, 1908); R. Neal, 'Liverpool shipping in the early nineteenth century', in J. R. Harris (ed.), *Liverpool and Merseyside*, pp. 147-81 (London, 1969); and R. C. Jarvis, 'Eighteenth-century London shipping' in *Studies in London History presented to Philip Edmund Jones*, pp. 403-25 (London, 1969).

[42] R. C. Jarvis, 'Liverpool statutory register of British merchant ships', *Trans. Hist. Soc. Lancs. & Chesh.*, Vol. CV (1953), p. 116.

[43] *Rise of the English Shipping Industry*, pp. 376, 378-9.

[44] Feinstein, loc. cit.

[45] After the development of open-hearth steelmaking, the prevailing price of iron and steel scrap played some part in determining the shipowner's decision to scrap tonnage.

[46] *Strictures on the necessity of inviolably maintaining the navigation and colonial system*, pp. 128f (London, 1806).

[47] PRO Cus. 17.

[48] *American encroachment on British rights*, p. lxxvi (London, 1808).

[49] *A Treatise on the coal trade*, p. 224 (London, 1813).

[50] *A Treatise on the wealth, power and resources of the British Empire*, p. 55 (London, 1814).

[51] *S.C. (H. of L.) on the Timber Trade*, BPP III (1820), App. XII.

[52] See 'The measurement of Ships', *Naval Science*, Vol. I (1872), pp. 388-400.

[53] These prices have been drawn from a number of sources, including Lord Sheffield, *Observations on the commerce of the American States*, pp. 87, 139f., 140f. (London, 1784); R. Davis, op. cit., p. 375.

[54] J. Phipps, *A guide to the commerce of Bengal*, p. 139 (Calcutta, 1823).

[55] I owe these figures to the kindness of Mr W. Salisbury.

[56] Lord Sheffield, *Observations*, p. 87.

[57] *Statistical Account of Scotland*, Vol. VII (1793), p. 22.

[58] *S.C. on British Shipping*, BPP VIII (1844), ev. of W. B. Cuming, p. 183.

[59] The differences between sailing and steam vessel gross and net tonnages under British registry in 1886, for example, were:

Sailing vessels		Steam vessels	
Gross tons	Net tons	Gross tons	Net tons
3,512,783	3,397,197	6,321,504	3,965,302

Discussants: S. D. Chapman, A. W. Coats, D. C. Coleman,
E. Cooney, P. Cotterell, R. Craig, D. W. Crossley, R. Davis,
M. Falkus, C. H. Feinstein, J. Ginarlis, J. L. Halstead, J. R. Harris,
N. B. Harte, J. Hibbert, J. P. P. Higgins, B. Hill, D. S. Landes,
W. Minchinton, B. R. Mitchell, C. Phillips, S. Pollard, M. Reed.

It was generally agreed by all discussants that it would be necessary to separate out repair and maintenance in order to arrive at 'gross' capital formation. One rough and ready method of doing this would be to pick out, for each canal company, the initial years of very heavy expenditure as representing the construction period, counting the later routine years, in which this type of expenditure was low, as devoted mainly to repairs. Sudden rises in expenditure figures in later years usually indicated some major new construction, such as a lengthening or widening of the system, and would be counted as such.

This would not, however, work very clearly for turnpikes. Some trusts, even as early as 1760, began operations by borrowing considerable sums on the security of the tolls and spent them apparently on a major reconstruction or improvement of their road. This was seldom very systematic or effective, and considerable annual expenditure was still required year by year afterwards. Nevertheless, the pattern of a large initial expenditure, followed by much routine spending, was there. There were many other trusts, however, who began by putting up a turnpike and perhaps filling in a few of the worst holes in the road, and as proceeds of the first tolls came in they undertook more repairs or road widening, gradually rebuilding their whole road system if they were successful. The profile of their annual expenditure curve is quite different from the first case, and maintenance cannot in their case be easily isolated. There were many such trusts, and the profile of a large initial investment followed by later routine maintenance came in only, as a general rule, with the McAdam revolution and it was an important aspect of that revolution. But over the history of turnpikes as a whole, what stands out was the enormous variation in practice among them.

In reply to further direct questions, Mr Ginarlis explained that it was not possible to establish the proportion of 'metalled' road mileage in the precise manner in which it would be possible today, since the distinctions were not so clear then between the different types of surface. As a rough guide, however, it was the turnpikes which had the good surfaces, while the parish roads were the by-roads. In 1816 there were 95,000 miles of parish roads and nearly 20,000 miles of turnpike roads, so that the latter formed about one sixth of the total. The Dukes of Devonshire and of Gloucester had supplied financial support for the Sheffield-Glossop road; this trust had been studied in detail by Dr Albert, and it appeared that these two noble investors had put a great deal of money into the trust, and were willing to provide tide-over loans in the hope of ultimate recovery of their investment, rather than see the trust go bankrupt. The purposes to which these loans were put were largely repairs of the road itself.

The determination of responsibility over a road could be a complex matter. As a rule, parishes had responsibility unless a turnpike trust existed, so that urban streets would normally come under the parish. Sometimes, however, Improvement Commissioners and similar ad hoc bodies were set up, and they might be made responsible for the pavements while the parish kept responsibility for the road surface, or they might have powers over lighting and scavenging, leaving to the parishes the surfaces of both roads and pavements. The exact division of functions would often depend on local pressures and interests. As regards railways, no work had as yet been done by members of the project, who hoped to make use of the work of Dr Mitchell and Dr Kenwood.

A lively discussion arose on the classification of the mobile assets of transport companies. There was little difficulty in regard to such items as barges or carriages (except those used for pleasure). They would be classified as stock, as vehicles are today, yielding annual services. It was, however, too early to say how large this item would turn out to be in relation to the fixed capital costs of canals and roads.

Horses, however, were much more difficult to classify. Unfortunately, however, even if horses used for pleasure riding only were omitted, the remainder would bulk extremely large in any calculation relating to the eighteenth and nineteenth centuries. For example, it was found that Pickford's in the eighteenth century allowed nearly £2 per annum for the shoeing of each horse; admittedly their horses would wear their shoes out faster than most, but on the other hand the company could be presumed to get very good terms from blacksmiths. Since there were well over half a million horses in use at any one time, the annual expenditure of over £1 million on horseshoes alone would completely dwarf the figures of investment in, say, cotton mill machinery. If the horse is the equivalent of the present day van or of its engine, his shoes would correspond to expenditure on tyres, and his hay to expenditure on petrol. The parallel could not, however, be taken too far, for the horse, after all, reproduced itself.

The problem is, therefore, basically that of livestock in general, which would have to be discussed in the final session. This is of major importance in present day national income statistics of such countries as Australia, as seen in the work of Butlin, and this is what one would also expect to find in eighteenth-century Britain. In the present-day national income estimate, livestock are included in stock rather than in fixed capital, but there would be little doubt about their classification as capital of some kind. A cow yielding milk was clearly a capital good, until the day of her slaughter, and so was a chicken producing eggs, at least if it survived for more than a year. If such animals were to be classified as consumption goods, they would have to be at least notionally slaughtered every year, and this was straining credulity too far.

Against this it was argued that cattle kept on a farm for fattening were not capital stock, but a consumer good in process of manufacture. Draught animals, however, were always considered capital goods, and people talked of horses as their capital stock, they talked of turning over their capital of horses at the end of the year, and they depreciated horses. The distinction between fat stock and draught animals would cause problems for the farm estimates, but it left a fair degree of agreement on the classification of horses used in transport.

Another issue which caused some controversy was the kind of sample to be used to determine the costs of road building, where the proportion of what was known was much smaller than in the case of canals. The opportunities for error were great, since the averages per mile varied enormously in the examples given. One suggestion was to rely heavily on statistical techniques, and to build up a picture of the national expenditure from a close study of the distribution of cost ranges in the sample, testing it perhaps by comparison with one small area which might be studied as a check on the accuracy of the method, and assuming the same proportional distribution for the national network as a whole.

The method used so far on the project had been to break the totals down into counties, and to find for each type of county two or three average costs of the main types of roads there, based on as wide a coverage of roads as possible, and in the case of the West Riding on every road. In this way it would be possible to build up sectional totals before these were combined into national totals.

The problem of the representativeness of samples, where total quantities were known but there were wide variations in unit costs, existed also in the case of ships. Mr Craig pointed out that statistical information on numbers and tonnage was probably better than in almost any other capital good. The official registration of shipping began in 1786, and thereafter there were annual official figures of ships built and added to the fleet. The registration from that year was very accurately done, as far as one could judge. There was much information available for the years 1780-8, and the age composition of the fleet as existing in 1789 was known, and if some reasonable – if crude – assumption were made about rates of losses and scrappings, it would be possible to reconstruct building figures for a good number of years before that. Given the excellence of the original sources, which include PRO, BT6/191, a list of the name, tonnage and port of registry of every vessel afloat in 1789, and the various surviving registers of shipping, it might in fact be possible to take the series back to 1750 with reasonable accuracy, as well as take it forward to 1850.

There were, of course, some difficulties. The further you got away from the really accurate stock list, the bigger the discrepancies were likely to be. At any given port, in Liverpool for example, where there were 400 to 500 ships on the register at any one time, the customs officers had a hard task keeping their lists up to date. There would be some unofficial information, derived from such sources as local newspapers, but little of it was wholly reliable. If a ship went missing, and many did, the officials were reluctant to write her off and get the widows of the crew appearing before them in their weeds while there was still a chance that the ship might turn up somewhere, as sometimes occurred. There are many pencilled remarks, memoranda and crossings out on the registrations themselves, inserted as information came in, was tentatively noted or perhaps contradicted, but such scraps of knowledge might then be forgotten – and ships did disappear, never to be heard of again, without a confirming entry in the books. There were the further difficulties of the big weeding out of the register in 1826-7, and the shipping built and/or registered in the colonies. Yet, on the whole, a series could be built up of tonnage terms, with a very fair degree of accuracy, and Mr Craig was hopeful that he could construct it with the information he had already, to form a homogeneous series from 1789.

The problem of translating tonnage into values was discussed to some extent in the paper, but needs further study. It cannot be assumed that there was a close correspondence between costs per ton of vessels of different sizes, although it is true that builders and shipowners tended to price ships in terms of so much per ton. From one point of view, the cost per ton ought to go down with increasing size, since the cost of building is the cost of building the hull and deck, etc., which increases as the square of the dimensions, while the tonnage (or cubic capacity) would increase as the cube of the dimensions.

Against this, there were considerable increases of costs with scale. First, there were diseconomies in the construction. Scantlings have to be larger, and, in the case of timber ships in particular, larger tree trunks are more than proportionately expensive, and beyond a certain size timber building becomes virtually impossible technically. Whereas a small ship may be built on the beach or in a back yard almost, larger ships need docks, cranes and berths.The larger ships also tend to be built for the longer voyages, and therefore the 'fitting out to sea' would be proportionately much more costly. There would also have to be larger quarters for crews, and in the case of steam ships a large part of the carrying capacity would have to be given up, though the tonnage regulations did in fact exclude the engine space from the tonnage measurement.

Thus, by the end of the nineteenth century shipbuilders would not quote a price per ton unless they had a fair idea what size and type of ship was required, and only within narrow ranges did the price per ton remain constant, – i.e. was the price directly proportionate to tonnage. For most of the eighteenth century, however, and for the first half of the nineteenth, the two tendencies of rising and falling costs with scale tended to cancel out quite well, and costs per ton of the same type of ship remained constant over very wide ranges. This is also borne out by Maywald's figures [1], which were, however, criticized by Mr Craig as being incorrectly formulated.

The real difficulty relates to the type of ship. There were many types and their proportions did not remain constant. East Indiamen, for example, formed a falling proportion of the total as the East India Company lost its monopoly of the China and India trade. Shipping altogether presents a very fluid kind of market, where old trades languish or disappear, new trades develop, new cargoes arise which determine the character or adaptation of a new type of ship, and besides this some owners indulge in some form of creative obsolesence. The varying fortunes of different trades might quickly change the relative prices of different types of ship, irrespective of their original cost, according to the supply and demand situation. Further, different owners would have different answers to the problem of whether to build a ship for a single trade cycle, say to last but seven years and make a quick profit, or to carry the loss years of the slump period in a life of twelve years or more. It is necessary to break the tonnage down into different categories and then attempt estimates of the comparative extent of these categories.

The important distinctions depend on the requirements of the trade and the ports, in the eighteenth and early ninteenth centuries. For example, a ship involved in the American trade has to contend with little rise of water in the ports, and most tideways in American ports happen to have deep water berths. A ship engaged in the British coastal and short-sea trades, on the other hand, met great tidal variations and lay aground a great deal, and therefore developed a flat bottomed and cranky shape. The very largest vessels, East Indiamen, were by far the most expensive per ton, but this was largely a matter of lack of effective competition and building without a very clear eye to cost.

A ship built for the gold rush to Australia, to sail between London and Melbourne or Sydney, might be built to be very efficient and economical for her trade, but only at the cost of making her virtually useless for any other trade if that boom should end; or she might be built partly with an eye to alternative runs. Costs would, therefore, depend on the owner's speculative assessment of the future.

Construction costs would also depend on other, sometimes temporary factors. For example, the loss of the East India Company's monopoly led to a drop in the price of teak. It was one of the objects of the shipbuilder to keep the specific gravity of his ships' timber as low as possible. The specific gravity of British oak, however, was high, and British vessels were therefore on the whole less efficient than their American counterparts, built of lighter softwood timber, which could carry more cargo on a given dimension. There were some foreign timbers, notably teak, which combined the advantages of strength while being of lower specific gravity than oak – but teak was very expensive while the East India Company kept its monopoly. As soon as this was broken, English shipping looking for return cargoes from the East loaded large quantities of teak in Rangoon, the price came tumbling down and ships could be built cheaper and stronger than with English oak.

Similarly, the survival rate, or the rate of capital consumption, depended greatly on the type and the temporary conditions of trade. In general, the life span was ten to twelve years for poorly built ships, and twenty to twenty-five years for well built ships – or, in other words, rates of capital consumption were 4 to 5 per cent and 8 to 10 per cent respectively. But the usage of a ship could be as important for its chances of survival as the quality of its construction. Thus a wooden sailing vessel employed in the Bilbao iron ore trade in the 1860s would have little chance of a long life, no matter what her construction, since she might typically spend much of her time bumping about on Bilbao Bar, and then lying aground with a heavy cargo at a tidal port such as Briton Ferry at the other end of her run.

In the early days of steam, the life of many sailing ships was also shortened by being run down by steamships whose speeds their masters miscalculated. Legislation also played a part, including the load line and the qualification of masters, and another factor was the development of navigational devices.

When a ship was withdrawn from one trade as being unseaworthy, she did not necessarily thereby disappear; very few vessels were broken up, as it was hardly worthwhile doing so for timber ships, though more so for iron ships. Such a vessel might, for example, be bought up by a Norwegian owner and sent out to bring home Canadian timber. She would be loaded up with timber, including a large deck cargo, and the hull and cargo together would be encompassed by chains, tightened up with screws, and old crates would be sent across the Atlantic like that on the assumption that, no matter what happened to them, they would not sink. When freights were falling it was often the better ships that were laid up while the old tubs still paid their way, as their capital had long since been written down and they were sailing with depleted crews and not bothering overmuch about Mr Plimsoll.

Problems abound in assessing pre-1786 shipping statistics and new methods will have to be tried to determine fluctuations in investment in shipping. One possible indicator which it will be worthwhile to investigate will be the trade statistics showing the value or quantity of imports of masts and spars. This might have some merit in revealing fluctuations in shipbuilding activity, but, on the other hand, the incidence of major storms or extensive damage by naval action in wartime might cause destruction on a scale which disguised fluctuations in shipbuilding itself. Nevertheless, Mr Craig had worked on the import figures for one boom, and believed it was possible that these figures might become a useful base for calculations.

The matter did not become much easier when steam replaced sail, and horse power was as imperfect a measure of investment in shipping as tonnage, for it was not very reliably related to tonnage. In the case of land-based steam engines, it was stated, there was a certain stability in the ratio, and one could assume, at least for two or three decades, that there would be about 1 h.p. for every 100 spindles in a cotton mill. For ships, however, there was a large difference between the common run of cargo ships, destined to sail at 7 to 9 knots, and the transatlantic liners, needing quite disproportionate power to sail faster, and perhaps to have some speed and power in reserve. Ferry steamers crossing the English or the Irish Channel would find it economically worthwhile to put in the kind of power which would have been pointless for the *John Bowes* or the *Q.E.D.*, the first two steamships in the coal trade. Even in the long distance trades, Alfred Holt settled for high h.p. for the Far Eastern trade, while the Booths had built ships of similar tonnage, but of much lower h.p. for their South American trade. Moreover, towards the end of the century, there was legislation that any vessel of more than 99 h.p. had to carry a second engineer, and in consequence large numbers of vessels were rated as having engines of exactly that power. Neither did a similar h.p. necessarily represent a similar investment. At first, engines were very inefficient, so that later ones cost less per h.p. Different power and construction was used for ships driven by paddles and those driven by propellers. At the same time, there were also diseconomies of size, both in the engine, and in the space it would use up for coal storage.

Finally, the Conference discussed the practical and theoretical problems of losses and acquisition of ships. A large proportion of ships was always built in the colonies and during the American Civil War, for example, something like 300,000 tons of American shipping was acquired by British owners. In each case, however, the tonnages and other details are known.

The matter was more difficult in relation to the taking and the losses of prizes, beside the losses through sinkings in wartime. This must be an almost unique example of large-scale loss or acquisition of capital assets by British owners. There were at least two problems here. First, throughout their ownership by other nationals, the ships depreciated in the normal manner. Secondly, large scale acquisition of prizes, for example in Liverpool, tended to depress the prices and values of the home-built ships, while the prize ships themselves were also acquired at less than their market value. Apart from the fact that the age distribution of the prize vessels is not known, the fleet would appear to be in some sense undervalued if a certain tonnage was lost, and a similar tonnage of equivalent value acquired but accounted at a lower price.

Even though, in this case, the insurance records have turned out to be of no help, there are some records of losses and gains by prizes for this period. The problem is how to fit them into the national income accounts. One could count the cost of acquiring prize ships, as the cost of fitting out the privateers, and this would be their cost of 'production'. Alternatively, and again from the national rather than the individual point of view, one could look at ships lost as exports – i.e. capital goods produced at home but not used at home – and prize ships acquired as imports, in the same way. The income from the captured ship would also have to be included in the national income estimate. The loss of a ship would be debited as its loss at the current value, which one could obtain from general tables of the values of secondhand ships.

From the point of view of the project, the important item was not so much the value of the fleet, as the value of the increment and, perhaps, the incremental capital/output ratio. If one were mainly interested in the national effort that went into capital formation, one would have to count in the cost of the ships built (even though lost during the war) and also count the cost of acquiring the prizes, as suggested above, for the ships gained – knowing that in between there was an element of capital destruction: the ships lost or sunk. In ships changing hands several times, only the net change would be counted in, but this was not likely to be numerically very significant. For net capital formation, one would balance ships lost as against ships gained, in terms of value rather than tonnage, and include the increment only.

There would, in fact, be interesting regional variations. Liverpool, for example, made heavy purchases of prizes so that it gained increments of capital at low cost. Another port at which an exceptional number of prizes was available for sale was Falmouth, since it was an easy port to reach by the prize crews and ships would be put up for auction there after condemnation, and bought up by owners from elsewhere.

NOTES

[1] K. Maywald, 'The construction costs and the value of the British merchant fleet, 1850-1938', *Scottish Journal of Political Economy*, III, No. 1, pp. 44-6.

5

Capital Formation in Agriculture

B. A. HOLDERNESS

Since I have only just begun the serious collection of data for capital formation, this paper contains few hard facts. However, the problems involved make an interesting study in themselves. Before 1866, there is a dearth of reliable information about the economics of British agriculture; even afterwards, when statistical series were annually compiled, there remain no precise data of capital formation. Only ten years ago, Colin Clark pointed out that important sectors of agricultural capital in Britain are still obscure, notably farm buildings [1]. It is therefore hardly surprising that, although we have reasonably accurate estimates of the output and income of British agriculture from the mid-nineteenth century, capital formation should have remained a largely neglected field of study [2]. It is unlikely that this omission can be fully remedied; the best to be hoped for is to achieve some estimate of gross capital formation from time to time during the period, by using the disparate source material available, public drainage and enclosure papers, private farm accounts and estate records, together with some of the abler contemporary expositions of capital investment in farming and the land, and, if possible, insurance data, loans for improvement, etc. The best approach to reconcile such diverse data is to find the level of investment per acre in agricultural land at different times. We cannot properly adopt the techniques of random sampling of surviving records, but it should eventually be possible to discover some measure of the rate of capital accumulation, at any rate of fixed capital formation, in British agriculture between the mid-eighteenth century and the beginning of the era of 'agricultural statistics'.

PROBLEMS OF DEFINITION

The various eighteenth- and nineteenth-century efforts to compute the growth of national capital from Petty to Giffen, although they give all due weight to agriculture in the British economy, are not applicable to the present problem [3]. They were subject to overmuch pure guesswork; they were too widely spaced in time from each other; and worst of all, nearly all contemporary estimates, even if one could

159

assume they had been independently derived, depended upon the capitalization of rents. No attempt was made to discover how far the computed national average of rents reflected an economic or 'Ricardian' interpretation of agricultural rent. To assume that the national rentroll was at rack overall in the eighteenth and nineteenth centuries was patently absurd, when rents were as often fixed upon traditional or social considerations as upon the desire to maximize the economic returns of land ownership [4]. From the nineteenth century controversy about agricultural rents, however, came a few potentially useful contributions to the present discussions, albeit of a limited nature and often seemingly by chance. Apologists of the system like E. P. Squarey and Albert Pell, in seeking to prove that rent was really the interest upon landlord's capital, attempted to calculate an average of capital investment required to raise virgin land to a state of cultivation [5]. To judge from the few data of actual costs which we already possess, these calculations were not wildly inaccurate. It is my hope that computations of this kind – of which there are others in various county agricultural reports of the 1790s and 1800s – may eventually act as a check upon data collected directly from manuscript sources.

Although the primary purpose of the study is to ascertain the growth of fixed capital, it is my intention to test the feasibility of including items other than the tangible fixed equipment for consideration. The range of this study is not easy to define at this stage, but it may be possible to include investment in increased livestock numbers [6] and tools, in improvements in existing land use, in permanent or semi-permanent conversions, and in improving breeds of livestock [7]. Fertilizers present a difficult problem, but in cases where the application of fertilizers or manures was intended to last beyond each twelve-month, their cost may be included as capital formation. Changes in the size and value of agricultural inventories would be interesting, but it seems unlikely that they can ever be calculated with sufficient precision for our purpose. The fixed capital of farms – drainage, enclosure, fencing, buildings, occupation roads – is easily distinguishable, though expenditure on repairs and maintenance appears seldom to have been separated from new investment in accounts of the time. However good the detailed evidence at my disposal, the end product will necessarily bear but a distant resemblance to modern data of agricultural capital formation.

In dealing with the flow of agricultural investment, some items which attracted rural funds will have to be omitted. In the interests of consistency with other sections of this project, expenditure such as legal and administrative fees incurred in the process of parliamentary enclosure cannot be admitted in evaluating its capital investment. To avoid trespassing also on others' territory, I intend to exclude all agrarian investment in improvements like canals, turnpikes — indeed, if possible, all public roads, although the largest share of the costs were often borne by landowners and farmers and the benefits equally accrued to the local agricultural community. This omission may well give a distorted view of capital formation in the agricultural sector at times, and it will certainly create problems in disentangling investment in improvements particularly on the great estates. For the same reason, it is desirable but may not be practicable to exclude horses not employed in agriculture, which were rapidly increasing in the eighteenth century.

Leaving aside the questions of overlapping interests, there remain several more specifically rural items of capital which need to be omitted as well. Rural housing presents the most difficult case, because farmers' houses were always included in the farmstead or farm buildings for the purpose of valuation. So, too, were at least some of the 'tied' cottages of their labourers [8]. Residential capital should really be given a separate analysis, but it is probable that contemporary evidence will allow no more than an approximate distinction between housing and occupational fixed capital in agriculture. One can make out a case for including such housing in the sector — not so the general run of village buildings. The latter only impinges upon our field when, for example, the landowning magnates chose to rebuild as model villages or to remove from their view existing communities, or alternatively rebuilt cottages for dependent labourers or retainers. Model villages or rows of improved cottages became an important manifestation of landlords' investment by the nineteenth century and most counties can show at least a few examples by 1850 [9]. Furthermore, the outlay on embellishing country mansions, parks and pleasure grounds often reached very considerable proportions in this period. Such 'conspicuous investment' bulked largely in the annual outgoings of most *rentier* estates, but added next to nothing to the capital formation of agriculture. Its importance is only hinted at in a recent calculation, in which it is shown that the parks of the 7,000 biggest country houses in England occupied 3 per cent of the total acreage of the country, but that half the national area of woodland lay in this parkland. The

expense per acre on these lands before 1870 was heavily disproportionate, both in relation to their area and to the productive use to
which they were applied [10].

One final problem needs to be raised in this section. With nearly
300,000 agricultural holdings (according to the Census data, 1831-61)
in Britain, a considerable proportion were small in size. Even the Census
figures, which underestimated the number of all smallholdings, gave
19,000 holdings under five acres in 1851. Of these a large number were
in the vicinity of industrial towns, especially in the counties of extreme
morcellement, Lancashire and the West Riding. In 1799, the West
Riding agricultural reporter declared that many of these small holdings
were only partly agricultural for one reason or another [11]. Many
such smallholders indeed invested little in their agricultural property,
preferring to rely upon it as an adjunct to industrial or commercial
employment. Nevertheless, there were many even on the periphery of
large towns whose agricultural functions were clearly defined and
important, as cow keepers, market gardeners, poultrymen, etc., who,
though on the edge of farming should still be included in the
agricultural sector. It is in fact on these 'ragged edges' of the industry
that the problems of capital formation are likely to be almost insoluble.

SOURCES AND METHODS

Enclosure

Enclosure makes a convenient starting point, not least because there are
already in print numerous examples of the costs of parliamentary
enclosure. To obtain an accurate impression it will be necessary to
re-examine at source the Awards which give details of costs incurred by
proprietors, but for the time being, all published material has been
sifted and tables to illustrate the changing level of expenditure through
time — expressed inevitably as yet in historic prices — have been drawn
up (Tables 1A and 1B) [12]. These tables are provisional, but it is
unlikely that further research will modify the trends that they reveal very
significantly. Only a comparatively small proportion of surviving
Enclosure Awards contains accounts or a schedule of costs, so we
cannot sample at random.

These tables demonstrate an interesting trend in total costs, but it is
far from being entirely satisfactory. The elimination of administrative
costs is accurate enough for present purposes [13]. Where there are no

TABLE 1A
Estimate of total cost per acre of parliamentary enclosure
in parishes with surviving accounts, 1740-1830

Period	No. accounts	Gross acreage	Total cost	Cost per acre in shillings
Before 1760	30	40,412	21,185	10.5
1760-69	76	112,747	71,315	12.7
1770-79	88	118,973	114,216	19.3
1780-89	34	56,032	53,858	19.2
1790-99	73	125,165	194,111	31.0
1800-15	17	34,054	72,831	42.8
1816-	8	9,094	30,589	67.3

TABLE 1B
Proportion of the total cost laid out in surveying and
capital improvement

Period	No. accounts	Percentage of total cost		Capital input per acre in shillings
Before 1760	9	26		2.7
1760-69	5	25.9		3.3
1770-79	8	40		7.7
1780-89	7	40.5		7.7
After 1790	14	49	1790-99	15.2
			1800-15	20.9
			1816-	33.0

N.B. Capital investment given only where accounted by the Enclosure Commissioners.

Sources and methods: see text.

detailed accounts to provide the necessary information, the various administrative costs were found by applying a derived average of the extant accounts. Surveying has been separately treated in Table 1B because whatever means was adopted of reallocating the land, a survey was essential: its inclusion with so-called 'improvements' as an item of capital formation, therefore, seemed to be justified. It is these 'improvements', however, which create most of the real difficulties. The term has been used to describe all outlays on the fixed equipment of the land, installed or ordered by the Commissioners, *and accounted by them.* But different Awards included different items in their 'public' expenditure. From the beginning, most Awards contained provision for the public 'out-fencing' of the tithe owners and sometimes also the manorial lords' allotments. Occasionally, the accounts also included the costs of all 'out-fencing', but it was more usual, as J. M. Marting pointed out, for the Commissioners to make no actual arrangements for fencing, but to stipulate that the 'out-fencing' be done often within two or three months of the Award's enrolment [14]. The realignment and fencing of roads were not always accounted for, but road-making became more commonly a feature of surviving accounts from the 1780s onwards, which goes some way to explain rising average costs. The public roads, in fact, almost certainly represented the largest single item of capital formation from parliamentary enclosures [15]. Surface drainage, similarly, was as a rule only installed on the tithe allotments until late in the eighteenth century.

However, much of the earlier parliamentary enclosure was in parishes with few proprietors and, as a general rule, in districts of relatively pervious soils, or on the lighter clays of the Midlands, which were immediately afterwards laid down to grass [16]. The provision of surface drains could safely be left to the owners' private fencing work. When areas of more difficult soils or parishes of more complicated landownership were concerned — when, for instance, large parts of the counties of Huntingdonshire and Cambridgeshire began their parliamentary enclosure — the Commissioners were more likely to provide for a considerable amount of public drainage. This was most obvious in cases of major public reclamation, as in the Fens, which are omitted from Tables 1A and 1B. Even in the generality of enclosures after the 1780s a somewhat larger quantity of new tangible equipment tended to be installed, but to how many cases this applied and what benefit it conferred upon the majority of allottees yet remain open questions.

When the Commissioners had laid out the funds which they had levied, the proprietors of new enclosures were faced with still more expense. The Commissioners usually ordered that a certain amount of fencing be done privately at the allottees' expense, to divide one property from the next, and most substantial proprietors also had to divide up their new allotments into viable closes. This obviously took time to accomplish, and in some instances the visible effects of enclosure were meagre [17]. On some estates, too, the rebuilding of farmsteads was undertaken, but by no means as a regular follow-up. All such developments were left to the individual proprietor, so that simply to calculate the expense of enclosure per acre gives a very limited view of the capital investment involved in this reorganization of the land. Each example should properly be examined in detail, since the economic after effects differed considerably from place to place. The notion that enclosure in the later eighteenth century comprehensively increased the capital applied in agriculture is misleading. Of the six million acres of parliamentary enclosure in the century after 1740, well over four million comprised land already cultivated and at least relatively productive. Moreover, perhaps half as much again for private enclosure in the period should be added to the total.

We have Dr Havinden's evidence from an earlier period that enclosure as such did not automatically raise productivity by encouraging improved methods of cultivation. The correlation of progressive farmers and enclosed farms, stressed by Arthur Young in particular, was never universal, and the bad agricultural practices to be found on many enclosed estates were criticized by less enthusiastic reporters to the Board in the 1790s and 1800s [18]. Opportunities for permanent improvements arising out of enclosure were often thrown away when landlords and farmers chose to economize upon the installation of new plant after the award had been made. Many of the agricultural reporters complained of the unwillingness of landlords to set up ring fences and build their farmsteads in the middle of the plot. Equally, many enclosures were not underdrained, often for one or two generations after the fences had been installed [19]. For tenant farmers the determination of landlords to raise rents almost immediately after enclosure, often two- or threefold, inhibited them from undertaking really important, but slowly maturing improvements of their own.

Parliamentary enclosure, therefore, represented merely the visible portion of a much greater volume of actual or potential capital investment. If the additional new capital were not supplied, the returns upon the original outlay on enclosure might have been considerably less than in parishes of the same type where this was provided. The estimates of capital formation in enclosure given in Table 2A tell us very little about the true capital requirements at the time. Hence it is essential to examine in detail numerous examples of enclosure and its after effects. In the meantime, it is possible to suggest a likely quantity of additional capital required for landlords to build upon the basis of the reorganization of the common fields, and this is attempted in Tables 2B and 2C.

Estimates of private hedging and ditching costs are plentiful enough, but are heavily biased towards the period 1780 to 1815, and they often give conflicting results, because many were obviously untypically extravagant [20]. However, in about 1800, we should probably add £3 to £4 an acre for hedges and ditches, and another £1 for gates and culverts; so that the basic cash requirement per acre of enclosure

TABLE 2A
*Provisional calculation of total outlay and
investment in parliamentary enclosure*

Period	A Approx. acres enclosed	B Total cost £	C Capital input £	D Ave column C per annum £
Before 1740	30,000	15,750	4,100	342 (1725-39)
1740-59	210,000	110,000	28,600	1,430
1760-69	520,000	330,000	85,800	8,580
1770-89	1,020,000	980,000	392,000	19,600
1790-99	740,000	1,150,000	563,500	56,350
1800-15	1,520,000	3,230,000	1,582,700	105,513
1816-44	250,000	768,000	376,300	12,976
1845-	190,000	c.570,000	c.340,000	c.10,700 (1845-74)
Total	4,480,000	6,853,000	3,371,000	

TABLE 2B
*Approximate estimates of necessary capital investment following
parliamentary enclosure (excluding new building, seeding and fertilizing)*

Based on costs quoted between 1794 and 1810 (see text)

High estimate (including underdrainage by bush or grip method)

	Acres	Additional cost per acre	Total cap. investment *	Total cap. per acre *
To 1770	760,000	60s	£2,398,000	63·0s
1770-89	1,020,000	85s	£4,727,000	92·7s
1790-1815	2,260,000	110s	£14,576,000	129·0s
1816-70	420,000	110s †	£3,030,000	143·0s
Total	4,460,000		£24,731,000	110·9s

* Including the capital input accounted by Commissioners
† Despite falling labour costs more expensive drainage probably kept overall
expenditure up. An estimate based on tile mole or pipe drainage would
enormously inflate these data.

TABLE 2C
Low estimate (without underdrainage)

	Acres	Additional cost per acre	Total cap. investment*	Total cap. per acre*
To 1770	760,000	45s	£1,828,500	48s
1770-89	1,020,000	60s	£3,452,000	67·7s
1790-1815	2,260,000	80s	£11,186,200	98·9s
1816-70	420,000	70s	£2,170,000	103s
Total	4,460,000		£18,636,700	83·6s

averaged about £6 in 1800. If underdrainage, even by the cheaper 'bush-drains' or grips, was undertaken, another 30s. an acre at the very least would be needed, and if new building were also contemplated, we must add another £3 to £4 an acre at a conservative estimate, to the total. Altogether, an enclosure undertaken about 1800 with new fixed plant fully installed by the landlord could easily cost him £12 an acre [21]. At this level, the apparently extortionate administrative costs of the parliamentary process no longer loom so large. In effect, by such an estimate we approach what the Americans call 'farm-making' costs, although most of the enclosure, as has just been said, was not concerned with virgin land. It is still unknown, and may indeed prove to be undiscoverable, on how many estates such comprehensive investment was needed; on a great many where it was required it was long delayed after the enclosure had taken place.

Reclamation and Enclosure of Waste

In dealing with the enclosure of waste, a much greater *quantum* of new capital equipment was obviously required. Of course, even some of the waste not associated with open field arable in its enclosure was cleared and fenced and then laid to existing farms. The larger tracts, however, needed more than mere reorganization. Since most of the waste was uncultivated because of difficulties in the way of piecemeal assarting, the costs involved in public action would obviously be greater than in already cultivated areas. But administrative costs still formed a large share of the totals, not least because most waste was common grazing and the intricacies of allocation held up proceedings. Tables 3A and 3B give some indication of the costs per acre of the parliamentary enclosure of wastes. It is difficult to say how typical are the examples quoted in Table 3A. Terrington Marsh was very expensive because some of the drainage and most of the embanking had to be done twice over, and the vast public works undertaking which was John Rennie's reclamation of the East, West and Wildmore Fens from 1801 onwards involved an enormous outlay on surface drains, many of which were large enough for canal traffic [22]. In general, however, the provisions were similar. Most wastes were swampy, and the greatest item of cost was nearly always drainage. Drains, highways, pumping engines, some fences and occasionally even the sites of new settlements were included in much of the public enclosure. 'In-fences', farm buildings, occupation roads and village housing were left to the allottees as usual, or to an entrepreneur as lessee of the Crown like John Parkinson in the West Fen of Lincolnshire, so the costs per acre given in the table still do not provide estimates of the investment required to bring virgin land into cultivation. Some of the examples of investment in reclamation given in contemporary works certainly included costs of building, marling and seeding the new lands. This may be the explanation of the estimated cost of £15 to £20 per acre for reclaiming Needwood and Cannock Chase, as the nearly contemporary enclosure of Charnwood detailed in Table 3A cost only £6 an acre [23]. It should be pointed out that reclamation of forest areas usually provided the proprietors or Commissioners with a saleable quantity of timber with which to offset part of the gross outlay.

TABLE 3A

Parliamentary enclosure costs of various wastes,
1760-1830

(1) Marshes		Acres	Cost	Cost p. acre		
Spaldingmoor, E. R.	1762 ff.	5,613	£14,000	£2	12	6
Holderness Level, E. R.	1762 ff.	11,211	£30,000	£2	13	6
Upper Witham Fens, Lincs.	1762 ff.	19,418	£77,672	£4	0	0
Eight Hundred Fen, Lincs.	1764 ff.	22,000	£50,600	£2	6	0
Terrington Marsh, N. F.	1790	868	£16,970*	£19	11	0
Anwick Fen, Lincs.	1791-3	1,097	£4,070	£3	14	0
Marshland Smeeth, Norf.	1795-8	6,343	£34,280	£5	9	0
Tattershall Fen, Lincs.	1796-8	892	£3,630	£4	1	6
Various E. Riding Fens	1790-1815	23,432	£206,600	£8	15	6
East, West & Wildmore						
Fens, Lincs.	1801 ff.	40,011	£400,000	£10	0	0
Sedgmoor, Somerset	1815-30	12,000	£60,000	£5	0	0

* The high cost of Terrington due to faulty construction of drains and banks, which had to be rebuilt.

(2)   Forest, Scrub, Fell, Warren, etc.

Wolsingham, Durham	1769 ff.	5,020	£12,550	£2	10	0
Haltwistle, Northumb.	1790s	10,000	c£40,000	£4	0	0
Cartmel, Lancs.	1795-9	12,516	£47,000	£3	15	0
Macclesfield Common,						
Cheshire	1796-1804	867	£5,433	£6	3	0
Charnwood, Leics.	1800s	c4,500	£27,000	£6	0	0
2 Lincs. Warrens*	1799-1805	1,216	5,562	£4	10	0
Ecclesfield, W. R.	1811	14,000	c£60,000	£4	6	0
Otmoor, Oxon.	1801-3	4,000	£26,000	£6	15	0

* The *private* enclosure of Driby warren and walks, Co. Lincoln, in 1779-80, about 1200 acres, cost less than £300, and Messingham waste, including a large warren, 1798-1804, by Parliamentary process only £2. 10s. 0d. an acre. Of the above, 350 acres were fenced internally and partially underdrained with tiles.

TABLE 3B
Suggested costs and capital investment in enclosing waste by parliamentary sanction 1727-1845

Period	Acres	Cost per acre	Total cost		Putative capital-input
Before 1760	74,500	40s	£149,000	50%	£74,500
1761-92	478,300	65s	£1,554,650	60%	£932,790
1793-1801	273,900	110s	£1,506,450	60%	£903,870
1802-1815	738,750	150s	£5,548,125	67%	£3,698,680
1816-1845	199,300	120s	£1,195,800	67%	£757,200
Total:	1,764,750	–	£9,954,025	–	£6,367,040

TABLE 3C
John Clutton's estimates of the cost of making cultivable four tracts of crown forest in the 1850s

Items	Hainault 2,255 Ac. £	Wychwood 3,016 Ac. £	Whittlebury 300 Ac. £	Delamere 1,554 Ac. £
Clearing, Grubbing	18,730	6,233	1,714	9,214
Marling	–	–	–	19,451
Draining	22,618 / 520	1,602	1,602	1,417
Fencing		1,506	220	1,397
Farm Roads	1,723	811	–	894
Buildings & Cotts.	15,070	14,337	2,014	14,337
Miscell.	836	–	–	–
Total	58,377	23,407	5,550	46,750
Receipts from Timber	55,000	14,080	5,800	17,815

Total Cost   £134,084;   Receipts from Timber   £92,695

Source: *Transactions of the Surveyors' Institution*, IV, 1871-2, p.17.

In the absence of definite evidence of 'farm-making' investment in the great phase of waste reclamation, John Clutton's information on the outlay in reclaiming 6,600 acres of Crown forest in the 1850s, although late, is invaluable. Clutton's data, summarized in Table 3C, did not include any expenditure on parliamentary enclosure or any other important administrative costs. His examples do, however, comprise both heavy and light soil areas. On the Essex clays of Hainault drainage was a major item; elsewhere it was of minor significance. In the first case the grubbing, drainage and fencing work cost £18 an acre; in Whittlebury, Wychwood and Delamere it averaged only five guineas an acre. The total investment, including buildings and in one case marling, cost £20 an acre, of which the Crown recouped 70 per cent by selling the timber [24]. Is it possible to assume that this figure was a fairly accurate reflexion of 'farm-making' costs in similar conditions in the previous sixty or so years? The only accurate calculation of costs from an earlier period which has been printed occurs in Vancouver's Survey of Devon. An assart of 140 acres in Blackdown at Loddiswell in fact cost no more than £6.15s.0d. an acre, including some building and seeding, although seventy acres had had to be cleared of rock [25]. Generalization is obviously dangerous with so few data. Most of the wastes which passed through the parliamentary process of enclosure obviously cost more than Loddiswell all told, but without more detailed research an average figure might lie anywhere between £10 and £20 an acre for the overall investment in improving waste lands.

How much virgin waste was brought permanently into production after 1740? The acreage subject to parliamentary enclosure is given as 1¾ million, which may be an underestimate, and much was reclaimed without parliamentary sanction, as had always been the case. In upland areas, landlords and farmers still tried to take in parcels of rough moorland to serve as better pasture. Private enclosure was also proceeding in scrubby areas where the soil was usually only marginally fertile, also in the carr-lands, along the flood plains of rivers, notably by warping, and most noticeably in reclamation from sea or estuarine saltings. Individuals such as John Wilkinson, the ironmaster, and Coke of Norfolk are recorded in this activity but there are numerous others up and down the country who accomplished similar intakes [26].

LANDLORD'S CAPITAL

According to the law defining the relationship between landowner and tenant, virtually all items of fixed capital in farming were, and are, held to form 'landlord's capital'. The phrase became a formula to describe the buildings, fences, ditches and drains and other fixed plant which were supposed to be handed over to each incoming tenant in a good and sufficient state of repair. In practice, individual arrangements between proprietors and tenants varied considerably, but before discussing interpretative problems, the two chief components of the landlord's capital — buildings and drainage — will be examined in more detail.

Farm buildings

For data on buildings we are heavily dependent upon the survival of farm and estate accounts. Evidence of new building on farms in the eighteenth and nineteenth centuries is at best piecemeal, and although many constructions of the period remain, or at least remained visible till within ten years or so, no survey of survivals has yet to be completed. An untried source which may prove fruitful and with which I am unfamiliar, is the record of fire insurance policies. For agriculture there are serious difficulties in such material. The growth in number of policies after 1780 can scarcely have reflected the rate or incidence of new farm building, since the number of farms remained fairly stable, and insurance only slowly became popular for existing properties. New building probably added an incentive to landlords or farmers to seek fire cover, but it cannot be assumed that the majority of new policies issued in this period of expanding business deals with farms on which any recent improvements had taken place. The comparative rarity of industrial or commercial premises makes it possible to obtain a reasonably accurate picture of fixed capital formation from the insurance data; but with 250,000 to 300,000 separate agricultural holdings at least, one third of which exceeded 100 acres in the census period, the results are likely to be less comprehensive for agriculture, because a large number of farms were still not insured in the early nineteenth century. However, it is possible that such source material may reveal more data when thoroughly examined than I have here suggested; insurance records remain a major line of inquiry.

There were important geographical differences in farm buildings, both in the uses to which they were applied in pastoral and arable districts, and also in the materials of which they were constructed. Most *model* farmyards were naturally built of brick and tile after 1750, although the materials remained expensive and many of the more conventional landlords and farmers continued to employ vernacular methods — lath and plaster, timber framing, clay lump, cob, etc. — until well into the nineteenth century, almost certainly longer than one would expect to judge from the propaganda of improvers like H. S. Thompson and J. Bailey Denton [27]. The survival of local traditions is important, not only because of their relative cheapness, but also because it implies that on perhaps a majority of farms in Britain no real break occurred in the pattern of farm building until the middle years of the nineteenth century, or even later. Adaptation and repair were perhaps more the order of things than any significant new construction of fixed plant.

The chronology of farm building is worthy of consideration at this point, since no modern study has yet been undertaken. The great phase of rural rebuilding noticed by W. G. Hoskins and M. W. Barley from the late sixteenth to the early eighteenth century suggests that there was a long drawn out period of active reconstruction [28]. Examined more closely, however, it seems clear that the rebuilding was mainly confined to residences with their attached outhouses. Probate inventories of the stock of testators in many regions infer that farmyards at any rate before the mid-eighteenth century, were often only semi-permanent, with many buildings put together out of wooden hurdles, posts and rails, thatch and straw, temporarily, so much so indeed that the 'hovels', or whatever local name was applied, were actually movable. In the context of fixed capital, farmsteads may in fact have been 'top-heavy' until the nineteenth century, with substantial farmhouses and expensive barns occupying a greater share of the capital equipment than was economically justifiable, especially in areas such as west Norfolk, where stored corn was traditionally kept indoors and not in open ricks [29]. According to various of the county reports in the 1790s and 1800s, and even the prize essays of the 1840s and 1850s, much new building was required all over the country [30]. In Northumberland and the Scottish Lowlands large, planned 'farmeries' were a feature of the landscape by 1800, but such farmsteads, like the model examples cited in propagandist literature, were impracticable for the general run of farmers in Britain, just as in the 1850s Bailey Denton's plans were conceived on an extravagant scale seldom adopted in practice. In some areas a great deal had already been accomplished by 1800 and, including the 'model farms', few districts were without new buildings, by that date.

Enclosure, of course, created the need for new buildings, although the number of buildings in which new construction work followed upon enclosure was limited. It was more frequent in the west Midlands, in west Norfolk and a few other regions than elsewhere [31]. The resiting of farmsteads to take advantage of the redistribution of land was not as usual as one might assume, and in some instances one or two generations were to pass before the new building was undertaken.

Improvement or extension of existing farmsteads, excluding complete rebuilding, were more frequently undertaken in the eighteenth century. The response to falling profits and abandoned holdings in the 1730s and 1740s, in the east Midlands, was for landowners to renovate and extend their farmyards to attract new tenants. At about the same time the Holkham estate showed an increase of expenditure on repairs and improvements, and this reaction to low prices may have been quite widespread [32]. Eighteenth-century farmhouses are quite common; immediately recognizable outbuildings of the same period rather less so, though this may simply indicate how important later amendment and rebuilding has been. It is, however, perhaps not unfair to state that new permanent farm building in the eighteenth and early nineteenth century was not so much a slow accretion according to need, but followed a sequence in which a long phase of inactivity (other than maintenance and repair) was interspersed by one or two bursts of large-scale capital renewal. Some landowners certainly developed their estates gradually as money became available or new ideas took root. The majority, however, apparently found it essential, or at least desirable, to install new farm buildings, often at one go, after 1820, and especially during a great phase of reconstruction from about 1840 to 1870, when the larger farmsteads in particular acquired the appearance of massive solidity which has persisted more or less to the present.

Between the early eighteenth century and 1870 most farms must have worn out at least one set of buildings, but since before the nineteenth century farmers in general had a much lower expectation of their farm buildings, the phasing of capital replacement is very difficult to estimate. To sum up, however, we can fairly assume a major transformation of farm buildings in Britain between about 1820 and 1870 — a transformation, that is, of older patterns of farm yard organization, layout and building capacity, and not merely involving a more extensive reconstruction of existing plant and requirements. It is significant, although not all-important, that the principles of scientific planning were first propagated by enthusiasts like Philip Pusey, H. S. Thompson and Bailey Denton in the 1840s and 1850s.

Most contemporary estimates of capital investment per acre in farm buildings assume a radical reconstruction of existing farmyards, or building on waste ground, so that before the 1820s they are of limited use in forming generalizations. Bailey Denton's extravagant, and therefore presumably untypical, estimates were the most thoroughly worked out before the 1870s. Obviously, as both he and the R.C. Report on Smallholdings demonstrated, the cost per acre varied inversely with the size of the farm. According to the Report a twelve acre holding required an outlay on buildings of £20 to £25 per acre, one of thirty acres £12 per acre, and another of fifty acres about £8. Bailey Denton gives the following: 1,000+ acres £4.10s. per annum; 500 to 999 £6;

200 to 499 £7. Denton was writing at the height of mid Victorian prosperity, and at the end of the nineteenth century a more economical calculation suggested £4.10s. for a 200 acre holding; about £3.10s. for a 400 acre holding and £3 for farms above 500 acres [33].

The question is how far was this last computation applicable to the period before the 1820 to 1870 phase of reconstruction. A common rule of thumb throughout the period, for enclosed farms, was to consider five years' rent as equivalent to the capital investment in new buildings for farms of 150 to 400 acres, which suggests something between £3 and £5 an acre for mixed farms in the Midlands in about 1800 [34]. Some landlords certainly equipped their farmsteads with buildings more cheaply, even using brick. Between 1780 and 1820, Sir Joseph Banks, a Lincolnshire landowner, was an active rebuilder. In 1799, he claimed to have provided tenants with new brick houses and offices – e.g. on a farm of £100 per annum for £480. His rents were strikingly low, averaging only 8s.6d. per acre at the time, so that his £100 farm was 220 acres in extent and the capital investment in building only £2.4s. per acre. Lincolnshire was remarked upon as a county in which new building was cheaply done. In Norfolk about the same time the cost was reckoned to be about double the example quoted for Lincoln [35].

These estimates are very imprecise, and mostly refer to the reconstruction of whole farmyards. Only by a detailed study of existing rentals and accounts can a more accurate picture be formed, and more work needs to be done before it becomes clear whether the estimates given above reflect the true state of affairs or not.

Drainage

Drainage was probably the most important form of investment in the fixed capital of agriculture during the period 1750 to 1900. It is likely overall to have incurred the greatest outlay, and, of course, as a touchstone by which good farming was distinguished from bad, its significance was fully brought home to farmers and landowners in the same period, although not all at once. There are few areas where no drainage took place after 1750, and none where the upkeep of drains did not represent a considerable tax on landlords' and farmers' incomes. It has already been said that the majority of cases of reclamation and enclosure was followed by drainage of one kind or another, usually because ditching was closely associated with fencing. Underdrainage was especially a major feature of the great phase of estate improvement during 1820 to 1880. But the *quantum,* layout and technical requirements of drainage on different soils varied so much that estimates of the cost per acre even in a brief span of time differ enormously [36].

Surface draining was intended to convey rainfall and standing water off the topsoil of agricultural land. In method it changed little in the eighteenth and nineteenth centuries. Whether a hedgerow ditch or a main drain in marshland were built, the principal item of cost was always labour because a great deal of spade work was required. The art lay not in the techniques involved, but in aligning the drain. Hence a competent piece of ditch-making, provided it was properly maintained, could last almost indefinitely. The real burden, therefore, lay in maintenance, especially in the great public drainage schemes, which explains the early development of communal responsibility in the Sewers Commissions [37]. Indeed, after the Restoration many marshland zones suffered greatly from poor maintenance of their drains and outfalls, and a great deal of rescue work had to be done after 1760, particularly between 1800 and 1860 [38]. Surface drains were of various kinds. At one extremity were the hedgerow ditches, which were little more than deep furrows; at the other, the great fenland drains were wide enough to be navigable, and could be used for drainage, irrigation or transport, according to need. However, underdrainage gave more spectacular returns and provided greater opportunities to perfect techniques.

Underdraining was intended to remove subsurface water, to relieve agricultural land of the accumulations of water on the stratum where impervious soils began. It was especially necessary on flat surfaces or on slopes where the spring-line reached the surface. Subterraneous water was originally removed simply by digging out a criss-cross of trenches which allowed the water to fall naturally into the field ditches. The disadvantages were obvious and by the eighteenth century, bush or ling 'grips' usually replaced open furrows. They were still mainly hand dug and required little in the way of purchased materials. At the bottom of the trench was put a clump of twigs, a dead bush or ling, packed with straw. The trench was then filled in, and the bushes left to act as filters. Obviously, such a method was short-lived, although it was generally expected to last a decade at least. before tile drainage became economically feasible for the majority of farmers, a constant input of labour was required to maintain or replace these underdrains. The Elkington method, widely propagated in the 1780s and 1790s was less a technical breakthrough than the perfection of existing underdrainage by improved methods of alignment. But by the 1790s, tile drains were already in widespread use among wealthier farmers and landowners. However, tile drainage did not become commonplace until after 1820, and it was still often regarded as prohibitively expensive. To reduce the cost, some landlords sank clay-pits to produce their own tiles, or sought an alternative in the use of mole-ploughs, which, though in effect less durable, reduced costs per acre quite markedly. Cheap underdrainage, using clay pipes, did not become practicable until after 1840, but in the next forty years pipe drainage steadily superseded the other systems [39].

The extent to which underdrainage really contributed to the progress of nineteenth century agriculture probably needs some qualification. By Caird's day, most of the lighter soils suitable for what Philip Pussy called 'high feeding' were already underdrained, if not always in the best manner. Much remained to be done in less forward looking areas, especially on heavy soils. The clays were hardly touched by the 1830s and 1840s, and even in 1880 it was calculated that only 16 per cent of land which needed draining had been effectively done [40]. Nevertheless, underdrainage contributed greatly to the total outlay of capital investment in the period, but, as with buildings, the actual outlay cannot accurately be estimated until the estate and farm accounts have been consulted.

By presenting a paper at the beginning and not at the end of a period of research one is denied the pleasure of forming conclusions which have permanent value. One can however, reasonably suggest that the definition of landlord's and tenant's capital in farming raises a fundamental problem of interpretation. How should one estimate the investment in repairs and new capital equipment, even of fixed plant like buildings and drains, when the formal relationships between landowners and tenants were diverse, and numerous different arrangements between the two existed for the upkeep and extension of capital equipment? There are several ways in which the relationship could be expressed:

(1) The landlord was entirely responsible for installation and maintenance of all fixed capital, while the tenant supplied the working capital — this was quite a rare arrangement.

(2) The landlord merely guaranteed security of tenure while the tenant was encouraged or permitted to install all the necessary plant as well as to provide the working capital.

(3) The tenant supplied the working capital and undertook to maintain the fixed equipment in tenantable repair, while the landlord did all the major alterations or extensions and put the farm into repair on its changing hands – this was probably the commonest agreement.

(4) The landlord gave a lease specifying the areas in which the tenant might improve the property in return for secure possession long enough to allow the costs of improvements to be discharged.

(5) The landlord reduced the rent of tenants who built new outhouses, constructed drains, applied marl; or alternatively charged interest on the landlord's outlay in improvement.

(6) On very rare occasions, the landlord even supplied the working capital.

(7) In altering or improving the fixed equipment the costs were shared equally.

(8) Alternatively, the landlord supplied the materials, the tenant the labour.

(9) As a variation on the last, the landlord sank clay-pits or built up stocks of useful materials which the tenant might employ for capital improvements.

Levels of investment

Farmers' accounts have in a few cases been printed, and Reading University has collected and catalogued as many of the unpublished accounts as are likely to come to light [41]. The yield is obviously disappointing, but they offer some scope for more research. Added to the small numbers, however, are disparities of methods used by working farmers. Few accounts were modelled on the best examples of the day, like those of Joseph Mechi, which were publicized in the mid-nineteenth century, and many run for periods essentially too short to give an accurate and reliable impression of the farms' capital structure. Mechi was always meticulous enough to complete accounts with opening and closing annual valuations, so that one can get some idea of the overall capital accumulation of his business in the 1860s, though it is not easy to distinguish his fixed capital. In his heyday, his capital grew at an average of 6 per cent of his annual income, but in good years the rate increased to 20 per cent. Mechi was altogether exceptional and his accounts are hardly representative of the wealthier farmers of the period, not least because he ended in bankruptcy. As a freeholder, his business itself was untypical [42]. The majority of other accounts concerned themselves chiefly with receipts and outgoings on a more casual basis. This does enable us to estimate the farmer's inputs, but capital formation per farm is impossible to calculate.

The records of the great magnates and the landowning gentry are equally diverse, and most suffer from antiquated methods of book-keeping or discontinuous compilation. Even on estates where a clear distinction between repairs and improvements and all other outgoings is maintained, the proportion of the *gross* income from rent devoted to *gross* capital formation fluctuated both from time to time and from one estate to another. In general, the outlay of *rentier* estates on repairs, etc., varied according to prosperity and depression. In periods of low prices, as in the 1730s and 1740s or from 1820 to 1850, such expenditure was relatively high on most estates whose accounts have so far been examined. In the eighteenth century, the Duke of Kingston laid out about 4 per cent of his gross rental on repairs and improvements before 1750; in the next decade this fell to 1.4 per cent and after 1760 to no more than 0.6 per cent. The Cokes of Holkham expended altogether greater sums: 1707-15 15 per cent of gross rent; 1735-44 21 per cent; 1778-87 11 per cent; 1807-16 17 per cent. The Holkham estates were certainly unusual and the majority of other estates in the period laid out proportions more in line with the Duke of Kingston's [43]. It will be very surprising if the generality of *rentier* estates is found to have laid out more than 5 per cent of gross rents at most .before 1790. In the war years expenditure to some extent increased, and then fell away after 1812 for about a decade. In the nineteenth century generally R. J. Thompson estimated that gross capital formation by landed estates averaged 25 per cent of the gross rentroll, which is clearly too large before the 1840s for the majority, though there were important exceptions like the Dukes of Bedford. It is possible that the gathering momentum of expenditure on repairs and improvements from the 1830s to the 1870s may have resulted in Thompson's average being achieved at the climax in the middle years of the century. Some Lincolnshire estates certainly laid out such a proportion after about 1830-40, and the best estate-owners of the day – Bedford, Northumberland, Leicester, Graham of Netherby, etc. – supplied a similar or greater total outlay. Repairs, of course, bulked very large, but in the mid-century much new building and drainage was undertaken. On most estates, however, it is very difficult to separate repairs from new investment, but where it has been done, it appears that new capital expenditure almost always formed the smaller part of the total outlay on the estate farms. An estate which seems typical of large and enlightened properties in eastern England, that of the Turnors in Lincolnshire, spent £155,000 on new capital equipment in the sixty years after 1830 — that is, about 8 per cent of average gross rents per annum [45]. Expressed in terms of acreage, which eventually will form the chief criterion of this study, expenditure clearly varied considerably because of the different requirements of different soils. The decision to invest was often intensely personal and the outlay per acre even on the great estates varied very widely in the nineteenth century, while it still remains for a careful examination to be made of the courses and consequences of these diverse levels of investment.

NOTES

[1] Colin Clark, 'Capital in agriculture', *Farm Economist*, IX, 1958, pp.28-34, being a review of A. Tostleben, *Capital in Agriculture, its Formation and Financing since 1870* (Princeton, 1957).

[2] The papers contributed to a discussion in *Farm Economist*, VII, 1952-3 may be consulted. Also, *inter alia*, L. Drescher, 'Development of agricultural production in Great Britain and Ireland from the early 19th century', *Manchester School*, XXIII, 1955; J. R. Bellerby, 'Farm and non-farm capital, 1867-1938', *Farm Economist*, VIII, 1955; J. R. Bellerby, 'National and agricultural income in 1851', *Econ. Journal*, LXIX, 1959; J. R. Bellerby, 'Distribution of farm income in U.K. 1867-1938' in W. E. Minchinton (Ed.), *Essays in Agricultural History*, Vol. II (Newton Abbot, 1968).

[3] S. Pollard, 'Growth and distribution of capital in Great Britain, 1770-1870', *Third International Conference of Economic History, 1965, Munich*, pp.336ff., P. Deane, 'Contemporary estimates of national income in the first half of the 19th century', *Econ. Hist. Rev.*, 2nd ser., VIII, 1956; R. Giffen, *Growth of Capital* (London, 1889); P. Deane and W. A. Cole, *British Economic Growth 1688-1959*, pp.269ff., esp. Table 70, p.271 (Cambridge, 1962).

[4] T. S. Ashton, *The Eighteenth Century*, p.45, on the subject of interest and the capital value of lands (London, 1955); R. J. Thompson, 'An inquiry into the rent of agricultural land in England and Wales during the 19th century', *J.R.S.S.*, LXX, 1907, pp.606ff.; F. M. L. Thompson, *English Landed Society in the 19th century*, pp.169-70, 206 (London, 1963), 'The land market in the 19th century', *Oxford Econ. Papers*, IX, 1957, passim.

[5] E. P. Squarey, 'Farm capital', *J.R.A.S.E.*, New ser., XIV, 1878; Albert Pell, 'The making of the land in England', *J.R.A.S.E.*, New ser., XXIII, 1887.

[6] Horses are particularly important in this context as providing the chief form of motive power in the agriculture of the period.

[7] The cost of conversions to grass or from grass to tillage was often quite considerable. In the 1880s the Duke of Bedford estimated the cost of laying down permanent pasture at £15 per acre, which was probably rather higher than the generality of farmers and landowners laid out at that period — see J. T. Coppock, 'Agricultural change in the Chilterns, 1875-1900', *Agr. Hist. Review*, IX, 1961, p.8. Long-term changes in land use in some regions were

more than once undertaken in the period 1750-1900, especially on gault or clay soils, e.g. W. Leics. See, *inter alia*, W. E. Minchington, 'Agricultural returns and the government during the Napoleonic wars', *Agr. Hist. Review*, I, 1953, pp.41-2; G. E. Fussell and M. Compton, 'Agricultural adjustments after the Napoleonic wars', *Economic History*, 1939, passim.

[8] Until the 1860s onwards, cottages on the farmsteads were scarce because of the fear of increasing pauperism by encouraging settlements, and many farm labourers had to live in 'open' villages and walk to work. Their landlords were reputedly non-agriculturalists, petty tradesmen, speculative builders, etc. See, e.g., *Report to the Poor Law Commission on Settlement and Removal*, P.P. 1850, XXVII, passim.

[9] In general, e.g., G. E. Fussell, *The English Rural Labourer*, Chs. V, IX (London, 1949).

[10] Jürgen Hohnholz, *Der Englishe Park als Landschaftliche Erscheinung* (Tübingen, 1964).

[11] R. Brown, *General View of the Agriculture of the West Riding*, pp. 77-8 (1799); James Caird, *English Agriculture in 1850-51*, p.287. In the series of agricultural statistics, 1867ff., over 130,000 holdings were returned in Britain under five acres, many of which were probably classified by the G.R.O. in the census data as labourers' occupations.

[12] Sources: Board of Agriculture, *General Report on Enclosure*, pp.321ff. (1808), which brings together evidence of costs from the Board's country surveys, notably Arthur Young, *Lincoln*, 1799, and *Norfolk*, 1804; T. Bachelor, *Bedfordshire*, 1808; W. Gooch, *Cambridgeshire*, 1813; J. Billingsley, *Somerset*, 1798; W. E. Tate, 'The cost of Parliamentary enclosure in England', *Econ. Hist. Rev.*, 2nd ser., V, 1952, pp.258-65; H. G. Hunt, 'The chronology of Leicestershire enclosures', *Econ. Hist. Review*, 2nd ser., X, 1957, p.269; J. M. Martin, 'Cost of parliamentary enclosure in Warwickshire', *Univ. Birmingham Hist. Jnl*, IX, 1964; T. H. Swales, 'The parliamentary enclosure of Lindsey', *Reports of the Archit. & Archaeol. Soc. of Lincs. & Northants*, XLII, 1936, and *Reports of the Lincs. Archit. & Archaeol. Soc.*, I, 1937; R. C. Russell, *The Enclosures of East Halton and North Kelsey* (W.E.A. Barton, Lincs.), and 'The enclosures of Bottesford and Yaddlethorpe, Messingham and Ashby', *J. Scunthorpe Museum Soc.*, I, 1964; J. D. Chambers, *Nottinghamshire in the Eighteenth Century*, p.178 (London, 1932); J. L. and B. Hammond, *The Village Labourer*, esp. App.A (London, 1911; paperback, 1966). N.B.: The costs of enclosure in several townships and regions of Lincolnshire, given by Arthur Young in 1799 (*Lincoln*, p.87) and often cited as examples by modern researchers, need amendment, since the acreages given are those of whole parishes, etc., and not of the part enclosed.

[13] Administrative costs certainly moved steadily upwards, but were subject apparently to sudden increases, as in 1765, when Henry Homer commented on it (*Nature and Methods of Ascertaining Specific Shares of Proprietors upon Enclosure of Common Fields*, p.105). Commissioners' fees, in particular, were subject to much variation as one would expect.

[14] J. M. Martin, loc. cit., p.146.

[15] See, e.g., E. C. K. Gonner, *Common Land and Enclosure*, pp.84-5 (London, 1912); *General Report, 1808*, p.90, indicated that road-making was generally a by-product of the act of enclosure, but often followed swiftly upon the Award.

[16] The geographical (or geological) determinist views on the course of enclosure expressed by M. Aurousseau in 'Neglected aspects of the enclosure movements', *Economic History*, I, 1926-9, need modification in

the light of much detailed research into the chronology of enclosure in particular counties, notably in W. E. Tate's unpublished *Domesday of Enclosures.*

[17] See, e.g., A. Harris, *Rural Landscape of the East Riding of Yorkshire*, p.68 (Hull, 1961).

[18] M. E. Havinden, 'Agricultural progress in open-field Oxfordshire', *Agr. Hist. Rev.*, IX, 1961, reprinted in E. L. Jones, *Agriculture and Economic Growth in England, 1660-1815* (London, 1967); T. Stone, *General View of Agriculture of Lincoln*, pp.38-46 (1794); I. Leatham, *General View of Agriculture of East Riding*, pp.42-3 (1794); Caird, op. cit., p.314; A. Harris, op. cit., pp.29-31, 61-2, 86-9; Bailey and Culley, *General View of Agriculture of Cumberland*, p.32 (1794); Lloyd and Turner, *General View of Agriculture of Cardiganshire*, p.29 (1794); W. Gooch, *General View of Agriculture of Cambridgeshire*, p.38 (1813).

[19] Thomas Stone op. cit., pp.40, 42; J. Tuke, *General View of Agriculture of North Riding*, p.33 (1799). A report by a Scottish factor on conditions of the home estate of the leading Lincolnshire magnate, Lord Gwydir (*quondam* of the Dukes of Ancester), at Grimesthorpe in 1809 indicated clearly that tenants were still living and farming as their predecessors had done at least a generation after enclosure. Lincolnshire C.R.O. 3 ANC 4/38.

[20] Estimates or actual costs are quoted in many of the County Agricultural Reports, in the *Communications* to the Board of Agriculture of the same period, in various numbers of Arthur Young's *Annals of Agriculture*, and in the writings of men like William Marshall and J. C. Loudon, spanning the years from the 1780s to the 1820s. Most of these disparate data have not been adequately sifted, but by way of example and to illustrate some of the variations in cost for the different improvements, William Pitt, *Leicestershire*, pp.68ff. (1809); Charles Vancouver, *Hampshire*, pp.334-5 (1810), and *Devon*, pp.89ff (1813); Bailey and Culley, *Northumberland*, pp.60-64, fencing (1804), Strickland, *East Riding*, pp.97ff (1812); Board of Agriculture, *Communications*, IV/1, pp.266ff., V/1, pp.163ff., VI/1, pp.42-3, VII/ii, pp.244ff (all drainage – usually by tiles and relatively expensive).

[21] F. M. L. Thompson, *England Landed Society in the 19th Century*, quotes an example from the Fitzwilliam estates (Alwalton, Hunts.) of 1806 in which enclosure and the provision of a new farm of 451 acres cost £16 an acre, p.223.

[22] A. Young, *Norfolk*, p.174, and *Lincoln*, pp.285ff., (1799); W. H. Wheeler, *The Fens of South Lincolnshire*, passim (2nd ed., 1896); see also H. E. Strickland, *East Riding*, pp.194-201 (1812).

[23] William Pitt, *General View of the Agriculture of Staffordshire* (1813); *General Report*, pp.144-7 (1808).

[24] In *Transactions of the Surveyors Institution*, IV, 1871-2, p.17; Clutton was perhaps the greatest of Victorian land agent/surveyors (F. M. L. Thompson, *English Landed Society in the 19th Century*, p.160); Pell and Squarey, loc. cit., pp.355, 431, suggest figures of £26 and £11.6s. respectively at about the same period, though these were clearly only estimates or guesses, based upon rather different calculations of landlords' capital.

[25] Charles Vancouver, *General View of the Agriculture of Devon*, pp.307-8 (1813).

[26] See, e.g., W. H. Chaloner, 'The agricultural activities of John Wilkinson', *Agr. Hist. Rev.*, V, 1957, pp.48ff.; J. D. Marshall, *Furness in the Industrial Revolution*, (Barrow), pp.63-5 (1958); C. Vancouver, *Devon*, p.296; E. Rogby, *Holkham and its Agriculture*, p.4 (1818); J. Thirsk, *English Peasant*

Farming, pp.219-20 (London, 1957); E. Oldfield, *History of Wainfleet and the Wapentake of Candleshoe* (Boston, 1829), *sub* Friskey.

[27] H. S. Thompson, 'Farm buildings', *J.R.A.S.E.*, XI, 1850; J. B. Denton, *Farm Homesteads of England* (1863); Nigel Harvey, *The Story of Farm Buildings* (Young Farmers' publication, 1955).

[28] W. G. Hoskins, *Provincial England*, pp.131-148 (London, 1963); M. W. Barley, *The English Farmhouse and Cottage*, passim (London, 1961), and 'English farmhouses and cottages, 1550-1725', *Econ. Hist. Rev.*, 2nd ser. VII, 1953.

[29] N. Kent, *Norfolk*, p.110.

[30] For a list, see Lord Ernle, *English Farming Past and Present*, Introduction by O. R. McGregor, XCIX-CIII (6th edition, London, 1961).

[31] J. M. Martin, *Social and Economic Changes in the Rural West Midlands*, Ch.III, unpublished M.Comm. thesis, Birmingham University; *Annals of Agriculture*, II 382, XIX 451; N. Kent, *Norfolk*, p.110 (1796); W. Marshall, *Rural Economy of Norfolk*, I, p.81.

[32] G. E. Mingay, 'The agricultural depression, 1730-50', *Econ. Hist. Rev.*, 2nd ser. VIII, 1956, reprinted in E. M. Carus Wilson (Ed.), *Essays in Economic History*, Vol.II, p.317; R. A. C. Parker, 'Coke of Norfolk and the agrarian revolution', in Carus Wilson, op. cit., pp.335-6; E. L. Jones, 'Changes in Hampshire chalk-land farming in the 18th century', *Agr. Hist. Rev.*, VIII, 1960: 'yet in these years (c.1730-50) there were estate outgoings which cannot be attributed entirely to the landlord's desire to prevent farms falling into land. Forty pounds were "Allowed towards building a New Rickhouse in 1738 as per Agreement on Farmer Morgans taking and (sic) Advanced Rent", and elsewhere smaller sums were spent on improvements notably in 1735 and 1736 . . ." (p.9).

[33] Denton, *Farm Homesteads of England* (London, 1863); Thomas Bright, *Agricultural Surveyor and Estate Agents' Handbook*, 1899; see also the evidence of the *R.C. Report on Buildings for Smallholdings*, Cd. 6708 (1913), although specific is still quite useful.

[34] See, e.g., T. Bachelor, *General View of the Agriculture of Bedfordshire*, p.20.

[35] A. Young, *General View of the Agriculture of Lincoln*, pp.33-4 (1799). Old materials were used by some landowners at least at that time: Young, *Norfolk*, pp.19ff.

[36] The cost of tile draining in about 1800 seems to have averaged about £10 to £16 an acre and bush draining or ditching only a fraction of this. Later, the costs were certainly much less as the art of field drainage developed. Good permanent underdrainage could be undertaken for £5 or less per acre in the 1830s and 1840s and, with the production of an unproved mole plough for subsoiling in the 1820s, less permanent but effective field drainage might cost as little as £4.10s.0d. per acre (see the ref. on p.165, note [21] above); F. M. L. Thompson, *English Landed Society in the 19th Century*, p.248; Lincoln C.R.O., 3 ANC 7/23/7/4; 3 ANC 7/23/13/13.

[37] See, e.g., A. M. Kirkus (Ed.), *Records of the Commissioners of Sewers of the Ports of Holland 1547-1603*, Lincoln Record Series, 54, 1, 1959, Introduction Pt II.

[38] T. Stone, *Review of Arthur Young's Corrected Survey of the Agriculture of Lincolnshire*, pp.248-53 (1800).

[39] Lord Ernle, op. cit., pp.364-7; G. E. Fussell, 'The evolution of field drainage', *J. Bath & West & Southern Counties Agric. Soc.*, 6th ser., IV, 1929-30; J. B. Denton, *Land Drainage* (London, 1855), in the midst of a controversy over the methods of underdrainage promoted respectively by

James Smith of Deanston, *Remarks on Thorough Draining and Deep Ploughing* (1831), and Josiah Parkes, *Essays on Land Drainage* (1848).

[40] J. Caird, op. cit., passim; Royal Commission on Agriculture 1880-2, *Minutes of Evidence*, I, pp.164-5 (J. Bailey Denton's deposition); also Caird, before S.C. House of Lords on Land Improvement, 1873, pp.343-4; in general, E. L. Jones and E. J. T. Collins, 'Sectoral advance in English agriculture, 1850-80', *Agr. Hist. Rev.*, XV, 1967; R. W. Sturgess, 'The agricultural revolution on the English clays', *Agr. Hist. Rev.*, XIV, 1966.

[41] University Library, Reading, 'Accessions of historical farm accounts up to December 1967'.

[42] D. N. B., *Profitable farming: Mr Mechi's latest Agricultural Sayings and Doings* (London, 1869); J. J. Mechi, *How to Farm Profitably*, passim (London, no date).

[43] G. E. Mingay, op. cit., p.317; R. A. C. Parker, op. cit., pp.335-6; G. E. Mingay, *English Landed Society in the 18th Century*, pp.56, 177ff. (London, 1963).

[44] R. J. Thompson, 'An inquiry into the rent of agricultural land in England and Wales during the 19th century', J.R.S.S., LXX, 1907, pp.600ff., esp. 604; D. B. Grigg, 'A note in agricultural rent and expenditure in 19th-century England', *Agricultural History*, p.391; F. M. L. Thompson, *English Landed Society*, pp.223-8, 247-54; D. Spring, 'A great agricultural estate: Netherby under Sir James Graham, 1820-45', *Agricultural History*, 29, 1955; B. A. Holderness, *Rural society in S. E. Lindsey, 1660-1840*, unpub. Ph.D. thesis, University of Nottingham, 1968, Ch. VII; F. M. L. Thompson, 'English landownership: The Ailesby Trust, 1932-56', *Econ. Hist. Rev.*, 2nd ser., XI, 1958, pp.130-2.

[45] H. Rider Haggard, *Rural England*, Vol. I, p.146 (London, 1902).

COMMENTS   *F. M. L. Thompson*

After Mr Holderness's admirable and most interesting run through the various items which ought to be included in an estimate of agricultural capital formation, and his exposition of most, or many, of the problems involved in arriving at any figures, there is not very much left to say. But it does seem that agriculture has reached the point where decisions have to be taken which are crucial to the whole project. It is perfectly clear that here we have a sector which certainly down to the early nineteenth century can easily be construed as dominating fixed capital formation, and it provides many areas where we can make extremely elastic estimates of what is involved, depending largely on what multiples it is decided to adopt in order to capitalize more or less known quantities.

Clearly there are some areas where one can work from what look like reasonably comprehensive figures – e.g. acreage affected by enclosure – and other areas where we can only make guesses by inference from partial data as to what sort of quantities of capital formation are involved. Even with something that looks like a reasonably identifiable quantity – acres enclosed – as Mr Holderness indicated, very considerable room for manoeuvre remains in terms of what average cost per acre one is going to select, and in particular which costs one is going to include. If one wants to inflate the total figures as much as possible, then on enclosure one ought to go to town on that part of it which was effectively extending the cultivated acreage, and add in as much as appears justifiable for all the consequential expenditure of equipping new farms with their new roads and their new sets of buildings, and so on. This sort of expenditure has evidently not, in fact, entered into Mr Holderness's Table 3A which isolates costs of enclosing wastes by parliamentary act, which themselves in 'per acre' terms do not differ very substantially from his 'high estimates' of cost per acre of enclosing land in general (including the already cultivated land, in Table 2B). Although the 'high estimate' of Table 2B may be overestimated as stated, by the inclusion of underdrainage, it seems a little unlikely that underdrainage of such significant cost (an average of 30s. per acre on 2¼ million acres is implied) was in fact so extensively undertaken on the new enclosed land of the 1790 to 1815 period. But leaving drainage in, the cost per acre in Table 2B is very similar to the cost per acre in Table 2A for enclosing waste. The latter is an operation effectively extending the cultivated acreage, which one would expect to be much more expensive than simple enclosure of cultivated land. I should have thought one ought to raise considerably the average cost per acre there. Quite how this is to be done realistically is foxing, unless one is going to have an enormous amount of time and labour at hand to go through a massive number of estate accounts; for the data can only be found in private accounts, since the Commissioners were not concerned with these consequential activities. If one is lucky, in individual estate accounts one will happen to come across this sort of operation taking place. In one or two that I have looked at, this kind of operation of effective extension of cultivated area, creation of wholly new farm holdings and all the rest of it, did in fact occur, and in the Napoleonic war period when this expenditure is added to the formal expenses of enclosure commissioners and the normal consequential expenses of building the internal boundary fences, and so on, one can easily come up with figures like £20 per acre as being the overall cost of more or less creating new farm land.

When one turns to other areas of capital formation, the openings for more or less inspired guesswork seem very much greater indeed, and it is perhaps in those areas mainly to do with capital employed by the farmers themselves (mainly tenant farmers) that the whole project really is most in need of a firm guidance, in terms of what is current practice in compiling the national accounts.

On tenants' farm capital, there is a desire to include as much as possible in terms, for example, of outlays on fertilizers and feeding stuffs. Certainly gross outlays on these would seem to be part of simple farm operating costs, and therefore not part of fixed capital under any definition. However, the part of these outlays which did not yield their return within twelve calendar months of being incurred presumably forms an addition to the stock of capital being employed in farming, and here is one of these areas open to imaginative calculations, which I have indulged in already myself for the 1815 to 1880 period: when something like a net addition to capital employed in the farming business in respect of these two major items of the order of £50,000,000, guesses have been made over those sixty-five years. To break this down into anything like an annual series would be an absurd operation, given the nature of the initial operations from which this guestimate is derived. Nevertheless, it is a figure which in total looks to be of some significance.

Livestock having been omitted from the tally, leaving animals destined for the table to other hands, I would like to make the point that whatever may be done in accounts of the modern industrialized and mechanized economy, in the economy of the late eighteenth and first half of the nineteenth century, the prime source of motive power ought somehow to be taken into account in the reckonings. After all, in taking prime draft power employed in farming, the intention seems to be to splice on to a series which itself counts farm tractors as part of capital stock in farming, and net increases in numbers of farm tractors as part of net capital formation. It is not clear why in agriculture, which was primarily a horse power agriculture, one should listen to argue-ments in favour of excluding the then equivalent of the tractor from the sort of calculations that are to be made. This is going to make a very substantial difference in terms of the size of the total figures that are likely to come up when the final addition sums are done, because the number of horses being used in British farming was very con-siderable. Horses were subject to one of the assessed taxes during the Napoleonic war period and, in principle it is possible, or ought to have been possible if the records had survived, to arrive at an annual series of horses used in husbandry over the period from about 1792, to the date of the abolition of this particular duty, which is about 1824. A complete run of these figures does not appear to exist in parliamentary papers; reference is made simply to the fire which destroyed the records in 1813, and it has not been possible to push these back earlier than about 1808. It might be possible to push them back to the beginning of this duty, in which case one might get an annual series covering a twenty-five to thirty year period. As it is, what they indicate is that, regardless of what the annual changes may have been, total stock of horses used in agriculture was of the order of 750,000 to 800,000.

These were definitely regarded by such farmers as kept accounts as part of the capital employed in their business, and here was a capital asset with a limited life, although in comparison with Mr Craig's remarks about ships of poorish quality, it was not all that limited. A horse's working life was something like ten to fifteen years. Now, if in general what the series is going to end up with is gross capital formation rather than net, one wants to know about gross horse formation, and gross horse formation is presumably of the order of 60,000 to 80,000 a year. A price has to be put on each farm horse; in the 1820s the relevant price for a farm horse was about £20, and presumably in most of the Napoleonic war period it was not less than this. So horses were valued at something like £1½ million a year, and the horses are liable to ride rough-shod over the figures in many other sectors where one is painfully adding up hundreds of pounds and ten thousands here and there. Whether capital formation in cotton mills totals £24,000 or £24,500 in a year would scarcely seem to matter in the global picture, if horses are going to total £1½ million plus per year in every year of the early part of one's series. This is where one needs a directive from Professor Pollard, not simply on the outline object of the whole exercise, but more specifically on the order of magnitude of the desired result. One might then want to take some arbitrary decision about horses if they seem to loom too large and say that this item of capital assets perhaps should be included as net horse formation rather than gross. But this would be discrepant with all the other figures that appear likely to come in from all the other sectors, where the accent all along has been on gross capital formation and not on net.

For this earlier period it is difficult to see any means by which one might arrive at anything that looked remotely reliable in the way of a figure for the net annual addition to the stock of horses used in husbandry. Later, right at the end of the relevant period, but within the 1850-70 period (which it appears Mr Holderness wants to include in these estimates for the agricultural sector as a whole) one might perhaps be able to do something about this, because it does seem that in these last twenty years after 1850 there was something of a tendency to substitute horse labour for manual labour. But whether one can find any sources from which one can quantify this is rather a different matter. The agricultural statistics themselves don't begin to give a return on these until right at the end of the 1860s. What of the rest of the horse population, that part of it which was used in business, industry and commerce, though not the part used for pleasure and personal transport, which ought by the same reckoning to be included, though not necessarily under the agricultural heading? The researchers could be more fortunate there, because one could get something that looked like a continuous time-series pretty well right through the period from about 1810 onwards, for by the juggling about with the assessed tax figures one could reckon on isolating out the element of the horse population which was being employed in the ordinary commercial carting business, and in drawing carriages for hire, and so on – the equivalent of the taxis and mini-cabs.

One could get some idea of the size of that segment of the horse population continuously over a very long period, but this presumably ought to get itself counted in under transport rather than under agriculture. On this point there seem to be one or two items which Mr

Holderness is anxious not to count under agriculture, which nevertheless it is desirable not to leave out, in case they find themselves not
counted at all. For instance, when you are desirous of excluding the
bulk of rural housing – assuming it should prove possible to do so from
the kind of individual estate account material one is liable to come
across – it does seem desirable that this should be included somewhere
else. We have not in fact, heard anything at all as yet about residential
building and what is being done about assembling figures on this, but
clearly investment in rural housing is part of domestic fixed capital
formation, as also presumably is investment in the great country
mansions. In fact, a series which could isolate out this one particular
component of country houses might be very valuable in itself for testing
one or two propositions which have been mentioned as to the
significance or insignificance of movements in country house investment in relation to releasing or not releasing funds for more productive
employment in industrial and commercial activities. So one hopes that
if figures for this sort of conspicuous investment exist in sources which
are being used, they will not simply be ignored. They ought to be
collected, even if finally they are going to be put into some other
category than the agricultural one.

I will end with a question about the type of source which could
be the only one from which one could get figures on this last point on
country house building – that is, estate accounts: How is one going to
set about getting a sample of these into one's net? After completing
some of my own work I realize that I ought to have started in an
entirely different way by conducting a systematic survey both of what
estates did exist at given points of time, and which ones of them had
records, and then employed some statistician to tell me which ones I
ought to have gone to in order to have been sure that I had studied a
sample that was representative. But, of course, I adopted no such
procedure. One simply goes on until one seems to have spent enough
time looking at what one happens to have heard of in the way of
records that happen to survive, and then draws a line and starts trying
to justify what one has done retrospectively. However, in this systematic project a different procedure is presumably going to be used, and
I would like to have information on how the sample of the account
material that is going to be drawn upon is going to be constructed.

COMMENTS *A. Harrison*

I am not a historian, but I am interested in current capital formation in agriculture, a number of aspects of which bear on the historical studies. Our work in this field is concerned with the identification of farm businesses, of farming costs and associated capital elements and with this examination of current records of investment in more permanent capital items. We are also studying the use made of capital provided in the past and whether or not it has been modified to meet modern technological requirements.

Part of our debate here has centred around what we understand by capital investment, for, although the definition of capital as produced goods which are going to be used in further production is acceptable, this leaves scope for debate as to what our definition embraces at the fringe, as it were, in order to keep in line with current accounting conventions at the Central Statistical Office or elsewhere, or because we do not have the resources to do all the counting which ought to be done. For our own part, questions of definition have proved less troublesome than those of statistical enumeration in the field, for we are operating in an environment of broadly agreed accounting conventions, although problems begin to arise in dealing with investment buildings. Thus, according to our definition, horses and livestock certainly are capital. In the case of fertilizers, however, one cannot equate expense and capital formation because this is a short-term resource which may be turned over and converted into output in less than a year. In the modern context, the same funds might be used to buy feeding stuffs for livestock, the livestock cashed, then converted into fertilizers turned again within the year, so the problem becomes that of calculating the rate of turnover which will convert expenses to investment per annum terms.

Our work on current records does lead us to a number of conclusions which are important. Thus, and this has already been emphasized, there are a lot of farmers, we do not know how many, but say 200,000 or 300,000; and aggregate capital formation is the result of the netting out of all the individual changes on these separate business units. In fact, if one was to calculate the percentage change in tenant's capital relative to the total investment for each farm and then plot the distribution of farms, one would get a normal curve distribution. The conclusion to be drawn from that is that one needs a large sample of farm accounts if one wishes to understand what is going on. We have looked at several hundreds, but even this does not add up to being satisfactory nationally. Sampling errors may be acceptable on a county basis if one looks at, say, 500 farm records. As historians we are unlikely to be able to operate on such a scale, however.

Moreover, there are large regional and farm-to-farm variations in performance and in the farming systems, or tenant's capital asset patterns, that are associated with fixed capital arrays. Thus, in studying fat lamb production recently we have found that the rate of return on the variable costs involved ranged from something like minus 30 per cent to plus 50 per cent on a sample of fifty to seventy flocks. With such great variations in systems, and in efficiencies of operation, there are clearly great risks in trying to relate output to capital on any average basis. Any capital series arrived at in the first instance, unless accompanied by a full study of associated tenant's capital, could yield markedly differing results.

Another point is that in farming currently (and also, we know, in the past), outside capital has been introduced from a number of sources on a large scale. In some areas we have studied intensively, 6 per cent of farmers have been found to be responsible for something like half of the additional capital formation largely by introducing outside funds. Again, it is clear that only a fairly large sample will make quite certain that one gets these active elements or that they alone do not produce a bias in the sample because of the non-random survival of material. Another conclusion to be drawn is that it is very dangerous to predict capital formation figures from income figures within only one sector of the economy.

Today, capital formation in farming is a family affair. It is the product of saving and investment by generation after generation. Also, to a large extent, and even more in the past, it is the result of family labour efforts, probably largely unrecorded – nevertheless undoubtedly an important effort. The period before 1894 precedes the introduction of the Agricultural Holdings Acts to govern the landlord-to-tenant relationship. Before that, strictly in terms of the law, the tenant was in the worst possible investment position, for, in attaching anything to the ground, he immediately transferred it to the landlord. That was the position at common law, but the position in practice was not so extreme and appears to have varied regionally.

One point about the study of farm records relates to the problem of where farming boundaries are drawn and how farming industry is defined. This is a problem which seems less obviously relevant for this project than for those large and multi-activity companies like Unilever which have gone into farming. However, some important sectors of change in farming — the poultry industry and pigs and beef production, for example — may get lost in the accounts of such large organizations. The current danger is that farming's boundaries will be too narrowly drawn. The historian's difficulty is to see that they are not cast too wide. While we agree that farming is the production of animals and crops, over the centuries it has also been concerned with the provision of transport and of domestic services and products of one sort and another. How much farm labour 200 years ago, for example, would have been devoted to the processing of feathers — just to take one farming product?

So much for the written records side which really covers most of our relevant experience. We have in addition, however, made visual inspections of buildings, with a view to calculating capital stock and particularly to get some sort of age profile of buildings. We have come up against the points already mentioned of regional variations in designs, differences in materials, and especially in their durability, and so on. Alterations to buildings to meet changed factor and product costs are far from easy to identify. This is particularly important in looking at houses. Furthermore, widely available plans tended to follow best practice, with poorest practice lagging well behind. Even when there is something concrete, like sets of initials and dates on walls, one can not be sure that they are right because they might commemorate a marriage and not when the house was built.   These various points seem to add up to a general conclusion that such historical data as are currently available will inevitably show wide fluctuations in the short term. Much more work is required on assembling and analysing basic records over as wide an area as possible if spurious conclusions are to be avoided.

DISCUSSION 5

Discussants: S. A. Broadbridge, S. D. Chapman, A. W. Coats, R. Davis, M. Falkus, A. Harrison, J. P. P. Higgins, B. Hill, B. A. Holderness, S. Pollard.

Most of the discussion was concerned with the statistical tables included in Dr Holderness's paper. One item which caused some misgivings was the classification of fertilizers as capital. This could be quite an important item in the aggregate, and it was more complex than appeared at first sight. Any manure spread for a particular crop must be considered as being used up by that crop within a single year and included in current, rather than capital costs. Some fertilizers, however, were intended for more long-term effects. Marl was perhaps the best example. Each application could be expected to improve the soil for three to seven years, or even longer, and this was clearly a form of investment. An application of perhaps seventy loads per acre per year might be considered current expenditure, but applications much larger than this were intended to fix the soil composition or the fertility of the soil and would take many years to work out. They should, therefore, be included, in the statistics of capital formation.

Horses were mentioned in almost every contribution, and were obviously of crucial importance in the agricultural economy, as well as in transport. The debate on horses following the papers on transport had been somewhat inconclusive. For agriculture, exactitude would be made even more difficult by the trend of substitution. In rough figures, for example, there might have been 800,000 horses on farms in 1820 and perhaps a million in 1870, and this looks like a substantial increase. At the same time, however, there was a decline in the numbers of draught oxen, and this may well have been even more substantial in the eighteenth century, so that the net change depended on a number of unknowns.

The main problem of agricultural statistics was the relative weakness of their base, and in particular, the scarcity of farm accounts. The proportion of large estates with surviving accounts was fairly satisfactory, but their total numbers were small. Farm accounts proper, however, survive in a very small percentage of cases only. Dr Eric Jones and his colleagues in Reading had made a sustained effort to collect farm accounts for this and earlier periods, and these represent much the best primary source available, yet even their total is very unrepresentative. There were altogether something like 300 sets available, scattered over several centuries, but most sets covered a very short period only, perhaps up to ten years, so that there were enormous difficulties in constructing a series out of them.

If the whole collection were taken as a sample, one would run the risk of lumping together enterprises that were most unlike. Farming was an occupation which varied enormously, according to individuals, areas and types of farming, not to mention the differences between periods which perhaps ought to emerge as a result of the study. If, on the other hand, the collection were split as to type of farming, which was undoubtedly the correct procedure, and an attempt were made to estimate capital formation ratios for each type, the sample on which each series was based would turn out to be too small for comfort. It might not even be possible to estimate the range of likely errors involved. Moreover, there was no uniformity at all in the way in which farm accounts were kept, and even those which survived tended to be unprofessional and idiosyncratic. Most farmers simply thought of balancing their annual expenditure. Some accounts start off with the total outlay on tenants' capital and work through for perhaps ten years, when there is a profit on the total working and the initial outlay is paid off. Others start from scratch and do not bother about any original inputs.

Nevertheless, the exercises were worth doing at least as a preliminary survey. At this stage of the investigation, they were intended as illustrations rather than as final results. It should be emphasized that it had been the original plan to hand the work on investment in the agricultural sector over to the University of Reading, but unfortunately our colleagues there had found it impossible to take on this task, so that Dr Holderness had been investigating this sector in Sheffield for a very brief period only, and was still very much at the beginning of his enquiries.

There remained some problems of detail. Table 2B, for example, was based on labour costs in the Napoleonic war period, a period of high wages, which therefore needed a subsequent adjustment of prices. The necessity for this adjustment was unfortunate, as it introduced possibilities of further errors, but the fact was that this was the period of the agricultural reports and it therefore had much the best figures. At the same time, there was an increasing proportion of materials costs later in the nineteenth century, compared with nearly all labour costs before 1800, for such works as underdrainage and other improvements to be found during the enclosure process.

The use of global figures of £24 or £25 million for all enclosure costs was for illustration only, and should not be taken to represent anything concrete since they were the sums of cumulated investment, undertaken at different price levels, and not of an investment at any one point in time.

There was some chance of double counting, when enclosure and other apparently agricultural improvements might improve the capital equipment of another industry, and be included under that sector as well. However, this was likely to be minimal, partly because enclosures were usually limited precisely to agricultural purposes, and partly because the odd investment for the purpose of opening up a quarry or even a small coal mine would not amount to a great deal.

Against these rather gloomy comments about the chances of obtaining some reliable agricultural series, two positive suggestions emerged from the discussion. One was the suggestion of using the concrete evidence of the farm buildings still surviving from the century 1750 to 1850, to improve the estimates of investment in farm buildings. Many buildings in that period were built of durable materials and in solid style, and little new building occurred on farms between 1850 and the very recent period, so that these buildings could be identified without difficulty. It is true that of the years before, say, 1830, only the larger structures would remain, but a great deal of the period 1830-50 has survived. Professor Hoskins, at Leicester, had taken a great interest in this source for the study of history, and had left behind him at Leicester a vernacular building group of scholars who might help in this sort of fact-finding and interpretation. In some areas and some estates, such as the Duke of Bedford's land, there was much well documented rebuilding in the late eighteenth century. There were also Clutton's estimates of farm building costs. But large structures, or structures put up at one go, rather than added to piecemeal, were not found everywhere, and where there were small holdings, or small additions to existing holdings, it would not be easy to identify actual dates and costs for buildings.

The other new approach suggested was the insurance records, which had already yielded such a rich harvest to Dr Chapman in his investigations of the cotton industry. There would be tens of thousands of valuations in the records of the Sun and the Royal Exchange and, as Mr Higgins confirmed, these specified all the main buildings separately on any farm, and data about them would be easy to include in the current search going on among these records for the general industrial series of this enquiry. They would, in fact, yield not only information on buildings, but also on stocks.

While it might be true that in some areas only the large farmers or the gentlemen farmers would insure their farms, this was by no means general. The impression was that the local coverage rather depended on the efficiency or drive of the local agent, so that in some areas one would not merely get a sample of farm buildings, but virtually all, as in the case of the cotton mills. Of course, the work would be enormously tedious and time consuming but it would produce quite reliable results.

Some doubt had been thrown on the value of insurance records because of their neglect of depreciation or other sophisticated methods of establishing the true value of the assets insured, at any one time. The fact of the matter was that insurance valuers tended to take historic costs as their basis, and continued to value at those costs until the asset was scrapped or replaced. This might lead to difficulties if we wanted to value the capital stock at any one time, but for this study, the method would produce the right answer, as long as we knew the dates of construction.

While this proposal was accepted as a valuable suggestion for the future, not all members were convinced that the coverage, particularly of the smaller of the 300,000 or so farms, would be anything like as good as the coverage of cotton mills, particularly after 1815 when falling prices led many farmers and landowners to save costs by allowing their insurance to lapse. There was also the relatively minor question of the date and age of the buildings when valued for first insurance. Some of these difficulties could be overcome by establishing the size distribution of farms from other sources, and then recalculating total values from appropriate weighted samples drawn from the insurance records.

Summing up, it was clear that the agricultural estimates of capital formation, like the agricultural sectors in today's national income estimates of agrarian economies, would be among the weakest and most doubtful series of the project, at least with the resources available today. In future, they might well offer the most promising area of improvement and extension of the work of the group, as had happened in the more recent statistics of such economies as the Japanese or the American over the past hundred years. Meanwhile, in spite of this weakness, the attempt will have to be made to arrive at the most plausible estimates consistent with the information available, and to integrate them with the aggregate figures for the other sectors of the economy.

Index

196

For Product Safety Concerns and Information please contact our
EU representative GPSR@taylorandfrancis.com Taylor & Francis
Verlag GmbH, Kaufingerstraße 24, 80331 München, Germany